EFFECTIVE OR WISE?

D1153625

Studies in the
Postmodern Theory of Education

Shirley R. Steinberg
General Editor

Vol. 447

The Counterpoints series is part of the Peter Lang Education list.
Every volume is peer reviewed and meets
the highest quality standards for content and production.

PETER LANG
New York • Bern • Frankfurt • Berlin
Brussels • Vienna • Oxford • Warsaw

EFFECTIVE OR WISE?

Teaching and the Meaning of Professional Dispositions in Education

EDITED BY
Julie A. Gorlewski . David A. Gorlewski
Jed Hopkins . Brad J. Porfilio

PETER LANG
New York • Bern • Frankfurt • Berlin
Brussels • Vienna • Oxford • Warsaw

Library of Congress Cataloging-in-Publication Data

Effective or wise?: teaching and the meaning of professional dispositions in education /
edited by Julie A. Gorlewski, David A. Gorlewski, Jed Hopkins, Brad J. Porfilio.
pages cm. — (Counterpoints: studies in the postmodern theory of education; Vol. 447)
Includes bibliographical references and index.
1. Teacher effectiveness—United States.
2. Effective teaching—United States. 3. Teachers—Training of.
4. Education—Standards—United States. I. Gorlewski, Julie A.
LB2838.E35   371.102—dc23   2014021273
ISBN 978-1-4331-2131-9 (hardcover)
ISBN 978-1-4331-2130-2 (paperback)
ISBN 978-1-4539-1342-0 (e-book)
ISSN 1058-1634

Bibliographic information published by **Die Deutsche Nationalbibliothek.**
Die Deutsche Nationalbibliothek lists this publication in the "Deutsche
Nationalbibliografie"; detailed bibliographic data are available
on the Internet at http://dnb.d-nb.de/.

The paper in this book meets the guidelines for permanence and durability
of the Committee on Production Guidelines for Book Longevity
of the Council of Library Resources.

© 2014 Peter Lang Publishing, Inc., New York
29 Broadway, 18th floor, New York, NY 10006
www.peterlang.com

All rights reserved.
Reprint or reproduction, even partially, in all forms such as microfilm,
xerography, microfiche, microcard, and offset strictly prohibited.

Printed in the United States of America

Table of Contents

Section Two: Imagination, Joy, and Wisdom

Section Three: Practicing What We Teach

Foreword

Wise or Effective? A 21st-Century Classroom Vignette

TIM SLEKAR

Mr. Rhodes walks into his fourth-grade classroom on Monday morning. He turns the lights on and looks at his classroom. The 28 desks are grouped in seven pods. Above each pod hangs a cardboard cutout of a jungle animal with the names of each child in the pod attached to the jungle animal.

On one wall, labeled prominently the "data wall," are all the charts and graphs that clearly demonstrate Mr. Rhodes's commitment to data-driven instruction. Mr. Rhodes's students know where they are and, most importantly, where they need to be—clearly written goals comprise another section of the "data wall."

Each child will walk into the classroom in the morning, look at the data wall, and see his or her individualized learning goal for the week clearly written on the wall. Also, just in case the child is interested, Mr. Rhodes includes the state standard that aligns with each child's goal (Mr. Rhodes's principal will surely be impressed). It is clear, to reiterate, that Mr. Rhodes wants his students to know where they are, where they are going, and where they need to be.

Mr. Rhodes walks over to the side of the room and turns on the 10 tablet computers, ensuring that each has the new math "simulation" ready to go so the children can get to work when the time is right.

And all around the room are inspiring posters reminding the children that there is "No Time for Failure," and exhorting them to "Shoot for the Stars" even as they "Listen Respectfully." Clearly Mr. Rhodes has set in motion a plan during which "effective" teaching will dominate the day.

However, is it possible that the children who enter Mr. Rhodes's classroom will spend the day demonstrating effectiveness but never really engaging in learning?

Even though Mr. Rhodes's practices seem to indicate that he is "effective," can we really be sure that his children will experience education? Will they listen to great stories and use their imagination? Will they get to think deeply about issues in their own community? Will the children "explore," "discuss," "discover," "dig up," "pretend," and "wonder?"

The answer to these questions can't really be determined because that would require regular visits to Mr. Rhodes's classroom. We would need to watch as the daily routine that is a school day takes on a life. However, without observing, we can be pretty sure that Mr. Rhodes has an "effective" classroom. And isn't that enough for today's technocratic, hyper-measurement-oriented, results-driven system of schooling?

I'm sure some would say, "yes." But what if some said, "no"?

In the pages that follow, you will have the rare opportunity to engage with scholars willing to push for more than "effective" as an acceptable descriptor for education.

Instead, the authors explore education that they call—*wise*.

Tim Slekar
Dean, School of Education
Edgewood College
January 15, 2014

Introduction

Wise vs. Effective

JED HOPKINS, DAVID GORLEWSKI, JULIE GORLEWSKI,
AND BRAD PORFILIO

For the last few years, Jed Hopkins has used this ice-breaker in his undergraduate and graduate courses. Students are seated in a circle and are asked to introduce themselves and then to share their response to this prompt:

> If you had to choose between these two alternatives—more precisely, if you had to place one in front of the other—which would you choose: (1) to be an effective educator, or (2) to be a wise educator?

It is emphasized that it has to be a choice; that you are disallowed the opportunity to have both *equally* (whatever that might mean). Instead, you have to put one in front of the other and volunteer an explanation for your preference. It is explained that the point of this thought experiment is to get us to identify which one is taken to be, in some sense, more fundamental. Of course the challenging nature of this activity makes for a good ice-breaker, setting the tone for a course that, it's hoped, will provide lots of opportunities for further reflection. But, additionally, the consolidated results from this activity are themselves particularly revealing about the way many of us tend to think about education. Pooling the responses of all the classes exposed to this particular ice-breaker reveals that, typically, 90% of the classes choose "effective." What follows is a discussion of the rationales the students provide.

For many, it's a struggle to come down on one side only. For example, some point out that perhaps you can't be wise without also being effective—and so they must, therefore, go together "in the end." Nevertheless, when pressed, "effective" is the popular choice because students reason that a wise educator is worse than useless if wisdom can't be effectively communicated, whereas someone who is effective at least gets something done. When asked to explain what made them think of associating wisdom with poor communication they often evoke images of the lone genius worthy of respect but possessing knowledge that is obscure to the majority (perhaps a negative experience with academic discourse has reinforced this). In contrast, "effectiveness" is a notion associated with wide and non-exclusive appreciation. For many students, then, "wisdom" is respected but restricted to an *individual's capacity* and, as a result, suffers from being confined to the few, or only to the person who is wise. "Effectiveness," on the other hand, connotes utility, getting the job done, or the objectives met—abstractable and generalizable *public events*—and therefore promises some sort of egality. Other explanations are given that employ similar connotative antagonisms, such as "effective" is collaborative while "wisdom" is self-centered; or "effective" is efficiency while "wisdom" is obscurity, if not impotence.

As we go around the circle, usually only one or two will be brave enough to admit support for "wisdom" over "effective." One popular rationale given here hinges on a semantic strategy; a definition of "wisdom" is provided that makes "effective" part of the definition. They'll say something like "wisdom *means* you can't be wise and not also effective and, furthermore, that it doesn't work the other way around: you can be effective and not wise." So, wisdom trumps effective because when "correctly defined," the two concepts are asymmetrically related.

Another given rationale, though rarer still, wants to recognize that "effective" isn't *necessarily* a moral category whereas "wisdom" is. Here, it's pointed out that concern with "effective" is a concern with the quality by which ends are achieved but not, necessarily, the ends themselves. "Effective" connotes a concern with means, while "wisdom" connotes a concern with *both* means and ends. This idea that wisdom is a moral category, while a concern with effectiveness can be morally neutral, explains why we feel comfortable admitting that Adolf Hitler's political techniques may have been quite effective (unfortunately for humanity) but would shudder to call him, in any way, wise. For a less dramatic example, but one more in line with our focus on education, it would explain why we could say that a method of teaching reading that may be very effective (at least according to a narrow source of publicly measurable results) should nevertheless be resisted by a wise teacher because, in this case, the method of the program tends to kill the joy of reading in the long term, and/or is restrictive about what reading makes possible, and so forth.

So, putting all this together, we could say that those few students who vote for "wise" over "effective" are being driven by the intuition that when we think about educational endeavors, we shouldn't separate out means from ends. *How* students learn is as important as *that* they learn, and *how* we teach is as important as any kind of measurable *result*. All of this is to suggest that when we consider teaching, in an educational context, we are not simply aiming towards pre-determined results (that can be measured) but something else. But, what is this "something else"? Whatever it is it seems to carry deep moral implications. (Let's hear it for wisdom!)

And, now let us come clean about our stand on all this; if it's a choice between "effective" and "wise," we too would recommend that we try to err on the side of wisdom when education is at stake. Hence, we want to argue that teaching reading, any kind of teaching in fact, is not a job primarily to be understood in terms of effective technicality but a job for wise educators (who, of course, will *also* need to possess some technical skill). But what is "wisdom"? How do we talk about education in ways that allow for this moral aspect to be given the attention it deserves? For though it may not be too surprising, the result of the thought experiment is disturbing, is it not? For the majority of in-service teachers, "effective" seems to be the overwhelmingly popular choice, while "wisdom" gets mostly a bad press, connoting such undesirable things as unconnectedness, obscurity, and perhaps even impotence. Just as worryingly, why does "effectiveness" often seem to connote *only* positive things—as though it were intrinsically a moral category? What can we do about the idea that professionality in education is increasingly being approached in terms of resource optimization and standardization rather than a matter of, say, sensibility and joy—words that sound oddly quaint, or out of place, in a context where "effectiveness" rules?

It might be an obvious claim that *professional educators*, if the phrase is to mean anything important, must take the core of their work as representative of, and advocating for, *education* rather than some distorted idea of it—whatever "it" is. And we know that for so long educational discourse has had a fairly predictable focus revolving around knowing—a concern with such things as what is to be known (think of the standards movement); how quickly and effectively it can be known (think of the search for and promotion of "best practices" and "effective instructional materials"); how it can be shown, by measurement, that knowledge is being mastered (think of standardized testing), as well as how to use measurements for making global estimates of the state of schooling at national, state, district, school, and teaching levels (think of the myriad legislated reform efforts). But, many of these foci are often pursued with unexamined assumptions about the meaning of education and the specific challenges and possibilities afforded to educators. So, perhaps a less obvious claim might be made to the effect that in order for teachers to represent and advocate for education, they must also become the intentional stewards of the richest discourse we can "grow" around it—a discourse that nurtures the possibilities of education.

This book is meant as a small contribution to such stewardship. In different ways, all the chapters invite us into the work of reinvigorating educational discourse. We believe this to be a crucial responsibility for all of us, especially when certain key concepts such as "education" suffer from the neglect of over-familiarity (Hopkins, *The Joy of Educating*), or when our understanding of "professional" might be damagingly influenced by its use in the media, restricting the more nuanced understanding we seek when we consider professionality in the context of authentic education (Gorlewski, Gorlewski, and Lalonde, *Practicing in the Panopticon: Teaching and Learning in the Surveillance Media Culture*).

In sum, this book contradicts the idea that being wise is only the province of the lone genius worthy of respect but possessing knowledge that is obscure to the majority. Instead, it asks us all to participate in the necessarily collaborative endeavor of discourse stewardship in—as grand as it may sound—the pursuit of wisdom.

ORGANIZATION AND CHAPTERS

Section 1: Myths, Lies, and Videotape

The first chapter of this section, *Practicing in the Panopticon: Teaching and Learning in the Surveillance Media Culture*, uses the framework of critical media literacy to analyze how representations of professionalism, particularly with respect to leadership, learning, and culture, relate to the identity development of educators. In this chapter, Julie Gorlewski, David Gorlewski, and Catherine Lalonde "investigate how selected reality television programs…portray the notion of professionalism, and how these portrayals relate to the experiences of teaching and learning." Situating contemporary television media representations against a backdrop of neoliberalism, the authors reveal how visual texts reinforce myths related to the cult of personality, meritocracy, and panopticism—myths that undermine the development of critical pedagogical practices in teachers and teacher candidates. Beyond theoretical considerations, the chapter argues that teacher preparation programs must reinforce skills and dispositions consistent with critical literacies in order to foster "lifelong critical social engagement."

In the second chapter in this section, *The Myth of the "Fully Qualified" Bright Young Teacher: Using the Haberman Star Teacher Pre-Screener to Teach and Assess Professional Dispositions*, Nicholas D. Hartlep, Sara McCubbins, and Grant B. Morgan report the results of research related to the Haberman STAR Pre-Screener assessment. The authors

> were interested in better situating what Haberman (2012) identified as the myth of the "fully qualified bright young teacher" in the context of teacher education professionalization generally, but specifically in the context of how or how not, the educational community thinks about dispositions.

Their study resulted in two implications. The first involves "revealing the myth of the 'fully qualified' bright young teacher" and the second involves the impact of graduate education on teacher effectiveness. In concluding their chapter, the authors claim that "It would be wise and highly effective to build pre-service teachers' dispositions and core beliefs so that they will be able to effectively teach and reach diverse students."

The third chapter in this section, *When the Obvious Isn't True: What's Really Wrong with Teacher Quality and Teacher Education?* P. L. Thomas argues that the debates around teacher quality

> are framed by three broad questions: (1) what are the bi-partisan claims and intentions of focusing solely or primarily on teacher quality as the central mechanism for education reform?; (2) what is the proper priority for addressing teacher quality within the larger reform needed in both society and education?; and (3) what's really wrong with teacher quality and teacher education?

To address these questions, Thomas investigates the meanings of teacher quality in relation to "high-stakes accountability, the credibility of Value Added Models (VAM), the reform movement's inverted focus on teacher quality, and finally, the authentic problems with teacher quality and teacher preparation." According to Thomas, it is essential for educators to speak out against education reforms that undermine the best interests of learners and, by extension, our society.

In the concluding chapter of this section, T. Jameson Brewer and Anthony Cody discuss the origins and prospects of *Teach For America, the Neoliberal Alternative to Teacher Professionalism*. The authors link positivist dispositional tendencies with the notion of "best practices," perspectives that promote a conception of teaching that is reduced to sets of strategies that can be scaled up and delivered as standardized methodologies. These ideas are consistent with deprofessionalizing neoliberal dispositions that undergird initiatives such as Teach For America (TFA), and Brewer and Cody "argue that this goal of de-skilling teachers via privatization of training and reductionist dispositions is best characterized by the alternative teacher training program Teach For America (TFA)." The authors trace the history of TFA, explicate links among neoliberalism, teacher professionalism, and TFA, and explain how it undermines public education. They conclude with a call for teacher autonomy as a means to "stabilize and strengthen struggling schools, and that means we must turn them into places where highly trained educators can make their careers."

Section 2: Imagination, Joy, and Wisdom

In the opening chapter of this section, Jed Hopkins explores and seeks to reclaim *The Joy of Educating*. An educational philosopher, Hopkins reveals how joy, far from being a superfluous aspect of education, "has concrete and practical application for the work we do as educators." Drawing on a vast array of historical and theoretical frames, he explains that "human practice is more than a mere assemblage of tasks and procedures—even if carried out effectively—and ultimately…teacher education might be best seen as the struggle to locate refreshing and hopeful ways of thinking about practices." Through careful attention to discourse, culture, and processes of learning, Hopkins argues that identity, education, and joy are inextricably interrelated, and that joy is essential to the art and craft of teaching and, therefore, to the act of preparing future teachers.

In the second chapter of this section, *Seeking the Authentic: Inquiry and Dispositions, Teacher Candidates, and Ourselves*, Pamela J. Hickey and Mary H. Sawyer "share discoveries from a semester in [their] on-going efforts to support the development of "inquiry" dispositions with future teachers even as [they] strive to grow in [their] own understandings and implementations of inquiry and teacher candidate support." As teacher educators, they embrace their obligation to encourage aspiring teachers to "look beyond the numbers and to create collaborative relationships with their greatest professional resources—their colleagues—within the context of an intentional learning community." Hickey and Sawyer make explicit the importance of the need to "walk the talk," modeling the inquiry dispositions they hope to foster, learning along with their teacher candidates and mentoring them in ways that they hope can be paralleled to benefit p-12 learners in future classrooms.

The third chapter in this section, *The Big "O": Occupying against Reductionism in Education Using Small and Sustained Actions* explicates

> What is largely unseen by the public—state mandates, initiatives that reduce teacher autonomy and create cultures of compliance created through public school policies and practices—is a web of causes and effects of lessening emphasis on human relationships in schools, and increased emphasis on control by profit-generating corporations.

To address the destructive forces and policies, Barbara Rose suggests that educators might apply the tenets of the grassroots "occupy" movements that have recently emerged. Focusing on the classrooms and communities in which teachers work, Rose argues, provides an optimal opportunity for a critique that can lead to transformative pedagogical experiences. Furthermore, the chapter extends past theoretical possibilities by providing concrete examples of

> small and sustained strategies (e.g., questioning practices and policies, exploring the cost and impact of accreditation culture, demanding data and transparency to support decisions and policies, developing student-centered pedagogy for curricula; exploring benefits and limitations of decisions) that can disrupt the impact of reductionism in teacher education.

In the final chapter in this section, *Ways of Being as an Alternative to the Limits of Teacher Dispositions*, Matthew J. Kruger-Ross applies the methodology of the researcher-bricoleur to define teaching dispositions in an alternative manner. Exploring alternative discourse around dispositions, the author develops and analyzes "two ways of being, teacher buy-in and fear towards technology...to identify the opportunities provided by using these ways of being to frame understanding the professional teacher." Kruger-Ross brings his chapter to a close by considering ramifications of his work and exploring prospects for future research.

Section 3: Practicing What We Teach

In the first chapter of this section, *Seeking Balance: Rethinking Who Decides the Role of Dispositions in Teacher Evaluation*, Mahoney and Ward provide critical insight as to the role dispositions are playing in education by examining who are the social actors currently determining "what dispositions matter for teaching." The authors begin the chapter by highlighting the historical trajectory of how theorists and scholars characterize dispositions in education from the "standpoint of standardization" to a "more teacher-centered framework of reflection." Unfortunately, according to the authors, the current trends "toward high-stakes teacher accountability have given the standards new power and influence over how the work of teaching is defined." Next, Mahoney and Ward argue the culture of standardization can be altered if "teachers and teacher educators" are committed to "reflection on dispositions as a critical component of meaningful evaluation." The authors also project "what the teacher accountability movement could mean in the near future" if the standardization movement continues to be embraced wholecloth in colleges and schools of education. After providing data from their empirical research that captures how beginning teachers were involved in an "interpretive search for who decides what dispositions matter," Mahoney and Ward conclude their chapter by arguing that the teaching profession can only be committed to students' intellectual and social development if "reflection and disposition development" are in "the hands of teachers, their students, and non-evaluating peers and coaches."

In the second chapter of this section, *Professional Dispositions for Teacher Candidates: From Standardization to Wisely Effective Classrooms*, Dunkle and Ahuna argue that schools of education must operate from a constructivist perspective if pre-service teachers are to generate their own understandings of the profession. The authors begin the chapter by detailing the nature of the five major models that are dedicated to "assessing professional dispositions" in teacher education and argue it is integral for schools of education to articulate what constitutes "dispositional intelligence." This process is needed if schoolteachers are able to support "notions of social justice and culturally responsive teaching." After explaining how education faculty can employ case studies and other real-life scenarios to guide pre-service teachers in becoming stewards of change, the authors conclude by arguing that professionalizing teaching is also vital for ensuring that future teachers are able to "meet the ever-evolving challenges before them."

In the third chapter of this section, *Teachers as Advocates for Democracy: Standardization of Public Education and Voter Participation*, Pineo-Jensen argues that teacher educators can guide pre-service teachers to become social justice advocates by activating their civic knowledge. According to the author, the process would consist of faculty positioning pre-service teachers to have the knowledge and skills to guide K-12 students to "participate in democracy at the most fundamental and most powerful level—by voting." After recounting "the historical rise and causes of educational standardization," the author "articulates the difference between standardization and differentiation in K-12 public education." Next, Pineo-Jensen highlights the "correlation between educational standardization and voter turnout for some recent years." She concludes the chapter by reminding teacher educators that teachers must have "the prerequisite thought processes and behaviors that foment voting" if K-12 classrooms are to become democratized during the 21st century.

In the fourth chapter of this section, *CSFE Principles: Wise and Effective Mechanisms to Translate Social Foundations Content to K-12 Classroom Practice*, Jacquelyn Benchik-Osborne examines the triadic connection among dispositions, standards, and the Social Foundations of Education (SFE) as a way to "help teachers" become multicultural educators and social-justice advocates. The chapter begins with the author articulating how "instructors apply the language of SFE to their instructional practice." Next, Benchik-Osborne looks specifically at how the Principles from the Council of Social Foundations of Education can become a vehicle "to demonstrate to student teachers how to combine the social world within teaching practice." After illuminating the importance of connecting democracy to the world of teaching and learning in K-12 classrooms, the author details the extent of the research that captures how the SFE improves "instructional delivery." Next, Benchik-Osborne shares her own research so as to caution us that the standards-based movement is sapping democratic impulses from many urban classrooms in the U.S. She states:

> Settings in which little or no connection to the CSFE Principles were evident, students engaged daily in isolated tasks. Teacher-led discussions, for example, focused exclusively on vocabulary from a basal reader in whole group format with little or no cultural connection. In one particular classroom, the fourth graders were failing numerous test assessments and the blame fell on the children. Little or no reflection as to the content delivery offered on the part of the teacher occurred.

The author concludes the chapter by giving us a sense of hope—hope that committed scholars and concerned educators can work collectively to ensure that schools of education take democracy, the SFE, and the needs of children seriously by producing good teachers.

In the final chapter, *Urban Teachers and Technology: Critical Reflections in the Age of Accountability*, Kate E. O'Hara culls data from her auto-ethnographic study of "the use and non-use of technology of urban teachers" and argues urban teachers' use of technology has the potential to "provide students with fair and equitable opportunities." She begins the chapter by documenting the numerous obstacles that schoolteachers face when implementing technology across the various content areas such as "economic factors, lack of professional development opportunities, and test driven practices." Next, the author illuminates how some schoolteachers, who believe in the potential of effective technology use on their students' learning, overcome obstacles to improve students' opportunities. For instance, her participants use:

> blogs, Wikis, and create digital projects that support the development of literacy, including digital and visual literacy; develop technology-based projects exposing students to issues related to copyright and fair use; engage in Internet research that uncovers multiple perspectives on a topic, and create videos and screencasts to aid in comprehension. And the examples do not end there. The teachers are often self-taught, using the technology as a true instructional tool, positively impacting and enhancing both their teaching and their students learning.

O'Hara concludes by generating ideas for using technology to facilitate culturally relevant and intellectually stimulating education, rather than employing technology as a means to control teachers' labor power and sap students' humanity.

Myths, Lies, AND Videotape

CHAPTER ONE

Practicing IN THE Panopticon

Teaching and Learning in the Surveillance Media Culture

JULIE GORLEWSKI, DAVID GORLEWSKI, AND CATHERINE LALONDE

INTRODUCTION

Like many educators, we embody our art, our craft, and our profession. We never stop thinking about teaching and learning—and thinking about how education influences, and is influenced by, the cultural constructions of identity and society that occur in everyday experiences. In this chapter, we explore the intersections among popular media culture, professional dispositions, and the field of education. Specifically, we investigate how selected reality television programs (*Frontline: The Education of Michelle Rhee*, the complete seven-episode run of *Teach Tony Danza*, and three episodes of *Undercover Boss)* portray the notion of professionalism, and how these portrayals relate to the experiences of teaching and learning.

The following research questions grounded our study: How is the concept of professionalism in the workplace represented in contemporary reality television? How do representations of professionalism, particularly with respect to leadership, learning, and culture, relate to the identity development of educators?

METHODOLOGY

The method of textual analysis is used to make explicit the social, political, and economic contexts in which the television episodes and documentary were produced, while also highlighting the messages about teachers, students, and educational sites embedded in each of the media artifacts (Bulman, 2005; Kellner, 1995). In the textual analyses, we situated the episodes and documentary in the social contexts in which they were produced by providing glimpses of the specific social, political, and economic landscapes surrounding each production. In relation to the television episodes, this analytical process helps to disrupt hyper-real (Baudrillard, 1983) representations of teachers and teaching in favor of a more critical perspective. Further, "[c]ultivation theory assumes that the 'television world' differs from our daily experiences, which leads heavy viewers to believe in the television world rather than real-world statistics" (Appel, 2008, p. 62). Contextualizing these episodes and the documentary is important in that we are better able to explore why these cultural artifacts were created in particular moments for particular purposes.

To address the concepts of education, professional dispositions, and media representations of these as expressed in our research question, we considered three programs: *Frontline: The Education of Michelle Rhee, Teach Tony Danza,* and *Undercover Boss. Frontline* provided a glimpse of leadership in K-12 schooling; *Teach Tony Danza* offered an on-the-ground depiction of an urban high school teaching experience; and *Undercover Boss* suggested a perspective on professionalism that reached beyond the field of education. Textual analysis of nearly 11 hours of video from these programs revealed three themes: the cult of personality, the ubiquity and influence of surveillance, and the persistence of the myth of meritocracy (represented as the American Dream).

RE-VIEWING *FRONTLINE: THE EDUCATION OF MICHELLE RHEE, TEACH TONY DANZA,* AND *UNDERCOVER BOSS*

Frontline: The Education of Michelle Rhee (2013) was promoted as an examination of "the legacy of one of America's most admired & reviled school reformers" (*Frontline*, 2013). As the tagline indicates, the 60-minute documentary claimed to have provided a complete portrait of Rhee, including biographical background as well as her professional experiences. Although it is not mentioned in the program, its airing coincided with the February 4, 2013, release of Rhee's book, *Radical: Fighting to Put Students First.* The *Frontline* documentary claimed that reporter John Merrow was given "unprecedented access" to Rhee during her tenure as chancellor of the Washington, D.C., public schools, so there is considerable footage of Rhee interacting with educators there. Although the piece raises gentle questions about the consequences, both positive and negative, of Rhee's influence, the validity of her celebrity status is never in doubt.

Teach Tony Danza (2010) is a reality television program featuring actor Tony Danza. The series focuses on the former star of the Emmy Award-winning sitcom *Taxi,* who uses his celebrity in order to fulfill his lifelong dream of being a teacher. The promos from the A&E network proclaim that Danza's newest endeavor, teaching, is "his toughest role yet." The actor, equipped only with a degree in History, is assigned a sophomore language arts class at Northeast High School in Philadelphia for a full school year. The seven one-hour episodes show Danza trying to juggle various aspects of teaching (e.g., engaging a diverse student population, lecturing, explaining course content, developing tests) with extracurricular activities, charity events, and interactions with administrators and colleagues. As the title implies, Tony Danza is being *taught* while serving as a teacher, and the viewers are often reminded of this.

Undercover Boss (2012) is another reality television program. Originating in the United Kingdom in 2009, *Undercover Boss* was first aired in the United States in February 2010. It received Emmy Award nominations in its first two seasons and won the "Outstanding Reality Program" award in 2012. In its weekly episodes, CEOs of large companies are followed on an individual basis when they pretend to be one of their own employees at different levels of their business. This enables them to infiltrate these levels, ostensibly to improve service and their profit margins. Each episode involves a brief exploration of the CEO's background (education, past and present family life, business experiences), a change in the CEO's appearance to "blend in" with their employees, the shadowing of four employees as they work, periodic introspective sequences when the CEO reflects on her/his experiences and, finally, a "big reveal," when the CEO meets with each employee and rewards or admonishes them for their work performance. The premise of *Undercover Boss* unites the three themes explored in this chapter, as the cult of personality of each CEO is manipulated through the process of layered surveillance to promote the meritocratic myth of the American Dream in the employees' lives.

The Cult of Personality: *The Education of Michelle Rhee*

A personality cult (or "cult of personality") is a system in which a leader is able to control a group of people through sheer force of his or her personality. Another aspect of the cult of personality is the individual's use of mass media to create an idealized, heroic, and, at times, god-like public image—resulting in what Max Weber (1978) called "charismatic authority." This portion of the chapter explores how the cult of personality manifests itself in the PBS *Frontline* documentary *The Education of Michelle Rhee.*

The narrator, correspondent John Merrow, begins the documentary by noting that "Michelle Rhee's journey to national prominence began in 2007," when she was selected by newly elected Washington, D.C., mayor Adrian Fenty to serve as the chancellor of the city's public schools. Though she had never run a school district, we learn that Rhee convinces Fenty that the sweeping changes she believes are needed "could be politically costly" and that she, as the chancellor and self-described "change agent," would absorb the political pushback. Rhee shares with viewers her initial conversation with the new mayor: "You are a politician. Your job is to keep the noise minimums to a level and to keep your constituents happy. I'm the change agent. And change doesn't come without significant pushback and opposition."

Though Michelle Rhee acknowledges that she never ran a school district, it should be pointed out that she never served in elected office either; yet she assumes to have an understanding of the political nature of her task, particularly in relation to Fenty, whose role as mayor she reduces to being "a politician" who merely has to keep his "constituents happy." It will be Rhee's self-assigned job to do the complex work of school reform. From the outset of the documentary, it is clear that Rhee is intent on creating a particular image of herself: reformer, crusader, challenger of the status quo—one that is quite distinct from Fenty's role.

Without having accomplished a single reform, Michelle Rhee presents herself as a "personality," someone unique to educational administration. The cameras begin rolling on the first day of school as Rhee introduces herself to the faculty and staff:

> I am Michelle Rhee. I'm the new chancellor of the D.C. public schools. And in case there was any confusion, I am, in fact, Korean. I am 37 years old. And, no, I have never run a school district before.

Given the cameras and her opening statement, Rhee sees herself as a focal point—someone (she assumes) that everyone is talking about. She takes this opportunity to clear up "any confusion" as if the entire school system is obsessed with her and her new position.

As Michelle Rhee's first months on the job unfold, cameras follow her everywhere. Narrator Merrow says: "Rhee met with each school principal one-on-one—*something no D.C. superintendent had ever done before* (emphasis added) — and had them (sic) commit to specific test score gains."

Later, based on teacher complaints that they were lacking supplies, Rhee goes personally to the district's warehouse. However, notes Merrow, "Recognizing a great photo opportunity, she invited the media to come along." There, Rhee finds science kits among many basic school supplies. Rhee's warehouse tour, says the narrator, "made the evening news and put central office bureaucrats on notice."

A portion of the documentary focuses on Rhee's "remarkably calm" personality as she closes schools and fights for (and wins) the right to fire principals. Says Merrow: "We saw that cool, detached side of Rhee several times; most notably, the afternoon she invited us to film this meeting with a principal." Though the

principal gave permission to film the meeting and though his face was intention-
ally obscured, he was totally unaware of the meeting's intent: Michelle Rhee had
decided to fire him on camera.

Afterwards, Merrow asks Rhee how it felt to terminate someone so publicly.
Rhee says, "I feel like I'm doing the right thing." She adds, "I have hired and fired
more people in my lifetime than almost anybody else."

The intentional use of the media (by filming selected portions of her day-
to-day job), the control of individuals (Mayor Fenty, legislators, principals), and the
making of god-like decisions (firing a principal on camera) present an irrefutable
case that Michelle Rhee uses the cult of personality as her primary operating tool.

In the end, Michelle Rhee could not separate her job from the world of politics and Mayor Adrian Fenty paid for it in the next election, suffering a crushing
defeat. With his ouster went Michelle Rhee, whose cultivation of celebrity and
personality has enabled her to command the attention, if not the admiration, of
millions of Americans.

The Cult of Personality: *Teach Tony Danza*

Though Michelle Rhee consciously cultivates the cult of personality by going from
an obscure school reformer to a national figure, Tony Danza enters the field of
education as a once famous television personality. Older viewers of the documentary
Teach Tony Danza remember him as the budding star in ABC's (and later, NBC's)
highly acclaimed sitcom, *Taxi*, which ran from 1978 to 1982, and as one of the main
characters in the ABC sitcom *Who's the Boss?*, which ran from 1984 to 1992.

In both sitcoms, Danza plays an athlete—a boxer with a losing record in *Taxi*
and a retired professional baseball player in *Who's the Boss?* The premise in *Teach
Tony Danza* is that the former television personality has decided that he wants to
"give back" to society by volunteering to become an English teacher in an inner
city Philadelphia high school for one year. Cameras follow him throughout the
day. After a time, it is apparent that Danza is teaching only one class (not five
classes, as is the typical load for a high school teacher) and that he is doing so
under the watchful eye of an assigned instructional coach.

It is evident from the outset that Tony Danza perceives himself not as a teacher trying to "give back" to society, but as a personality who sees his former fame as
the key to success in his new position. In the first episode, called "Back to School,"
Danza is seen working with the varsity football players as a volunteer coach. In
a voice-over, he says, "I'm from Malibu Beach. What am I doing here?" Though
Danza volunteered for this assignment, in this scene, the viewer is expected to
reflect on the horrible situation in which Danza finds himself, that is, a celebrity
from Malibu stuck in Philadelphia. In the same episode, he is seen bringing in a
birthday cake to the building principal and singing "Happy Birthday" to her in

the corridor in front of numerous students and staff. In fact, Danza's singing and dancing skills are exhibited in almost every episode.

In the third episode, entitled, "Just Say No," Danza says, "I'm spreading myself a little thin." The viewers learn that he has been asked by the mayor of Philadelphia to serve as master of ceremonies at an upcoming function. In the meantime, Danza has also been asked (or he volunteers; the viewer is never sure) to choreograph a musical production *and* to help coach the football team. Implicit in the requests for Danza's time is that his celebrity and concomitant talents make him both a hero (tapping into his skill set) and a victim (everyone wants a piece of him).

In these episodes, we also see Danza trying to teach. He reads aloud (and quite theatrically) from a student's paper; he attempts to teach the plot of Steinbeck's *Of Mice and Men*; and he administers his first quiz (the results of which are dismal). But his celebrity and personality do not translate as easily in the classroom. Unlike the adults who request Danza's services, the students do not know Danza as a television star. Because they were born a decade *after* Danza's last sitcom went off the air, he appears to them to be nothing more than a struggling teacher. And we know he is struggling because his voice-overs continuously allude to his daily difficulties. But the cult of personality does not allow Danza to point the finger of failure at himself (with his lack of teacher training and lack of content knowledge). Instead, Danza blames student failure exclusively on the students. He tells the viewers that special education students have been told, "they can't do it" (as if effort alone could offset special needs). He says that the "teachable moment is when we learn that hard work pays off."

In the fourth episode, "Homesick," Danza inserts himself into yet another school activity: the marching band. He is also seen walking through the corridors and interacting with virtually everyone he sees; but the interactions are all "one-way," with Danza making jokes and comments, and asking rhetorical questions; but he is never seen *listening*. When he does allow for others to speak (as he does when he meets with administrators), his eyes are lifeless, he makes no eye contact, and he comes across as profoundly disengaged; he doesn't nod his head or provide any visual indicators that he understands what is being communicated. It is as if he is thinking: as a high profile personality, what could these professional educators possibly tell me that I don't already know?

In that same episode, Danza organizes an after-school study group, which is attended by four female students. The review session quickly moves off-topic with Danza telling the (captive audience) students how he proposed to his future wife. How this anecdote is related to review for the upcoming test (which is the *purpose* of the study group) is lost on the viewers. Later, when one of Danza's high-achieving students asks why he did so poorly on the unit test, Danza says, "Well, first of all, you didn't go to the study group." The implication is that compliance (attending the study group) enhanced the chances of a better grade.

Perhaps the most telling aspect of Danza's celebrity status occurred in the sixth episode, "To Cheat or Not to Cheat." After months on the job, the camera shows Danza struggling. Some of his students, particularly the boys, seem withdrawn, and various conflicts emerge between and among individuals and groups. At one point, Danza, frustrated with the noise level and complete lack of attention, says, "That's it. I give up." And he leaves the room. He then positions himself in the corridor where he receives maximum attention from anyone who passes by. Subsequently, several students are seen putting together a huge "I'm Sorry" card, which they all sign and present to him to apparently make up for their bad behavior. Danza is moved by this gesture and takes it as an indicator that he has "gotten through to them." The cult of personality wins again.

In the final episode, "Teacher's Pet," Danza is shown to have a difficult time teaching students how to write a five-paragraph essay. But this lesson is merely the back-drop for the personality/celebrity-driven climax: a musical production called *Extravadanza*. While having his students work in the school library on their essays, Danza comments on how uncomfortably hot the room is. He then decides to organize a fundraiser to purchase an air conditioning system for the library. Danza even makes a production of the announcement by having a Dave Lennox (the air conditioning symbol) character appear in an assembly. Throughout the episode, it is evident that Danza knows a great deal about singing and dancing—and very little about how to teach the five-paragraph essay. Clips of students working on their essays are mixed with after-school practice sessions for the *Extravadanza* production. The difference is stark: As a teacher, Danza's celebrity buys him nothing of substance; but as the producer and director of *Extravadanza*, he is in his element.

On the surface, the clever title, *Teach Tony Danza*, is meant to show how much the former television star had learned by teaching for a year in an urban high school. But, in reality, the cult of personality never allows Danza to learn much of anything. He never really identifies with his co-workers; he merely gives the *impression* of identifying with them. In many respects, he also gives a superficial representation of what a teacher is and what a teacher does. In the end, Tony Danza was not a teacher; he simply played one on TV.

The Cult of Personality: *Undercover Boss*

Given the premise of this reality television program, that a "boss" is "undercover," three points should be noted: The first is that the boss is so well known and so very different from the average employee, that he/she must be *disguised* in order to learn about the intricacies of the organization. The second is related to the type of disguise. In other words, specifically how are these bosses disguised to make them look like the average employee? And third, during the episode's dramatic conclusion, how does the boss reveal his/her identity? These aspects of *Undercover Boss* are revealed in three episodes analyzed in this study: "Mood Media," "Cinnabon," and "Moe's Southwest Grill—Atlanta," and, collectively, they offer insights into the cult of personality.

"Mood Media" follows the undercover activities of CEO Lorne Abony, who presents himself as a self-made man raised by a "single mom"; a man whose father was a "no-show" at Lorne's various graduations (we are told he has two law degrees and a master's degree from Columbia Business School).

Much is made of Abony's disguise. To make him look like a "regular" employee, Abony grows a beard, is outfitted with fake tattoos, and dons a wig and a pair of dark-framed glasses. When fully disguised, the viewers see Abony Skyping with his wife and young daughter and son the morning of his first day on the job. He is now officially an employee named Beau. Noting the quizzical look on his daughter's face, Abony asks, "Does daddy look funny?" Later, an employee named Leila comments on Abony's teeth, noting that she had never worked with anyone with such white teeth. "You've got the look; you've got the attitude," she says, giving her personal assessment of her temporary colleague. Here, the viewer is shown that, even when disguised, the true personality of the boss (charismatic, commanding) emerges.

In "Cinnabon," viewers meet company president Kat Cole who, like Lorne Abony, is a product of a broken home and, in her case, a dysfunctional (Vietnam veteran) father. Her particular disguise is a badly fitting blonde wig, which features a hard-to-miss pink stripe along the left side.

In "Moe's Southwest Grill—Atlanta," CEO Paul Damico is transformed into employee "Mark Richards" by adding a wig and a tattoo, along with a set of tacky sideburns and a goatee. This, the viewers are to assume, is what typical employees look like.

The conclusion of all *Undercover Boss* episodes, as the voice-over tells us, is called "The Boss Reveals His Identity." Despite the unique natures of the respective businesses, the "boss reveals" segments are strikingly similar. In the three episodes studied, the show culminates in the employees being summoned to corporate headquarters. At these meetings, the "boss" reveals his/her identity and, as a staple of the show, proceeds to offer assistance to the employees in the form of cash, services, or training, all of which are consistent with the needs revealed by those employees during their one-on-one interactions earlier in the program.

What is most interesting about these segments is the *way* the identity is revealed; that is, the *circumstances* under which the true identity is made known to the employees. In each episode, the employee is filmed seated in a waiting room outside the boss's office (no secretary is visible). There is a pervasive sense of isolation and dread. The narrated voice-over gives a refresher on the employee's name, and video snippets are played showing the employee interacting with the boss from earlier in the show. With no transition, we see the employee walking into the boss's office (somewhat sheepishly since they are unsure of the purpose of the meeting); no one greets them at the door or leads them into the office; as they enter, they see the boss seated behind a desk in a clearly imperious fashion. The point, of course, is to shock the employees, a few of whom recognize the boss immediately while the majority has to be told explicitly. Typically, bosses are heard asking, "Do you know who I am?" Discomfort, fear, and uncertainty are maximized. When the recognition occurs, viewers are treated to the understandably surprised reactions of the employees. The circumstances surrounding this segment seem to run counter to every other aspect of the show's overriding message, which is to be customer-centered and service-oriented. The various bosses expect their employees to make customers feel comfortable and welcomed; yet, in this segment, the viewer gets the sense that we are witnessing the convergence of two wildly disparate social classes—that power and wealth is summoning the working class to offer a pat on the head and token rewards for their efforts. The "personality" here is virtual royalty dispensing gifts to the poor. And, somehow, that is supposed to represent the manager/worker relationship in America today.

MERITOCRACY AND INDIVIDUALISM

Identities are constructed in a social context and are affected by the discursive messages that saturate social interactions. Professional identities, as one aspect of a person's sense of self, are influenced by ideologies perpetuated in popular media. In the U.S. today, the norms of identity and professionalism represented in popular media "model the normative neoliberal worker and learner—roles which are increasingly drawn together" (Windle, 2010, p. 251).

A society shaped by neoliberal norms is focused on the drive to meet the ever-increasing demands of a capitalistic economic structure; an outgrowth of this focus is the need to develop workers who are "supple, adaptable and willing learner(s)" (Windle, 2010, p. 251).

Vassallo (2013) explained:

> Neoliberalism is an economic philosophy underpinned by the logic that a free market best supports economic prosperity and well-being. Researchers argue that in order for the free market to function properly subjectivities must be constituted in ways that legitimize neoliberal relations (Apple, 2006; Fitzsimons, 2011). That is, the subject must be (re)defined in terms of human capital and self-management, and must be guided by an imperative to pursue a kind of self-improvement that is aligned with an economic rationality. (n.p.)

The representations of participants in the television productions analyzed serve as what Windle (2010) called ideological exemplars for the management of disappointment, the cultivation of hope and the maintenance of belief in meritocracy. Compliance, effort, just desserts, and luck are emphasised in programs that offer viewers self-narratives that allow them to account for both their own circumstances and wider inequalities. (p. 251)

One who believes in the power of meritocracy adheres to the notion that "anyone from anywhere can succeed, if they are bright enough, based solely on their individual talent and effort" (Tannock, 2009, p. 202). While the meritocratic ideals are portrayed as beneficial in terms of social mobility, talent development, and technological progress, Tannock is dubious about its roots and effects: "Global meritocracy, as currently invoked, is a transparently elite project: it promotes corporate interests, elevates competition and pursuit of competitiveness as central organizing principles of world society, and reinforces the neoliberal agenda of liberalizing world labor markets" (p. 202).

Analyses of *Frontline: The Education of Michelle Rhee, Teach Tony Danza*, and *Undercover Boss* reveal echoes of meritocracy consistent with the neoliberal agenda. Although messages are various and plentiful, this section of the chapter will focus on compliance, effort, and competition—all of which reinforce the idea that if workers try hard, they will be richly rewarded.

Frontline: The Education of Michelle Rhee

Two aspects of the *Frontline* documentary relate directly to meritocracy. First, a meritocracy differs from a democracy; democratic principles do not require individuals to compete in order to have a voice. Second, Michelle Rhee righteously promotes competition as the means to school improvement. Both of these messages are established in the documentary.

At the outset, Rhee refers to the need to take charge of Washington, D.C.'s, school reform initiative, stating that, "We're not running this school district through the democratic process.... No, it's not a democracy." She proclaims this with great pride, the assumption being that *she* knows best and that democracy (where *everyone* has a voice) is deficient in terms of conceiving and implementing school improvement. This echoes Giroux's (2013) points about violence and the culture of cruelty that contributes to the construction of a pedagogy of violence:

Representations of violence dominate the media and often parade before viewers less as an object of critique than as a for-profit spectacle, just as the language of violence and punishment now shapes the U.S. culture—with various registers of violence now informing school zero-tolerance policies, a bulging prison-industrial complex, and the growing militarization of everyday life. There is also the fact that as neoliberalism and its culture of cruelty weaves its way through the culture, it makes the work place, schools, and other public spheres sites of rage, anger, humiliation, and misery, creating the foundation for blind rebellion against what might be termed intolerable conditions.

> Accepting the logic of radical individual responsibility, too many Americans blame themselves for being unemployed, homeless, and isolated and end up perceiving their misery as an individual failing and hence are vulnerable to forms of existential depression and collective rage. (p. 2)

In sharp contrast to Freire's liberatory pedagogy, Rhee's words and actions represent a public pedagogy of violence consistent with neoliberalism.

Competition is another critical aspect of Rhee's school reform initiative. She sets up a system in which schools must compete in order to show improvement (with "improvement" being determined exclusively through student achievement on standardized tests). "Winning" schools are publicly recognized and receive monetary rewards; educators in "losing" schools are subject to punishments that include involuntary transfers and possible job loss. Although close examination of these consequences reveals a certain dissonance from meritocracy (since students' scores—over which teachers have limited influence—are the only accepted metric for success), the message is powerful: there are winners and losers. Winners are rewarded with money and recognition, and losers are subject to humiliation and penalties.

Teach Tony Danza

In the *Frontline* program, host John Merrow explains Rhee's approach:

> Rhee brought those high expectations to her new job, but now she was aiming them at school principals. If you didn't measure up to her standards, you'd be out. By the end of the first year, she fired 24 of them.

This notion of high standards and the constant threat of removal also exist throughout *Teach Tony Danza*. In the first episode, the school principal says to Danza: "If this doesn't work out, you're outta here!" (this exchange recurs as a promotional clip throughout the episode). The precarious nature of Danza's position is emphasized from his first moments on the job when he is summoned over the PA system to report to the main office where an assistant principal scolds him for not "signing in" when he arrived in the morning. The assistant principal's attitude and diction is demeaning; Danza is unnerved and repeatedly messes up the simple task of signing in, putting his name in the wrong spot. The incident ends with the assistant principal admonishing Danza for being "vain" and instructing him to put on his glasses. While Danza's position in the school might be deservedly uncertain—since his qualifications are dubious—his introduction to the school (and the audience for the program) undoubtedly highlights the subordinate nature of his role as teacher. It is evident that if he doesn't measure up—regardless of the arbitrary, capricious, and sometimes unstated standards—he will be dismissed. In this case, since no instructional abilities were involved in this particular event, Danza is being reminded of the importance of compliance.

Danza's approach to special education is informative. When the special education students in his class ask him if they could complete their tests in an alternate location, as mandated in their individual education plans, Danza denies their request. He openly disregards the need for resource room assistance, referring to it as "a crutch" and stating that he believes that the students should "try harder." He claims that the real challenge for special education students is their poor attitude, which, he believes, contributes to a lack of effort: "That's what's wrong with these kids—they don't think they can do it." He also asserts, in the presence of certified special education teachers, that "effort will almost eliminate the learning disability." At one point, in reference to his deficient teaching skills, Danza states, "I hate not being good at something. It's driving me nuts!" This is ironic, since he insists that his students just need to "try harder," but he never questions his own effort as it relates to his teaching ability.

In the episode "Tested," over half of the students fail Danza's quiz. The comments of two students indicate that these results might reflect Danza's abilities. One student suggests: "If he's a first-time teacher, who knows if he can even make a test?" Another is more definitive: "If more than half the class did horrible, then obviously it's something the teacher did." Tony, confident in the meritocratic belief that his own effort will produce higher student achievement, responds to these dismal results by saying, "Most kids don't wanna read" and "I'm sure it's not me. What bothers me is their lack of effort."

In this neoliberal version of the realities of teaching and learning, the implication is that effort is regulated through a hierarchical process; that is, supervisors (and those with surveillance capacities) must continuously ensure that their workers are fully exerting themselves. This interpretation of the ideological framework explains why Danza doubts his students' efforts while simultaneously trumpeting the virtues of his own work ethic, as demonstrated by his remark at the end of the first episode: "This is the hardest thing I've ever done in my life."

The opposite of the meritocratic belief in effort leading to success is the notion that failure is blamed on the individual. This idea is illustrated in an episode entitled "Teacher's Pet." There, Danza tries to counsel students who are chronically absent and, consequently, suspended from classes. In one exchange with a male student, Danza suggests that the student should assume responsibility as a first step toward turning his life around:

Danza: Have some self-discipline!
Student: I had to sit in jail while my mom died.
Danza: Whose fault is that?

Danza's response is deceptively simple. On the surface, he is asking the student to take responsibility for being in jail. However, this interpretation of the exchange omits the multifaceted nature of power and agency in society. It might be worth applying the "whose fault is that?" query to the other parts of the student's statement. For example, whose fault is it that his mom died (while he was in jail)? Would self-discipline have changed the loss of a parent? Moreover, decades of research have corroborated the inequities of the criminal justice system; the question of blame does not include any contextual nuance.

Undercover Boss

This series, which originated in the United Kingdom and has since been replicated in the United States, Austria, Canada, France, Germany, and Norway, follows a formula that represents a storyboard for a meritocratic plot. In this show, CEOs are portrayed as so dedicated to their corporate standards (usually framed in terms of customer satisfaction), that they are willing to assume the identities of ordinary workers in order to learn how the organization works from the ground level. At the end of each episode, as noted earlier, some employees are rewarded and others are offered additional training or improved working conditions. The characteristics of rewarded employees are consistent across episodes: to reap the greatest gift from the CEO, workers must exhibit behaviors and attitudes that *mirror those that the CEO attributes to his or her own success*. Like the CEO, workers seen as exemplary are extraordinarily hard-working and ambitious, and utterly committed to maintaining (and often raising) the standards of the corporation—however menial their positions may be. In addition, "winners" in this worker lottery are also optimistic, virtuous, and kind; they are portrayed as nurturing providers who care for children, parents, co-workers, and even—often as part of the boss's transformative experience—the CEO him/herself. Examples of features that promote a meritocratic perspective are numerous, so one from each of the three analyzed episodes is provided.

In *Undercover Boss*, Season 4, in an episode entitled, "Cinnabon," CEO Kat Cole describes the "mantras" that shape her life. Two of them are "Make it happen" and "Figure it out." Highly reflective of a meritocratic belief system, these creeds illustrate the belief that individuals control their own destinies. A third mantra is "Some people may be left behind," a doctrine that acknowledges two aspects of meritocracy. First, it is accepted as unavoidable that the system is a competitive endeavor that will result in winners and losers (in contrast to notions of solidarity or community). This principle echoes the "if you can't cut it, you're outta here" idea that was reinforced in both *The Education of Michelle Rhee* and *Teach Tony Danza*. Extending this viewpoint, Cole reveals her perspective toward her workers: "Be sure you really are as hungry as you say you are. I might be able to find someone hungrier." This highlights the need for workers to demonstrate continuous, ongoing effort as well as the notion that deserving workers are highly motivated and ambitious in the service of the corporation.

Each *Undercover Boss* episode features a "How I Grew Up" segment, which offers a glimpse into the events and relationships that have influenced the respective CEO's development. In discussing her background, Cole explains that she had to "step up and be responsible" and says, "people who grew up like me have a desire to be successful." An underlying message is that workers whose lives and characteristics resemble those of the CEO are lauded and rewarded. Cole's childhood included a largely absent father and circumstances bordering on poverty. Cole pursued a climb up the corporate ladder of Hooters by dropping out of college at age 19 and making that restaurant chain her exclusive focus. This enabled her to become vice-president of the company by age 26. As part of presenting background about Cole, her mentor (who was the focus of a previous *Undercover Boss* episode) tells her, "You are very good at what you do, which is why you are where you are." This pull-yourself-up-by-your- bootstraps perspective echoes the idea of a meritocracy, because through effort, ability, and grit, Cole lives the rags-to-riches American dream. In Cole's case, however, education is not prized in this process.

Emphasizing the individualism that is a central motif of the series, all the CEOs are initially presented to their co-workers as entry-level employees who are seeking a fresh start. Typically, they are portrayed as "failed" business owners or striving career-changers. Further cementing the dramatic irony, workers are informed that they will be judging the "new employees" and determining whether their dreams will come true. In reality, of course, the workers are being evaluated without their knowledge. As bit players in the drama in which the CEO is clearly the protagonist, the workers "play" themselves and are assessed on the basis of personal dispositions and professional behaviors. The primary focus of the program is to reveal the bosses' transformative experience, an experience that includes transforming the lives of the workers. The theme that is repeated at the start of each show (that "s/he will discover the truth") stresses the program's focus on the boss as proxy for the corporation. Throughout the series, each corporation is humanized through the boss who is often shown as fallible at simple tasks but ultimately revealed as virtuous, humane, and philanthropic.

Commenting on his *Undercover Boss* experience, Cole's mentor adds, "It's not as easy as people think. It's not scripted; it's real. Doing the show was amazing— not the business part, the emotional part." Regarding the workers that Cole will interact with, he explains, "This is their livelihood. Emotionally, it will be different. You'll be a different person when it's over." It is interesting that, for the workers, what is filmed *is* undeniably real; the jobs *are* their livelihood and, presumably, if they don't perform well they could be fired. For the boss, however, the experience is surreal: the stakes are low and mainly involve being filmed in embarrassing situations such as being unable to keep up with the physical demands of their jobs (conditions that might be expected as a brand new trainee). The more meaningful aspect of the experience for the bosses exists on a different plane; it concerns improving the business by understanding it better and, in the process, having *their* lives transformed. The deserving workers are given material wealth to transform their lives, but the boss is supposed to be transformed *emotionally*.

Perhaps the strongest example of meritocracy across any of the analyzed episodes is linked with Miguel, a Cinnabon employee who is working hard to earn money to purchase his own franchise. As a result of Cole's recognition of his hard work, he will now get one. Miguel's quote after discovering this underscores meritocratic principles. He tells the viewers: "Never give up. Always believe, believe, believe in your dreams. Hard work will *always* pay off."

SURVEILLANCE: TOWERING OVER CELLS

American society has been monitoring teachers' professional behavior and performance for decades via popular culture (Hollywood movies, television shows, etc.) and standardized testing processes, the latter of which have reached a fever pitch through legislation such as *No Child Left Behind* and *Race to the Top* (Wood, 2004). In relation to movie- and television-based portrayals of teachers, we usually see "good" teachers pitted against "bad" teachers, with teacher identities tending to be constructed more as black-and-white caricatures and less as fallible human beings living and working in contextualized gray spaces. "Put another way, the fact that we see teachers in such extreme terms—as angelically good, as horrifyingly bad—may in fact be an indication that we don't see them at all" (Alsop, 2012, para. 16). By analyzing a documentary based on Michelle Rhee, episodes of *Teach Tony Danza*, and episodes of *Undercover Boss*, what connections can be made between perceptions of "professional educators" and American workers in the service industry in the context of neoliberal-based systems of surveillance? What layers of surveillance are evident throughout individual and broad interactions in the documentary and television episodes, and in what ways do celebrity and self-surveillance come into play?

Frontline: The Education of Michelle Rhee

Michelle Rhee began her tenure as Chancellor of Education in Washington, D.C., with the knowledge that the schools there had been consistently struggling. Her solution was to use an annual standardized test called the D.C. Comprehensive Assessment System (CAS) to track students' academic achievement based on these scores—and to use the scores to gauge teachers' and administrators' (specifically, principals) performance, ultimately determining whether or not to retain these critical school personnel. This process of surveillance effectively positioned teach-ers and administrators as "under the gun," which led to responses ranging from resistance to using the test scores as evaluative measures of teacher performance, to accusations of "test erasures," wherein teachers allegedly altered students' tests to increase scores (these remain accusations only, as they have not been confirmed through multiple investigations—another level of surveillance).

While Rhee found ongoing support from the mayor who hired her for the Chancellor position, she met resistance not only from teachers and administrators but also from community members, especially when a plan surfaced that reflected her intention to close about two dozen schools and redistribute resources to other schools. One parent and community member, Philip Blair, stated,

> You can't yank them out of the ground they're in and move them somewhere else and expect that program to work! I'm telling you that you are not being serious about taking parent and community input into account.... It is a done deal. Now, I understand this situ-ation. (http://www.pbs.org/wgbh/pages/frontline/education/education-of-michelle-rhee/transcript-35/)

In this parent's statement, we see his realization of the panopticon at work, posi-tioning him firmly in place as a "cell" to Rhee's "tower" of authoritarian control, and he ultimately becomes disinvested in the situation and succumbs to that power as a form of self-surveillance.

Teach Tony Danza

From the first episode of *Teach Tony Danza*, Danza positions himself as constantly surveilling *himself* in relation to being a teacher and not a celebrity, drawing on stories from his struggles in school rather than those associated with his celebrity status. He is not alone in this respect, as his celebrity status, amplified by the cameras that follow him everywhere, constantly reminds everyone around him to engage in an ongoing evaluation of his "performance" as a teacher. As noted ear-lier, Danza is introduced to one of the official layers of the panopticon at work in schools by one of the assistant principals, who calls him to the office via the P.A. system and proceeds to chastise him for not signing in upon arriving, culminating in the comment, "Don't be vain, Mr. Danza," when noting that he should put on his eyeglasses to facilitate signing his name. The latter comment can certainly be tied to Danza's perceived vanity in relation to his celebrity status, but the other interactions likely reflect the standard approach with all school personnel at that institution—namely, being positioned as a worker in relation to a body of rules for procedures and "professional" conduct. "As an ideology, teacher professionalism succeeds, but structurally, teaching is not a profession" (Altenbaugh, 1991, as cited in Bushnell, 2003, p. 267), as is evidenced by the assistant principal's interaction with Danza. However, when students hear a teacher called to the office over the P.A. system and perhaps see the individual chastised by the school's administration, this works to limit the teacher's power, both in and out of the classroom. Hence, we "need to consider how surveillance restricts the power of school workers and constructs teaching as a semiprofession" (Bushnell, 2003, p. 252). Through the *consistent* use of these kinds of surveillance with teachers, the strength needed to call these aspects of the panopticon into question gradually wanes to the level of struggling to survive.

Danza's students also analyze his teaching abilities and performance as a professional educator. During the third episode, his students critique his lateness to a charity event as unprofessional, calling into question his dedication to these activities and to them. In this way, we see the power shift to the cells in the panopticon, rather than resting with Danza or the administration; this isn't just the "tower of Tony" trained on the students, because those students are processing media images of teachers as well as engaging with other teachers in school on a daily basis. In this and other instances where the students question Danza's professionalism and engagement in the classroom, they are highlighting the idea that "even people who hold positive professional dispositions must continually combine knowledge, skills and reflection to find ways that make sense when confronted with challenging classroom [or other school-related] experiences" (Tindle et al., 2011, p. 32). In this way, rather than using the same or similar approach to disengaged or struggling students, or compromising the success of school-related events, Danza's students are indicating the importance of generating skills that will enable teachers to reflect on and respond to contextualized circumstances.

Not all student-related comments about Danza and his teaching performance can lead to those more nuanced teaching practices outlined in the previous paragraph, as the presence of the camera during their classroom lessons and other school-related interactions clearly influence their responses to Danza and his teaching methods. For instance, in the sixth episode, Danza has a particularly challenging time trying to engage his students, so he leaves the classroom crying toward the end of that session. While the students begin chastising themselves ("Oh my god, we are horrible people!" "I feel so bad."), a critical viewer should be concerned that these students are being manipulated and exploited to feed other viewers' interest in the television show. Also, the students seem to play into the presence of the camera, with one female student motivating the others to help her create an "I'm Sorry" card, sign it and present it to Danza as an apology for his emotional outburst. We are given a glimpse of how "unreal" this response is when the instructional coach, who observes each of Danza's classes, notes that he never received a similar card following one of his rare frustrated outbursts. It is important to note in relation to this series of interactions that "[t]he identities of teachers are constructed not only by individuals themselves but also through how others view them and through their interactions with others, including students, their own families, other educators, and the general public" (Bushnell, 2003, p. 257). Whether the camera was present or not, the panopticon would be at work in Danza's classroom, but it adds another layer, a window to an unknown audience, of which students are aware—students who are also in danger of being exploited by that same open connection.

The "student layer" of surveillance is complicated when analyzing perceptions of students as a whole versus individual students. In relation to all students at the school, Danza notes in the first episode that he is there to learn specifically about "urban schools." The perceptions embodied in "urban" are made clear during the fifth episode (which focused on implementing a new school uniform policy) and the sixth episode (during which Danza chaperones a dance). In both episodes, the viewer is presented with stereotypical perceptions of "urban youth," in that female students, in particular, are expected to violate the new school uniform policy on multiple levels that reflect sexualized attire, and that all students are expected to engage in "risqué" dancing at the school dance. Giroux (1996) would refer to these representations as reflecting the "crisis of youth," with youth understood "as a social and political category in an age of increasing symbolic, material, and institutional violence, and the crisis of youth is represented through the imagery and discourse of popular culture" (p. 10). While a few students weigh in on the new school uniforms (offering both support and opposition to them), the majority of commentary about the school dance is gathered from school personnel.

Undercover Boss

Throughout the *Undercover Boss* episodes reviewed ("Cinnabon," "Mood Media," and "Moe's Southwest Grill"), surveillance is reflected in the storylines by the CEOs' evaluations of their workers at each site, as well as by the camera that tracks these interactions. Surveillance is also reflected by the producers of the show with their highly edited and stylized workers' stories of meritocracy (that are meant to produce compliant responses from workers among the television viewing audiences). The CEOs dress according to what they (and likely the producers) perceive to be blue collar workers' attire, which tends to fall short of convincing their employees. For instance, during the "Moe's Southwest Grill" episode, Tito, a manager at one of the franchises, perceives Damico's tattoos as reflecting how Damico "wants to be younger," rather than blending in with his colleagues.

Another aspect of surveillance moving throughout each episode is exemplified at the end of the "Mood Media" episode, when the CEO reunites with his long-estranged father. In this culminating reunion, we see how "the commodified circulation of affect, as well as generating direct profits for television producers, plays a role in socialization [sic] that was previously the preserve of family, schooling, church and civil society" (Clough, 2003; Skeggs & Wood, 2008a, as cited in Windle, 2010, p. 254). Hence, we find that the seemingly harmless reunion of a father and son becomes an opportunity for television producers to parlay this affective scene into "selling" meritocratic notions of business- *and* family-oriented success, wrapping up the episode's storyline with a bow that producers *know* viewers are avidly watching and buying into, thereby mobilizing the "normal" happy ending typically associated with the panopticon in *Undercover Boss*.

CONCLUSION

Using critical media literacy to focus the method of textual analysis enables a deeper understanding of how visual texts reinforce particular perceptions about teaching, professional dispositions, and power relationships. Here, we have used this critical lens to expose the cult of personality, meritocracy and panopticism flowing through the documentary *Frontline: The Education of Michelle Rhee*, and from episodes of *Teach Tony Danza* and *Undercover Boss*. For instance, the premise of *Undercover Boss* unites the three themes explored in this chapter, as the cult of personality of each CEO is manipulated through the process of layered surveillance to promote the meritocratic myth of the American Dream in the employees' lives.

While we selected these visual texts to amplify the central issues of this chapter, critical citizens should subject any visual artifacts or other cultural forms of entertainment (e.g., music, performance art, theater, digital media) to this kind of contextual analysis, for "[w]ithout critique, visual media may perpetuate commodification of the historical and cultural 'other,' even when this is the very discourse a film aims to undermine" (Bellino, 2011, p. 105). In the face of persistent neoliberal policies and practices, critical media analysis should be a part of the P-12 curriculum at all levels, and especially among teacher candidates, to lay the groundwork for sustained critical analysis of visual texts and other artifacts in order to promote democratic political engagement among a citizenry. Further, this ability should be considered a part of educators' professional dispositions as "media literacy is more effectively conceptualized as a lifelong 'thinking disposition' that facilitates critical consumption and inquiry of all media forms in all consumption contexts" (Bellino, 2011, p. 102). If we help our teacher candidates develop this skill, then they can use it to question (and possibly disrupt) cultural artifacts in their own lives *and* help their P-12 students develop this ability, potentially leading to more widespread, critical movement in society. In this way, classrooms become spaces for uniting teachers and students; and "[c]ollectively critiquing popular films for their flaws and inaccuracies invites students to build on socially acquired knowledge, challenge unexplored assumptions, resist the seduction of daily visual media exposure, and engage in the act of historical thinking" (Bellino, 2011, p. 109). As teachers consistently reinforce these critical skills and dispositions, students would then be able to apply them outside the classroom, turning their critical lenses on their own communities, and possibly leading to lifelong critical social engagement.

REFERENCES

Alsop, E. (2012). Not so hot for teacher. *The New York Times*. Retrieved from http://www.nytimes.com/2012/09/16/magazine/not-so-hot-for-teacher.html?_r=1&emc=etal

Appel, M. (2008). Fictional narratives cultivate just-world beliefs. *Journal of Communication, 58*, 62–83.

Baudrillard, J. (1983). *Simulations*. New York, NY: Semiotext(e).

Bellino, M. (Spring/Summer, 2011). Historical understanding and media literacy: A dispositional alignment. *International Journal of Social Education, 23*(1), 99–117.

Bulman, R. C. (2005). *Hollywood goes to high school: Cinema, schools, and American culture*. New York, NY: Worth.

Bushnell, M. (2003). Teachers in the schoolhouse panopticon: Complicity and resistance. *Education and Urban Society, 35*, 251–72. doi: 10.1177/0013124503035003001

Frontline: The education of Michelle Rhee (2013). Retrieved from http://www.pbs.org/wgbh/pages/frontline/education-of-michelle-rhee/

Giroux, H. A. (1996). *Fugitive cultures: Race, violence, and youth*. New York, NY: Routledge.

Infinito, J. (Spring, 2003). Ethical self-formation: A look at the later Foucault. *Educational Theory, 53*(2), 155–71.

Kellner, D. (1995). *Media culture: Cultural studies, identity and politics between the modern and the postmodern*. New York, NY: Routledge.

Kitchens, J. (2009). Situated pedagogy and the situationist international: Countering a pedagogy of placelessness. *Educational Studies, 45*, 240–61. doi: 10.1080/00131940902910958

McKnight, D. (Summer, 2004). An inquiry of NCATE's move into virtue ethics by way of dispositions (is this what Aristotle meant?). *Educational Studies, 35*(3), 212–30. doi: 10.1207/s15326993es3503_2

Tindle, K., Freund, M., Belknap, B., Green, C., & Shotel, J. (Spring, 2011). The urban teacher residency program: A recursive process to develop professional dispositions, knowledge, and skills of candidates to teach diverse students. *Educational Considerations, 38*(2), 28–35.

Weber, Max. (1978). *Economy and Society: An Outline of Interpretive Sociology*. (2 vols.). Edited by Guenther Roth and Claus Wittich, translated by a number of scholars. Berkeley, CA: University of California Press.

Winfrey Freeburg, B., & Workman, J. E. (2010). Media frames regarding teacher dress: Implications for career and technical education teacher preparation. *Career and Technical Education Research, 35*(1), 29–45. doi: 10.5328/cter35.103

Wood, G. (2004). A view from the field: NCLB's effects on classrooms and schools. In D. Meier & G. Wood (Eds.), *Many children left behind: How the No Child Left Behind Act is damaging our children and our schools* (pp. 33–50). Boston, MA: Beacon Press.

FILMOGRAPHY

Fanning, D. (Executive producer). (January 8, 2013). The education of Michelle Rhee [Television episode]. *Frontline*. New York, NY: PBS.

Jackson, D. (Director). (2010). Back to school [Television series episode 1]. In N. Briscoe (Producer), *Teach: Tony Danza*. Beverly Hills, CA: The Greif Company.

Jackson, D. (Director). (2010). Tested [Television series episode 2]. In N. Briscoe (Producer), *Teach: Tony Danza*. Beverly Hills, CA: The Greif Company.

Jackson, D. (Director). (2010). Just say no [Television series episode 3]. In N. Briscoe (Producer), *Teach: Tony Danza*. Beverly Hills, CA: The Greif Company.

Jackson, D. (Director). (2010). Homesick [Television series episode 4]. In N. Briscoe (Producer), *Teach: Tony Danza*. Beverly Hills, CA: The Greif Company.

Jackson, D. (Director). (2010). Solidarity [Television series episode 5]. In N. Briscoe (Producer), *Teach: Tony Danza*. Beverly Hills, CA: The Greif Company.

Jackson, D. (Director). (2010). To cheat or not to cheat [Television series episode 6]. In N. Briscoe (Producer), *Teach: Tony Danza*. Beverly Hills, CA: The Greif Company.

Jackson, D. (Director). (2010). Teacher's pet [Television series episode 7]. In N. Briscoe (Producer), *Teach: Tony Danza*. Beverly Hills, CA: The Greif Company.

Lambert, S. (Writer), & Gonzales, A. (Director). (2012). Cinnabon [Television series episode 3]. In C. Carlson (Executive producer), *Undercover boss*. New York, NY: CBS.

Lambert, S. (Writer), & Gonzales, A. (Director). (2013). Mood Media [Television series episode 6]. In C. Carlson (Executive producer), *Undercover boss*. New York, NY: CBS.

Lambert, S. (Writer), & Gonzales, A. (Director). (2013). Moe's Southwest Grill [Television series episode 8]. In C. Carlson (Executive producer), *Undercover boss*. New York, NY: CBS.

CHAPTER TWO

The Myth OF THE "Fully Qualified" Bright Young Teacher

Using Haberman Star Teacher Pre-Screener to Teach and Assess Professional Dispositions

NICHOLAS D. HARTLEP, SARA MCCUBBINS AND
GRANT B. MORGAN

INTRODUCTION

Picture this: a young female pre-service teacher is about to embark on her first journey into the classroom. She quickly learns that teaching is not what she expected. The students have to deal with violence, the school lacks resources, and this new teacher feels like nothing is being done to change the situation. So, she takes on the challenge to change things all by herself. She is met with student and staff resistance, but in the end she is wildly successful and everyone praises her efforts, including her building administrator. This scenario is not new. Hollywood, beginning as early as the 1990s, has perpetuated the idea that a bright young teacher, usually White and usually unmarried, can radically turn around a classroom or even a school. Movies such as *Dangerous Minds* (1995), *Music of the Heart* (1999), *Freedom Writers* (2007), and *Won't Back Down* (2012) perpetuate a deleterious myth: that young, unseasoned teachers can have greater instructional impact than veteran teachers. That's not the only myth that this story is perpetuating and perhaps not the most deleterious, either. It is also perpetuating the myth that authentic social change—the kind that is needed for a sustainable educational experience—can be achieved by the efforts of a single person. That's a dangerous myth, which ignores how the social and cultural play a central role in conditioning what we are, how knowledge is generated, and how we come to feel an appreciative understanding of something.

The authors of this chapter, one a former urban elementary teacher and now professor of educational foundations, one a current curriculum and instruction doctoral student, and one a professor, were interested in better situating what Haberman (2012) identified as the myth of the "fully qualified bright young teacher" in the context of teacher education professionalization generally, but specifically in the context of how the educational community does, or does not, think about dispositions.

Part of the "professionalization" movement within education is the notion that teachers must have professional and clinical knowledge of teaching and learning gained through a teacher preparation program of some sort. The "professionalization" movement has been an important aspect of reform in the U.S. education system since the early 19th century (Popkewitz, 1994). In fact, the concept that educators serve as professionals with technical expertise and knowledge of children's learning has often been a motivation of the occupation and has contributed to teacher dispositions (Labaree, 1992; Mintrop, 2012; Popkewitz, 1994). However, the professionalization movement can also be an overly simplistic mentality, since it may consider teaching to be more of a science than an art. Moreover, under the professionalization movement, teachers are sometimes conceived to be educational technicians, resulting in the belief that teachers may not need to study curriculum, instruction, and pedagogy in order to be effective in the classroom. Is this effective or wise?

In response to this question, we feel that substituting prepared teachers with trained college students, such as in the case of Teach For America (TFA), is problematic. Consequently, we have sought to examine the likelihood that "older" and "more-experienced" in-service teachers at a selective enrollment public school in Illinois would answer the Haberman Star Teacher Pre-Screener correctly. This is important, since Haberman's (2012) "research, conducted over a period of 55 years, indicates that of those over 30 who claim they want to teach diverse children and youth in poverty, approximately one in three passes Conversely, "Of those under 25 who say they would like to teach diverse children and youth in poverty, the pass rate is one in 10" (p. 927).

THE HABERMAN STAR TEACHER PRE-SCREENER

The Haberman Star Teacher Pre-Screener has been used by suburban and urban school districts across the United States to identify prospective teachers who will be successful in the classroom (Rockoff, Jacob, Kane, & Staiger, 2008). The Star Teacher survey instrument uses 50 multiple-choice items to assess 10 different attributes: (1) persistence, (2) organization and planning, (3) beliefs about the value of students' learning, (4) approach to students, (5) approach to at-risk students, (6) ability to connect theory to practice, (7) ability to survive in a bureaucracy, (8) fallibility, (9) explanation of students' success, and (10) explanation of teacher success.

The present study focused on teacher disposition and core beliefs. Particularly, the researchers were most interested in how the predictive nature of the Haberman Star Teacher Pre-Screener (henceforward STAR Pre-Screener) might align with teacher disposition and core beliefs.

PURPOSE OF STUDY

The purpose of this study was to examine potential relationships between dimensions of teachers' dispositions, knowledge, and skills on the STAR Pre-Screener and teachers' background characteristics.

LITERATURE REVIEW

In order to analyze the data collected in this study, a literature review was done on the following topics: Teacher Effectiveness, Teacher Dispositions and Core Beliefs, and the Haberman STAR Pre-Screener.

Teacher Effectiveness

Many factors contribute to teacher effectiveness, including age/experience, national board certification, advanced degree completion, certification, and more. Yet teacher effectiveness is almost exclusively measured by student performance on high-stakes standardized achievement tests, although the push for additional measurement methods such as performance-based evaluations, observations, and merit-pay is increasingly gaining attention. In the literature, teacher effectiveness—or what makes an effective teacher—is defined in numerous, but consistently similar, ways. Morrison (2006) described effective teachers as those who: "accept responsibility for teaching, allocate most of their time to instruction, organize their classroom for effective instruction...maintain a pleasant learning environment that is student centered, and provide opportunities for practice and feedback on performance" (p. 13). Another definition was provided by Wong and Wong (2005), who defined an effective teacher as "one who has positive expectations for student success, is an extremely good classroom manager, and knows how to design lessons for student mastery" (as cited in Aleccia, 2011, p. 87). Some researchers break down the definition even further, separating teacher effectiveness into distinct categories. According to Aleccia (2011), there are four criteria for being an effective teacher and/or teacher educator. They are: (1) be clear about your professional mission; (2) have the appropriate background/training; (3) keep current in your classroom practice by bridging theory with practice; and (4) model what it means to be an "accomplished teacher" for pre-service teachers, including getting your National Board certification (p. 87). All four of these criteria require experience, suggesting that older and more experienced educators would be more effective teachers than younger and inexperienced educators.

The literature says a lot about the role experience plays in teacher effectiveness. While many scholars have found it difficult to identify the factors that correlate well with teacher effectiveness, the one factor that *has* been regularly correlated with teacher effectiveness is experience from on-the-job training (Chingos & Peterson, 2011). This correlation, however, is weak over time. Some recent studies have suggested that the value of on-the-job experience eventually decays and becomes negative after five to 10 years of teaching (Chingos & Peterson, 2011; Clotfelter, Ladd, & Vigdor, 2006; Harris & Sass, 2008; Kane, Rockoff, & Staiger, 2008; Rivkin, Hanushek, & Kain, 2005; Staiger & Rockoff, 2010). In a study by Rivkin et al. (2005), the researchers noticed some improvements in teaching initially, but concluded "there is little evidence that improvements continue after the first three years" (p. 449). Although these studies have indicated a leveling out, or even a decline, in teacher effectiveness, no previous study has detected the point at which that decline occurs, which is particularly of interest in terms of policy given that teacher salary schedules tend to reward teachers for additional years of experience (Chingos & Peterson, 2011).

The other factor affecting the validity of the relationship between experience and teacher effectiveness is the potential bias that is inherent in the data. A study of Florida teachers by Chignos and Peterson (2011) analyzed student reading and mathematics scores on a state standardized achievement test. The scores were analyzed from 2002–2009 and adjusted for demographic characteristics in addition to matching the individual students' scores with each teacher. The results showed a positive relationship between student achievement and the number of years teaching, although the authors noted that a potential bias exists given the higher attrition rate of less effective teachers (p. 458). Nonetheless, the literature points to a clear, albeit small, correlation between age/experience and teacher effectiveness, part of which might be related to the development over time of teaching self-efficacy. As teachers increase their own personal teaching efficacy—the belief in themselves that they are effective teachers and can produce desired student outcomes—they often become more effective teachers because they are less concerned about the demands of teacher tasks and more likely to adopt innovative approaches that support diverse learning needs (Ghaith & Yaghi, 1997; Ng, Nicholas, & Williams, 2010; Wertheim & Leyser, 2002). This efficacy is directly related to teaching experience and therefore impacts teacher effectiveness.

Another factor that is often said to increase teacher effectiveness is the completion of an advanced or terminal degree. Yet, the research literature does not support this conclusion. Although most teacher pay scales reward the attainment of an advanced degree, literature on teacher effectiveness shows that holding a master's degree does not increase teacher effectiveness (Aaronson, Barrow, & Sander, 2007; Clotfelter, Ladd, & Vigdor, 2006; Ehrenberg & Brewer, 1994; Kane, Rockoff, & Staiger, 2008; Summers & Wolfe, 1977). Additionally, Chingos and Peterson (2011) found that "teachers with master's degrees are no more effective in the classroom than those without an advanced degree" (p. 464). This does not mean that teachers with advanced degrees are not effective; in fact, they are highly effective teachers because they also tend to be those teachers with more experience. The completion of that degree alone, however, does not increase the already high level of effectiveness that these teachers demonstrate. In other words, the lack of change in teacher effectiveness could, in part, be due to the fact that teachers who are already effective are more likely to seek advanced degrees and certificates.

Part of the reason for identifying effective teachers is to develop reward systems that promote effective teaching practices, and that is exactly what the National Board for Professional Teaching Standards (NBPTS) aimed to do with the creation of the National Board Certification process. Established in 1987, the National Board was founded as a voluntary process for advanced certification. The NBPTS outlined Five Core Propositions for the program: (1) commitment to students and learning, (2) knowledge of subject matter and how to teach those subjects to students, (3) ability to manage and monitor student learning, (4) ability to systematically think about teaching and learn from experience, (5) become a member of learning communities (National Board for Professional Teaching Standards, 1987). In fact, one of the main reasons for creating the National Board certification process was to professionalize teaching and provide external motivation for accomplished teachers (National Research Council, 2008). Now, this certification process is highly regarded because, as Chingos and Peterson (2011) explained, it involves many components that are intended to increase teacher effectiveness by developing reflective practices such as displaying lesson plans and other evidence of teaching methods, and providing videos of classroom instruction (p. 452). Thus, it has become "the gold standard of accomplished classroom teaching" (Aleccia, 2011, p. 88).

Many studies have examined teacher effectiveness in relation to National Board (NB) certification as well as the underlying motivational factors behind attaining the goal of becoming NB certified. Chingos and Peterson (2011), for example, found that "teachers certified by NBPTS are more effective than those not so certified" (Chingos & Peterson, 2011, p. 450). Many other studies have also suggested that National Board Certified teachers are more effective than their non-NB certified peers (Clotfelter, Ladd, & Vigdor, 2007; Goldhaber & Anthony, 2004; Harris & Sass, 2007). And when it comes to motivation, it often has to do with professionalization.

Hildebrandt and Eom (2011) explained that the motivation for a teacher to move towards professionalization, which they defined as achieving National Board certification, can be broken down into five main components: (1) a desire to improve teaching, (2) external validation, (3) the opportunity for financial gain, (4) increased collaboration, and (5) internal validation (pp. 419–420). Given that these motivational factors as well as the fact that teachers completing National Board certification are often mid-career teachers in their mid-thirties and forties, experience/age can again be directly linked to teacher effectiveness. Overall, the literature has shown that teacher effectiveness can be correlated with experience/age, which can be explicitly seen in the attainment of advanced degrees, and National Board certification.

Teacher Dispositions and Core Beliefs

Linked to teacher effectiveness are teacher dispositions and core beliefs. A study conducted by Masunaga and Lewis (2011) supported the notion that "positive teacher dispositions predict effective, successful teaching" (p. 44). Furthermore, we tend to use dispositions to define teacher effectiveness. When discussing "good" versus "bad" teachers, the focus tends to be on dispositions rather than skills or pedagogy. "Good" teachers are generally described as encouraging, stimulating, and so on, whereas "bad" teachers are categorized as impatient, and remote, among other things (Katz & Raths, 1985). To understand dispositions, we must look at the moral and reflective domains of how we think and act for a variety of experiences (Dewey, 1904; Johnson & Reiman, 2007; Shulman, 1998). However, defining dispositions can be tricky as many variations of the term appear in the literature. There are many competing definitions of dispositions, but generally they reflect beliefs and attitudes about specific knowledge or they represent belief statements that define the individual teacher (Welch et al., 2010). The most commonly cited definition comes from the National Council for Accreditation of Teacher Education (NCATE, 2008), which defined dispositions as the "professional attitudes, values, and beliefs demonstrated through both verbal and non-verbal behaviors as educators interact with students, families, colleagues, and communities" (pp. 89–90). This tends to be the focus of the literature because it is the definition connected with the NCATE standards for accreditation.

Other definitions for dispositions can also be found in the literature. Thornton (2006) presented two different definitions of dispositions, related to how these dispositions appear "in action" or in the classroom setting. The first is what she called *responsive* dispositions, which reflect "a way of thinking about teacher and learning that is…responsive to the needs and actions of the learner, their developmental characteristics, their cultural background and experiences, (and) their levels of understanding" (p. 61). The second is what she called *technical* dispositions, which represents the notion of "teacher as technician focusing on how to successfully employ the skills of teaching" resulting in little variation (p. 62). Thornton argued that more effective teachers exhibit responsive dispositions. Katz and Raths (1985), on the other hand, defined a disposition as "an attributed characteristic of a teacher, one that summarizes the trend of a teacher's actions in particular contexts" (p. 301). The authors go on to say that "the acts that constitute a disposition may be conscious and deliberate or so habitual and "automatic" that they seem intuitive or spontaneous" (p. 301). Furthermore, they emphasize that dispositions involve not just having a particular skill or behavior, but rather the likelihood and frequency of using that skill or behavior. Thus, dispositions can be distinguished from traits, habits, attitudes, and skills (pp. 302–303).

In the end, sometimes dispositions are defined merely as beliefs or behaviors (NCATE, 2008), and other times they are defined in relation to whether those beliefs and behaviors are prevalent in the classroom (Katz & Raths, 1985; Masunaga & Lewis, 2011; Thornton, 2006; Villegas, 2007). Perhaps more important is the fact that dispositions can be either positive (cultural-consciousness, self-awareness, and social justice) or negative (close-mindedness, impatience, and intolerance) in the context of teaching (Ros-Voseles & Moss, 2007). Regardless, these dispositions have an effect in the classroom. Talbert-Johnson (2006) explained that "the personal belief systems of teachers significantly influence the behaviors displayed in the classroom and the instructional decisions teachers make" (p. 152). Therefore, understanding dispositions is important in relation to student learning and teacher effectiveness.

The history of teacher dispositions is a long one. John Dewey (1904), one of the most influential thinkers on education, believed that one of the primary challenges for teachers was the "development of dispositions toward reflection, inquiry, ethical judgments, and orientation towards the multifaceted processes of students" (as cited in Johnson & Reiman, 2007, p. 686). The push for understanding dispositions really came in the early 1990s when the Interstate New Teacher Assessment and Support Consortium (INTASC) outlined 10 dispositions that all teachers should have. According to INTASC (1992), teachers should have dispositions towards: (1) being a lifelong learner; (2) having healthy relationships with children; (3) understanding and appreciating diversity; (4) using creativity, problem solving, and divergent thinking; (5) promoting positive social interactions; (6) maintaining effective communication; (7) planning, organizing, and goal-setting; (8) recognizing and promoting growth in others; (9) self-reflection and self-development; and (10) integrity and collaboration for student advocacy. The importance of dispositions becomes clearer when we examine teachers with the same skills, content, and pedagogical knowledge who still vary in their effectiveness. Thornton (2006) argued not only that we need to examine why these differences occur, but also that "dispositions may be the key" (p. 67). Given this paradox, most research surrounding teacher dispositions focuses on teacher candidates, and the nature of these dispositions has been studied extensively (Darling-Hammond & Bransford, 2005; Katz & Raths, 1985; Villegas, 2007; Welch et al., 2010).

With such a long history and with so many competing definitions of dispositions, measuring these dispositions becomes very difficult. Yet, NCATE mandated that teacher candidates must reflect appropriate dispositions for accreditation. According to Welch et al. (2010), the measurement tool most commonly used to gauge dispositions tends to be observations. Given that the measurement occurs only when a certain behavior or disposition is observed, the dispositions seen during observation might not reflect that teacher's typical affective and social behaviors, making the measurement tool problematic (p. 181). Still, a vast amount of research has been conducted on teacher dispositions and its relationship to effective teaching. For example, reflection is one of the key dispositions, according to INTASC (1992), and plays a large role in teacher effectiveness. In Thornton's (2006) study of middle school teachers in a specialized program, the teachers who did not reflect on their own teaching—those who felt the instruction was continuous among all the teachers and did not contain variation based on who was teaching—were the ones who were identified by other teachers, observers, and students as been less effective (p. 61). The lack of self-reflection, which can be seen as a negative disposition, had an impact on teacher effectiveness.

Another large area of focus in the disposition literature is on social consciousness. Mueller and Hindin (2011) defined social consciousness in respect to teachers as those who "act as stewards and leaders; understand, respect, and value diversity; and apply what they have learned about teaching to support diverse learners" (p. 18). Furthermore, Villegas and Lucas (2002) outlined six characteristics of socially and culturally responsive teachers—teachers who: (1) are conscious of their own way of perceiving reality based on their background, (2) are positive and have high expectations for all students, (3) have high efficacy, (4) understand and can support how students build knowledge, (5) care about students' lives, and (6) create opportunities for students that build on prior knowledge and promote future growth. In particular, dispositions towards race and ethnicity are of growing importance given that the population of students of color is growing. According to Gollnick and Chin (2009), by the year 2020, more than half the student population will be students of color, whereas teachers will remain predominantly white and female. These dispositions are important because they can affect student learning. Teachers are more likely to adopt new ideas if they are compatible with their beliefs and dispositions; however, those ideas that contradict or challenge their dispositions are generally dismissed for being too theoretical, impractical, or wrong (Raths, 2011).

Haberman STAR Pre-Screener

One of the ways researchers have answered the call for a focus on teacher dispositions is through the development of measurement tools such as the Haberman STAR Pre-Screener, which intends to identify people with the dispositions that have been shown to lead to effective teaching. Martin Haberman spent decades of his life devoted to teaching children in poverty and learning about what makes teachers successful in urban schools. As Hart and Rowley (1999) explained, "few educators have the passion for teaching children in poverty that has defined the life and career of Martin Haberman" (p. 204). In order to understand the STAR Pre-screener, we must first look at how Haberman developed his definition of a STAR teacher. Star Teachers are those who "are so effective that the adverse conditions of working in failing schools or school districts do not prevent them from being successful teachers" (Haberman, 2004, p. 53). According to Haberman (2004), some of the qualities that STAR teachers possess include:

> their persistence, their physical and emotional stamina, their caring relationships with students, their commitment to acknowledging and appreciating student effort, their willingness to admit mistakes, their focus on deep learning, their commitment to inclusion, and their organization skills. They also protect student learning, translate theory and research into practice, cope with the bureaucracy, create student ownership, engage parents and caregivers as partners in student learning, and support accountability for at-risk students. (p. 53)

In an interview conducted by Shaugnessy et al. (1999), Haberman described star teachers as those who "manifest an ideology based on a set of predispositions to act which is derived from their life experiences" (p. 198). He went on to explain that "their ideology requires them to integrate ethical concerns in everything they teach" (p. 199) and that star teachers "think of themselves as using various forms of content to make better people" (p. 201).

Haberman's concept of the STAR teacher is often seen in contradiction to those who typically complete teacher education preparation programs. The majority of pre-service teachers are full-time undergraduates under 25 years of age, with a small but growing number of college graduates age 30 and older. According to an interview conducted by Shaugnessy et al. (1999), Haberman believed this trend needed to be reversed—that the majority of new teachers should be those who are over 30 and already have life experiences and a college degree (p. 198).

One of the critical problems with teacher training programs, according to Haberman, is that they try to prepare pre-service teachers for urban school settings without any background or context in teaching in those settings. As Haberman explained,

> those who themselves have not been successful teachers of children in poverty for sustained periods cannot teach others to do so. By ignoring this rule, we have a traditional system in which the ignorant are teaching the fearful to do the irrelevant. (p. 199)

Additionally, teacher-training programs cannot change if they continue to accept the same candidates. "If teacher preparation programs would like candidates with different visions of what teaching might become, then candidates would have to be identified and proactively recruited, rather than self-selected" (Haberman, in an interview with Shaugnessy et al., 1999, p. 200).

From all of this experience with STAR teachers, Haberman recognized the need for a tool that could identify candidates who would be successful in urban education settings. Haberman (1993) believed that "what matters most is the quality of the teachers," (p. 1) and that when it comes to the quality of our schools, "a school district's most critical decision is who to hire. No decision is more important in determining the quality of schools" (p. 2). Thus, the Haberman STAR Pre-Screener was developed to identify those potential teachers who exhibit the STAR attributes. As Sawchuk (2012a) explained, "The (Haberman Star Pre-Screener) tool, used in districts across the country, is meant to determine which teacher-candidates have the dispositions for working with poor and minority schoolchildren" (p. 5). Based on Haberman's identified STAR teacher traits, the pre-screener uses these attributes to "predict the effectiveness and staying power of teachers serving diverse students in low-income urban schools" (Haberman, 2004, p. 53). And this tool is proving to be successful, based on the literature of studies that have used the Pre-Screener as well as schools that have implemented it as a hiring mechanism.

Many schools and districts across the country have made use of Haberman's methods for identifying star teachers and their dispositions, but the impact of Haberman is not just limited to K-12 schools. Universities have also used Haberman's methods to supplement their teacher training programs. Though Haberman is a strong proponent of alternative certification methods, some institutions have also tried to bring his theories into their traditional undergraduate teacher education programs. For example, Hart and Rowley (1999) used Haberman's idea of star teachers to develop a video series using case scenarios that each reflected one of the star teacher functions identified by Haberman. These case scenarios used urban students, star teachers, administrators, and urban school support personnel to provide a realistic virtual world of urban teaching for pre-service teachers, based on the expertise and reflections of actual star urban teachers (Hart & Rowley,

1999, p. 207). Additionally, a study conducted by Rockoff et al. (2008) examined the teacher characteristics associated with the Haberman STAR Pre-Screener and then looked at whether performance on the pre-screener predicted any teacher or student outcomes. They found that teachers who had one standard deviation score higher tended to also have an increase in math achievement of their students (p. 65). The study also showed a small but significant positive relationship between the Pre-screener score and the tendency of the teacher to return to teaching the following year (p. 65). As is apparent from the literature, the Haberman STAR Pre-Screener has proven successful in schools, districts, and higher education institutions across the country.

METHODOLOGY

Participants and Setting

This study took place in a selective enrollment K-8 public elementary school in the state of Illinois: Meadowbrook Elementary School (a pseudonym). Initially attempting to survey all licensed staff members in the building (n = 35), 31 Meadowbrook licensed staff formed the analytical sample for this study, provided that they completed both survey instruments—the STAR Pre-Screener and a Survey Monkey background survey created by the researchers. This represented an 89% response rate. In order for readers to understand what type of school Meadowbrook is, Table 1 below highlights comparisons made between the school and the State of Illinois.

Meadowbrook Elementary staff. All 31 elementary school teachers who participated in this study self-identified as being White and the majority were over the age of 44 (see Table 2.). The racial and sexual composition of the Meadowbrook teaching staff should not be surprising. Toldson (2011) analyzed census data and concluded that 80% of America's K-12 teachers in 2010 were White and 90% were female. Meanwhile, compared to State of Illinois averages, Meadowbrook is considered to be a school that is highly White. Again, this should not be surprising. According to Sawchuk (2012b), writing in *Education Week*, Illinois ranks 49th out of 51 (the 50 U.S. states plus the District of Columbia) for having the largest percentage point difference between non-White teachers and students. In other words, 46% of the student body in Illinois is non-White while 11% of its teachers are non-White, resulting in a 35% discrepancy between students and staff.

Further, 54.84% (n = 17) of Meadowbrook Elementary teacher participants were over the age of 41. There was only one teacher that was younger than 27. Haberman (2012) pointed out that teachers who are age 25 and younger may lack the life experience and maturity necessary to be effective classroom teachers, despite impressive grades and achievement while in colleges of education.

Table 1. Meadowbrook Elementary vs. State of Illinois.

Factor	Meadowbrook	State of Illinois
School Enrollment	(K-5) 246 (K-8) 387	
Grade 3 Class Size	21.5	22.3
School Low Income	n/a	49.0
School Demographics	67.7% White 8.8% Black 9.3% Hispanic 8.3% Asian 0.0% American Indian 5.9% Multiracial	51.4% White 18.3% Black 23.0% Hispanic 4.1% Asian 0.3% American Indian 2.8% Multiracial
Grade 3 ISAT (2010–2011) Meets or Exceeds	Reading: 100 Math: 100 Science: n/a	Reading: 74.7 Math: 87.3 Science: n/a
Grade 4 ISAT (2010–2011) Meets or Exceeds	Reading: 100 Math: 100 Science: 100	Reading: 74.7 Math: 87.7 Science: 79.3
Grade 5 ISAT (2010–2011) Meets or Exceeds	Reading: 100 Math: 97.9 Science: n/a	Reading: 76.4 Math: 84.0 Science: n/a
Grade 6 ISAT (2010–2011) Meets or Exceeds	Reading: 100 Math: 100 Science: n/a	Reading: 84.1 Math: 84.0 Science: n/a
Grade 7 ISAT (2010–2011) Meets or Exceeds	Reading: 93.5 Math: 100 Science: 95.7	Reading: 78.8 Math: 84.3 Science: 81.9
Grade 8 ISAT (2010–2011) Meets or Exceeds	Reading: 98.0 Math: 100 Science: n/a	Reading: 85.0 Math: 86.3 Science: n/a
Attendance	96.5	94
LEP	n/a	8.8
IEP	n/a	14

Sources: Illinois State Board of Education (2012) and Meadowbrook School Principal

RESULTS

This chapter sought to examine potential relationships between dimensions of teachers' dispositions, knowledge, and skills on the STAR Pre-Screener and teachers' background characteristics. To this end, we used descriptive and graphical analyses to explore these relationships within this sample (n = 31) of teachers.

Table 2. Meadowbrook Elementary Teacher Age Information (n = 31).

Teacher Age Range	Frequency	% Meadowbrook Total
18–20	0	0.00%
21–23	1	3.23%
24–26	0	0.00%
27–29	2	6.45%
30–32	2	6.45%
33–35	6	19.35%
36–38	2	6.45%
39–41	1	3.23%
42–44	1	3.23%
45–47	3	9.68%
48–50	3	9.68%
51+	10	32.26%
	n = 31	100%

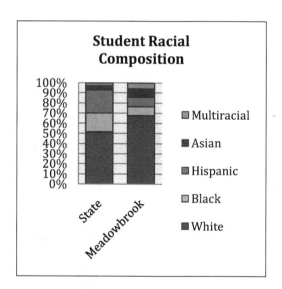

Fig 1. Meadowbrook Elementary School vs. State of Illinois Racial Composition.

We did not conduct inferential analysis, which is typically used to make broader statements about a target population based on the information provided by a sample, for the following reasons. First, the teachers who provided data for this study were not randomly sampled. Therefore, we could not assess the representativeness of this sample to the general teacher population. Second, data configuration and structure were not conducive to inferential tests. For example, most inferential procedures require one or more assumptions to be met in order for the results to be trustworthy. Given the size and unbalanced nature of the comparison groups, the assumptions for procedures, such as analysis of variance or chi-square, were not met.

For certain comparisons in these data, the chances of making an accurate inference would have been at least five times greater by flipping a coin rather than conducting an inferential test. Consequently, in order to avoid making an incorrect decision based on untrustworthy information, we used descriptive statistics and graphical displays to represent real data collected from actual teachers.

Years of Experience and "Persistence"

In his book *Star Teachers*, Haberman (2010, p. 131) referred to "persistence" as a teacher's ability to problem-solve with students. In other words, persistence refers to a teacher's responsibility to make the classroom climate interesting and engaging so that students' educational needs are met, ensuring that all students learn.

We found that all teachers who had 30+ years of teaching experience ($n = 5$) scored high on "persistence" (see Figure 2). The "persistence" dimension that is

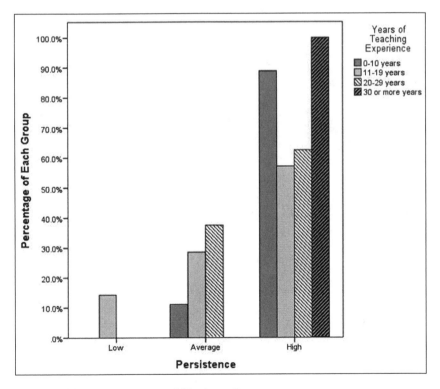

Fig 2. Years of Teaching Experience and "Persistence".

assessed by the Haberman STAR Pre-Screener predicts the propensity to work with children who present learning and behavioral problems on a daily basis without giving up on them for the full school year.

We also found that all teachers who held (n = 3) or were in the process (n = 3) of obtaining their National Board Certificate scored high on the "persistence" dimension (see Figure 3).

EDUCATION LEVEL AND "PERSISTENCE"

Lastly, we found that teachers who completed education past the baccalaureate level were not at a relative advantage for scoring higher on "persistence" dimension (see Figure 4). Stated differently, while a greater percentage of teachers who

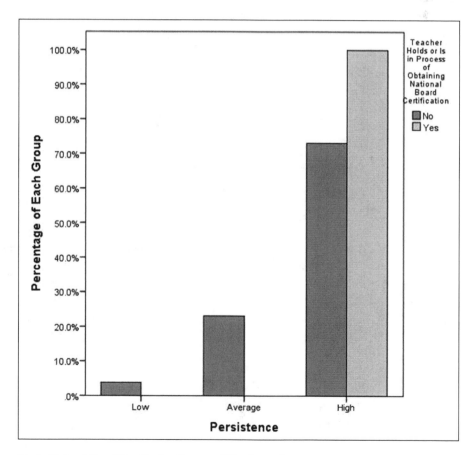

Fig 3. National Board Certification Status and "Persistence".

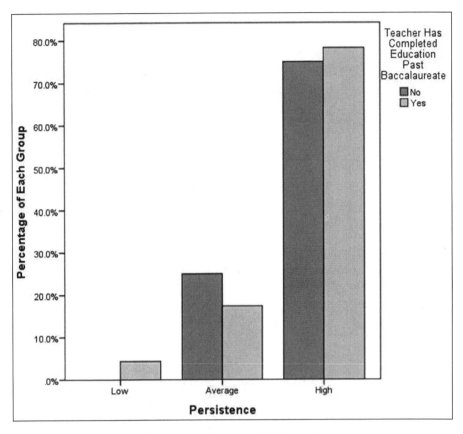

Fig 4. Completed Education Past the Baccalaureate and "Persistence".

completed education past the baccalaureate level scored high on the "persistence" dimension, there were no teachers with just a bachelor's degree who scored low on the persistence dimension (compared to those who completed higher than a baccalaureate).

DISCUSSION

In paying honor to the work of the late Dr. Martin Haberman, this chapter shared the findings of preliminary fieldwork done in the state of Illinois, in Meadowbrook Elementary, a selective enrollment K-8 public school that sought to examine potential relationships between dimensions of teachers' dispositions, knowledge, and skills on the STAR Pre-Screener and teachers' background characteristics. This study revealed three salient findings: (1) elementary teachers who had more years of teaching experience (e.g., 30+ years) scored higher on the "persistence" dimension of the Haberman STAR Pre-Screener, (2) elementary teachers who held, or were in the process of obtaining, their National Board Certification scored higher on the "persistence" dimension than those teachers to whom this did not apply, and (3) elementary teachers who completed education past the baccalaureate level were not at a relative advantage for scoring higher on "persistence" dimension compared to colleagues with just a bachelor's degree.

IMPLICATIONS

The results of this small-scale study yield two interesting implications for the "professionalization" movement within (teacher) education and for teacher dispositions. The first is the importance and need for revealing the myth of the "fully qualified" bright young teacher. Teaching experience matters much. According to our findings, seasoned teachers appear equipped to be more effective in the classroom as measured on the diagnostic STAR pre-screener. The second implication is that formal education might matter, but further studies ought to examine the effect that graduate education training has on teachers' impact in the elementary school classroom. Specifically, the ways in which graduate education can teach dispositions and core beliefs that lead to student engagement and overall success.

This small-scale study also found that National Board Certified and National Board Certification candidates, were most likely to be found to persist in the classroom. This begs the questions: What sorts of dispositions are cultivated during the National Board Certification process? What sorts of training do Nationally Board Certified Teachers have? How does their training positively impact their professional disposition and how does it positively impact students' learning? The professionalization movement, we believe, has, in some ways, created space in the teacher preparation arena, which can be used effectively and wisely. It would be wise and highly effective to develop pre-service teachers' dispositions and core beliefs so that they will be able to effectively teach and reach diverse students.

REFERENCES

Aleccia, V. (2011). Walking our talk: The imperative of teacher educator modeling. *The Clearing House, 84,* 87–90.

Chingos, M. M., & Peterson, P. E. (2011). It's easier to pick a good teacher than to train one: Familiar and new results on the correlates of teacher effectiveness. *Economics of Education Review, 30,* 449–465.

Clotfelter, T., Ladd, H. F., & Vigdor, J. L. (2006). *Teacher-student matching and the assessment of teacher effectiveness* (Working Paper No. 11936). Retrieved from National Bureau of Economic Research website: http://www.nber.org/papers/w11936

Darling-Hammond, L., & Bransford, J. (Eds.). (2005). *Preparing teachers for a changing world: What teachers should learn and be able to do.* San Francisco, CA: Jossey-Bass.

Dewey, J. (1904). The relation of theory to practice in education. In C. McMurry (Ed.), *The third yearbook of the National Society for the Scientific Study of Education, part I: The relation of theory to practice in the education of teachers* (pp. 9–30). Chicago, IL: University of Chicago Press.

Ehrenberg, R. G., & Brewer, D. J. (1994). Do school and teacher characteristics matter? Evidence from high school and beyond. *Economics of Education Review, 13*(1), 1–17.

Ghaith, G., & Yaghi, M. (1997). Relationships among experience, teacher efficacy, and attitudes toward the implementation of instructional innovation. *Teaching and Teacher Education, 13,* 451–458.

Goldhaber, D., & Anthony, E. (2004). *Can teacher quality be effectively assessed?* Retrieved from the Urban Institute website: http://www.urban.org/publications/410958.html

Gollnick, D., & Chin, P. C. (2009). *Multicultural education in a pluralistic society.* Boston, MA: Pearson Merrill.

Haberman, M. (1993). Predicting the success of urban teachers (the Milwaukee trials). *Action in Teacher Education, 15*(3), 1–5.

Haberman, M. (2004). Can Star Teachers create learning communities? *Educational Leadership, 61*(8), 52–56.

Haberman, M. (2010). *Star Teachers: The ideology and best practice of effective teachers of diverse children and youth in poverty.* Houston, TX: The Haberman Educational Foundation.

Haberman, M. (2012). The myth of the "fully qualified" bright young teacher. *American Behavioral Scientist, 56*(7), 926–940.

Harris, D. N., & Sass, T. R. (2007). *What makes for a good teacher and who can tell?* Florida State University, Department of Economics. Retrieved from http://www.urban.org/publications/1001431.html.

Harris, D. N., & Sass, T. R. (2008). *Teacher training, teacher quality, and student achievement.* Florida State University, Department of Economics.

Hart, P. M., & Rowley, J. B. (1999). Origins of Star Teachers: Implications and challenges for teacher education. *Journal for a Just and Caring Education, 5*(2), 203–208.

Hildebrandt, S. A., & Eom, M. (2011). Teacher professionalization: Motivational factors and the influence of age. *Teaching and Teacher Education, 27,* 416–423.

Illinois State Board of Education. (2012). Interactive school report card. Retrieved from http://iirc.niu.edu/

Interstate New Teacher Assessment and Support Consortium (INTASC). (1992). *Model Standards for Beginning Teacher Licensure and Development: A Resource for State Dialogue.* Washington, DC: Council of Chief State School Officers. Retrieved from https://goed.american.edu/docs/INTASC_standards(7).pdf

Johnson, L. E., & Reiman, A. J. (2007). Beginning teacher disposition: Examining the moral/ethical domain. *Teaching and Teacher Education, 23,* 676–687.

Kane, T. J., Rockoff, J. E., & Staiger, D.O, (2008). What does certification tell us about teacher effectiveness? Evidence from New York City. *Economics of Education Review, 27*(6), 615–631.

Katz, L. G., & Raths, J. D. (1985). Dispositions as goals for teacher education. *Teaching & Teacher Education, 1*(4), 301–307.

Labaree, D. (1992). Power, knowledge, and the rationalization of teaching: A genealogy of the movement to professionalize teaching. *Harvard Educational Review, 62*(2), 123–134.

Masunaga, H., & Lewis, T. (2011). Self-perceived dispositions that predict challenges during student teaching: A data mining analysis. *Issues in Teacher Education, 20*(1), 35–49.

Mintrop, H. (2012). Bridging accountability obligations, professional values and (perceived) student needs with integrity. *Journal of Educational Administration, 50*(5), 695–726.

Morrison, G. S. (2006). *Teaching in America* (4th ed). Upper Saddle River, NJ: Merrill-Pearson.

Mueller, M., & Hindin, A. (2011). An analysis of factors that influence preservice elementary teachers' developing dispositions about teaching all children. *Issues in Teacher Education, 20*(1), 17–34.

National Board for Professional Teaching Standards (1987). *The Five Core Propositions*. Retrieved from http://www.nbpts.org/five-core-propositions

National Council for Accreditation of Teacher Education (NCATE). (2008). *Professional Standards for the Accreditation of Teacher Preparation Institutions*. Retrieved from http://www.ncate.org/Portals/0/documents/Standards/NCATE%20standards%202008.pdf

National Research Council (2008). *Assessing accomplished teaching: Advanced level certification programs*. Washington, DC: The National Academies Press.

Ng, W., Nicholas, H., & Williams, A. (2010). School experience influences on pre-service teachers' evolving beliefs about effective teaching. *Teaching and Teacher Education, 26*, 278–289.

Popkewitz, T. S. (1994). Professionalization in teaching and teacher education: Some notes on its history, ideology, and potential. *Teaching & Teacher Education, 10*(1), 1–14.

Raths, J. (2001). Teachers' beliefs and teaching beliefs. *Early Childhood Research and Practice, 3*(1). Retrieved from http://ecrp.uiuc.edu/v3n1/raths.html

Rivkin, S. G., Hanushek, E. A., & Kain, J. F. (2005). Teachers, schools, and academic achievement. *Econometrica, 73*(2), 417–458.

Rockoff, J. E., Jacob, B. A., Kane, T. J., & Staiger, D. O. (2008). *Can you recognize an effective teacher when you recruit one?* Cambridge, MA: National Bureau of Economic Research.

Ros-Voseles, D. D., & Moss, L. (2007). The role of dispositions in the education of future teachers. *YC Young Children, 62*(5), 90–97.

Sawchuk, S. (2012a, January 18). Advocate for access to quality teaching dies at age 79. *Education Week, 31*(17), 5.

Sawchuk, S. (2012b, October 10). Wanted: More diverse teaching. *Education Week, 32*(7), 1, 14–15.

Shaugnessy, M., Melancon, B., & Abebe, S. (1999). An interview with Martin Haberman. *Journal for a Just and Caring Education, 5*(2), 196–202.

Shulman, L. S. (1998). Theory, practice, and the education of professionals. *The Elementary School Journal, 98*(5), 511–526.

Staiger, D. O., & Rockoff, J. E. (2010). Searching for effective teachers with imperfect information. *Journal of Economic Perspectives, 24*(3), 97–118.

Summers, A., & Wolfe, B. (1977). Do schools make a difference? *American Economic Review, 67*(4), 639–652.

Talbert-Johnson, C. (2006). Preparing highly qualified teacher candidates for urban schools. *Education and Urban Society, 39*(1), 147–160.

Thompson, S., Rousseau, C., & Ransdell, M. (2005). Effective teachers in urban school settings: Linking teacher disposition and student performance on standardized tests. *Journal of Authentic Learning, 2*(1), 22–36.

Thornton, H. (2006). Dispositions in action: Do dispositions make a difference in practice? *Teacher Education Quarterly, 33*(2), 53–68.

Toldson, I. (2011). Diversifying the United States' teaching force: Where are we now? Where do we need to go? How do we get there? *The Journal of Negro Education, 80*(3), 183–186.

Villegas, A. M. (2007). Dispositions in teacher education: A look at social justice. *Journal of Teacher Education, 58*(5), 370–380.

Villegas, A. M., & Lucas, T. (2002). Preparing culturally responsive teachers: Rethinking the curriculum. *Journal of Teacher Education, 53*(1), 20–32.

Welch, F. C., Pitts, R. E., Tenini, K. J., Kuenlen, M. G., & Wood, S. G. (2010). Significant issues in defining and assessing teacher dispositions. *The Teacher Educator, 45*, 179–201.

Wertheim, C., & Leyser, Y. (2002). Efficacy beliefs, background variable, and differentiated instruction of Israeli prospective teachers. *The Journal of Educational Research, 96*, 54–63.

CHAPTER THREE

When THE Obvious Isn't True

What's Really Wrong with Teacher Quality and Teacher Education?[1]

P. L. THOMAS

After teaching music for 30 years, including being recognized as Michigan Teacher of the Year in 1993, Nancy Flanagan (2013, February 1) wrote a post on her blog, "Teacher in a Strange Land," at Education Week/Teacher (http://blogs.edweek.org/teachers/teacher_in_a_strange_land/), to address a call for a bar exam for teachers (Sanchez, 2013): "I'm going to step out on a limb here and declare that I kind of like the idea of a bar exam for teachers. Depending, of course, on what the exam looks like." Flanagan's post prompted one reader, [Mark Ahiness] (2013, February 2), to comment:

> Any current discussion about teaching quality is bogus. It assumes two myths: 1) there is a problem in US education, and 2) the problem is teachers. Any discussion about teacher quality perpetuates both of those myths. I refuse to even enter into a discussion about it, because of the supposed gravitas it lends to the issue. More people talking about a myth does not make that myth true.

[Ahiness's] (2013, February 2) comment represents the increased tension that exists between the political/public focus on teacher quality and the reactionary stance of many, if not most, practitioners—whose voices Flanagan tends to reflect. To this comment, however, Flanagan (2013, February 3) responded:

> Shouldn't we all be looking—continuously—to improve our schools? Granted, due to federal policy and grasping desire to tap into the previously untapped K-12 education

market, policy-makers are currently looking in all the wrong places. But I can't believe that saying everything is fine is the answer.

Nor do I believe that "the problem" is teachers—but that doesn't address the millions of teachers who are constantly striving, on their own, to be better practitioners. Or the insidious practice of replacing career teachers with attractive but untrained "temps."

If we want teaching to be regarded as a profession, we need to identify markers of quality (shouldn't be hard to do, as even the school in the most wretched neighborhood has pockets of excellent instruction). We need to pursue those markers. Not to "prove" that there's nothing wrong with US education. But because we love the kids we're teaching, and they deserve the best possible teachers.

Flanagan's (2013, February 1) blog post and subsequent online discussion characterize the paradox in which educators and educational scholars find themselves, trapped as they are between pursuits of professional recognition and the misguided and possibly disingenuous focus on teacher quality in education reform, political and public discourse, and the media.

The first decade of the twenty-first century has included some powerful and harsh narratives about U.S. public education and its teachers: Public schools are failing, particularly in international comparisons; that failure is primarily caused by "bad" teachers (Bessie, 2010b) and corrupt teachers' unions; and teacher education, historically weak, does little to help correct the low quality of the teacher workforce. These enduring and compelling claims were central to the 2010 documentary *Waiting for "Superman,"* but they are also behind public policy and commitments at the federal and state levels throughout the U.S.—notably Race to the Top, opting out of No Child Left Behind (NCLB), increasing funding for Teach For America (TFA), implementing value-added methods (VAM) for evaluating teachers, and expanding the charter school movement.

Yet, my three decades in education—18 years teaching high school English in rural South Carolina and over 10 years in teacher education—and as an education scholar have proven to me that these narratives are essentially false or at best distortions of what is true. I have made the case that the rush to embrace charter schools, for example, fails to start with what education problem we are trying to solve (Thomas, 2012d) in order to insure our solutions match our problems, and below I make a similar argument about teacher quality and teacher education: *Teacher quality matters and teacher education needs to be reformed, but not in the ways currently being argued.*

As with the charter school debate, seeking solutions to teacher quality and teacher education must start with clearly defined problems, goals, and conditions, or the arguments slip into mere ideological advocacy—free market advocates chanting their mantra at union advocates (Casey, 2013a, 2013b), prompting union advocates to chant in reply. For example, *Waiting for "Superman"* included and perpetuated the claim that U.S. education failure should be placed at the feet of "bad" teachers protected by corrupt teachers' unions (Bessie, 2010b), prompting union advocates to note that unionized states correlate positively with higher test scores. All the while, real problems and potential solutions to raising the quality of public schoolteachers and improving teacher preparation are lost in argument-for-argument's-sake. If the political agenda and public genuinely want to raise the quality of public schoolteachers and teacher preparation, they must start with some clear problems and conditions at the root of both, including the context of teaching and learning, as that is couched in the lives of students and teachers as well as the communities within which schools sit (Thomas, 2013b).

Here, the teacher quality and teacher education debates are framed by three broad questions: (1) What are the bi-partisan claims and intentions of focusing solely or primarily on teacher quality as the central mechanism for education reform? (2) What is the proper priority for addressing teacher quality within the larger reform needed in both society and education? (3) What's really wrong with teacher quality and teacher education? To answer these questions, the discussion below examines teacher quality in an era of high-stakes accountability, the credibility of VAM, the reform movement's inverted focus on teacher quality, and finally, the authentic problems with teacher quality and teacher preparation.

DRIVEN TO DISTRACTION: TEACHER QUALITY IN AN ERA OF HIGH-STAKES ACCOUNTABILITY[2]

Over the past 30 years of high-stakes accountability education reform has become a bi-partisan issue, represented by the passing of NCLB and the nearly seamless transition between George W. Bush and Barack Obama in the U.S. Department of Education. The messages, claims, and polices of Republicans and Democrats, conservatives and progressives are essentially identical, especially in the narratives about teacher quality (Thomas, 2012c).

In the early 1980s, the current accountability era was spurred by a flawed and politically corrupt report, *A Nation at Risk* (Bracey, 2003; Holton, 2003; Ravitch, 2010). The early focus of high-stakes accountability based on standards and testing, however, was directed at schools and students (initially through exit exams for graduation) while being implemented at the state level. That pattern cycled through several versions for about 20 years before NCLB lifted accountability to the federal level. Within another decade, the accountability focus has shifted to include the same standards and high-stakes testing paradigm applied to teachers at the individual classroom level. Again, these policies and claims are bi-partisan and compelling among the public.

As a typical example, the League of Women Voters of South Carolina released a report entitled "How to Evaluate and Retain Effective Teachers" (2011–2013) with the identified purpose "to examine the growing movement toward 'results based' evaluation nationally and in South Carolina" (p. 1). The LWVSC report represents both the patterns of focusing on teacher quality at the political and public levels, along with a relatively progressive organization embracing and promoting ideologies, policies, and claims that are essentially indistinguishable from conservative, neoliberal, and corporate agendas.

Before examining the substance of the report to reveal the patterns concerning teacher quality, several problems with the larger context of teacher evaluation and retention as they intersect with important challenges facing education need to be identified:

- Typical of calls for addressing teacher quality, the LWVSC report fails to clarify and provide evidence that teacher quality and retention are *primary* problems facing the education system. Without a clear and evidence-based problem, solutions are rendered less credible. However, one ignored but identified problem with teacher quality is *teacher assignment*: students of color, students from poverty, English-language learners (ELL), and students with special needs are disproportionately assigned to un-/under-certified and inexperienced teachers (Peskey & Haycock, 2006). As well, the implied problem of the report marginalizes the greatest obstacles facing public schools: poverty and the concentration of poverty. *Without identifying problems, goals, and the contexts of teaching and learning, claims about teacher quality are likely misguided and flawed.*
- The LWVSC report compiles and bases claims on a selection of references that are not representative of the body of research on teacher quality and VAM or performance-based systems of identifying teacher quality. As detailed below, the claims and research included in this report misrepresent the cited studies themselves as well as the current knowledge base on teacher quality and retention. *The teacher quality debate, along with ignoring evidence, is often marred by cherry-picking data or misrepresenting research that has garnered the status of urban legend in political and public discourse.*

In that context, the LWVSC report fails the larger education reform needs facing public education as well as the stated purpose of the study. The report opens with the assertion that "the most important school-based factor is an effective teacher" ("How to Evaluate," 2011–2013, p. 1), and then goes on to cite Hanushek (who perpetuates misleading claims about school funding [Heilig, 2013] and teacher quality although his own work shows teacher quality is only about 13–17% of measurable student outcomes [Hanushek, 2010; Jersey Jazzman, 2013]), among others. While the report is careful to note teacher quality is an important in-school factor, it repeatedly overstates teacher quality's impact, with terms such as "overwhelming" (p. 2), and fails to clarify that in-school factors are dwarfed by out-of-school factors. As represented in this report, two key aspects of the teacher quality debate include: (1) many advocates for addressing teacher quality do not qualify the importance of teacher quality, omitting "in-school" in their claims, and (2) when that qualification is made, few clearly acknowledge the disproportionate influence of out-of-school factors on measurable student outcomes.

Thus, teacher quality must be framed in the context of all influences on measurable student outcomes. Di Carlo (2010) offered a balanced picture of the *proportional impact* of teacher quality, including an accurate interpretation of many of the references cited in the LWVSC report (such as Hanushek):

> But in the big picture, roughly 60 percent of achievement outcomes is explained by student and family background characteristics (most are unobserved, but likely pertain to income/poverty). Observable and unobservable schooling factors explain roughly 20 percent, most of this (10–15 percent) being teacher effects. The rest of the variation (about 20 percent) is unexplained (error). In other words, though precise estimates vary, the preponderance of evidence shows that achievement differences between students are overwhelmingly attributable to factors outside of schools and classrooms (see Hanushek et al., 1998; Rockoff, 200[4]; Goldhaber et al., 1999; Rowan et al., 2002; Nye et al., 2004).[3]

As well, Di Carlo (2010) clarified that the data on teacher quality is a metric necessarily limited to measurable student outcomes (test scores) in the complicated context of teaching and learning:

> Now, to be clear: this does not mean that teachers aren't really important, nor that increasing teacher quality can only generate tiny improvements…. More practically, school-related factors are the only ones that education policy can directly address.

> So, teachers matter, and there are effective and less effective ones. And less effective ones can be made better, which would improve student performance. I dare say that teachers would agree completely.

> *Yet anyone reading or hearing the endless repetition of the standard teacher impact argument may very well think that teachers are all that matters* [emphasis added]. They might not spot, in the case of the blueprint's version, the twist of phrase ("at every level of our education system") that limits the scope to schooling factors. And even if they do, they may not be aware of how much schooling matters compared with non-school factors.

> As a result, they may also be more likely to unfairly blame teachers for the huge proportion of variation that is "out of their hands," instead of the extremely important factors, such as poverty and early childhood development, which we need to address at the same time. These people will also have unreasonable expectations for teacher quality policies. They'll expect immediate, miraculous progress, when real improvements are gradual and sustained.

Public and policy discussions of teacher quality, then, often contribute more to misunderstanding teacher quality and its importance than clarifying either how teacher quality matters or what the whole picture of needed education reform entails. Along with misrepresenting the impact of teacher quality on measurable student outcomes, the LWVSC report exposes that teacher quality claims often lend further credibility to misrepresented and flawed studies that have gained credibility through distorted media coverage; for example, a study by Chetty, Friendam, and Rockoff (2011) is cited in the LWVSC report in the exact ways that Di Carlo (2012e) warned against: "[T]hose using the results of this paper to argue forcefully for specific policies are drawing unsupported conclusions from otherwise very important empirical findings." As well, Baker (2012b) offered a similar warning:

> These are interesting findings. It's a really cool academic study. It's a freakin' amazing data set! But these findings cannot be immediately translated into what the headlines have suggested—that immediate use of value-added metrics to reshape the teacher workforce can lift the economy, and increase wages across the board! The headlines and media spin have been dreadfully overstated and deceptive. Other headlines and editorial commentary has been simply ignorant and irresponsible. (No, Mr. Moran, this one study did not, does not, cannot negate the vast array of concerns that have been raised about using value-added estimates as blunt, heavily weighted instruments in personnel policy in school systems.)

Along with misrepresenting the connection between teacher quality and future earning potential by students (the media-created narrative around the Chetty, Friendam, and Rockoff study), the LWVSC report perpetuates another popular and agenda-driven research myth—the need for consecutive years of high-quality teachers; yet again, this claim is inaccurate and should not drive policy, as explained by Di Carlo (2011b):

> [T]he "X consecutive teachers" argument only carries concrete policy implications if we can *accurately identify* the "top" teachers. *In reality, though, the ability to do so is still extremely limited* [emphasis added].

> So, in the context of policy debates, the argument proves almost nothing. All it really does—in a rather overblown, misleading fashion—is illustrate that teacher quality is important and should be improved, not that policies like merit pay, higher salaries, or charter schools will improve it.

> This represents a fundamental problem that I have discussed before: The conflation of the important finding that teachers matter—that they vary in their effectiveness—with the assumption that teacher effects can be measured accurately at the level of the individual teacher [see Di Carlo, 2011c, for a quick analogy explaining this dichotomy].

> But the "X consecutive teachers" argument doesn't help us evaluate whether this or anything else is a good idea. Using it in this fashion is both misleading and counterproductive.

It makes huge promises that cannot be fulfilled, while also serving as justification for policies that it cannot justify. Teacher quality is a target, not an arrow.

Teacher quality is directly linked to student earning power and *having high-quality teachers several years in a row* are both common claims in the teacher quality debate, but the only real thing the two claims share is that they are inaccurate and thus harmful to addressing teacher quality. Addressing oversimplified metrics related to teacher quality can and will reduce teacher quality in the same way as accountability based on standards and high-stakes testing has asked less of students.

Further, another implied and cited reason for addressing teacher quality and retention rests on widespread criticism of traditional teacher evaluation policies and practices. The LWVSC report lends a great deal of credibility to those criticisms while relying on *The Widget Effect* from The New Teacher Project (TNTP) (Di Carlo, 2011a). However, a typical pattern of think tank reports endorsing the focus on teacher quality includes that the media covers (and often misrepresents) the report but fails to acknowledge subsequent reviews that challenge or reject the credibility of the initial report. For example, a review of TNTP's publication calls into question, again, the credibility of the study's claims as well as using it as a basis for policy decisions:

> Overall, the report portrays current practices in teacher evaluation as a broken system perpetuated by a culture that refuses to recognize and deal with incompetence and that fails to reward excellence. However, omissions in the report's description of its methodology (e.g., sampling strategy, survey response rates) and its sample lead to questions about the generalizability of the report's findings. (Pecheone & Wei, 2009)

Di Carlo (2012b) has also documented that TNTP continues to misrepresent and overstate the impact of teacher quality and the effectiveness of identifying high-quality teachers, suggesting all stakeholders must be cautious, if not skeptical, about think tank reports:

> I just want to make one quick (and, in many respects, semantic) point about the manner in which TNTP identifies high-performing teachers, as I think it illustrates larger issues. In my view, the term "irreplaceable" doesn't apply, and I think it would have been a better analysis without it.
>
> Based on single-year estimates in math and reading, a full 43 percent of the NYC teachers classified as "irreplaceable" in 2009 were not classified as such in 2010. (In fairness, the year-to-year stability may be a bit higher using the other district-specific definitions.)
>
> Such instability and misclassification are inevitable no matter how the term is defined and how much data are available—it's all a matter of degree—but, in general, one must be cautious when interpreting single-year estimates.
>
> Perhaps more importantly, if you look at how they actually sorted teachers into categories, the label "irreplaceable," at least as I interpret it, seems inappropriate no matter how much data are available.

The LWVSC report does not highlight what is wrong with teacher quality or how teacher quality should be viewed by the public or addressed by policy, but it does expose the misleading claims made about teacher quality and the failure of the media and think tanks in that debate. Another significant element in the teacher quality discourse is the role of VAM and other metrics-based teacher evaluation systems, also reflected in the LWVSC report.

PERFORMANCE-BASED TEACHER EVALUATIONS: IS VAM CREDIBLE?

One of the most distracting threads of the teacher quality debate is the argument over VAM—most of that being how to make VAM work (usually wonkish discussions among statisticians that ignore larger foundational questions about if and why VAM is needed) or what percentage of revised teacher evaluation formulas should include VAM data. Those arguments, of course, help mask the larger questions about reform: The inherent flaws with using test scores in any high-stakes environment to label, rank, and sort students, teachers, and schools.

Typically, a significant portion of the LWVSC report makes claims about value-added methods (VAM) of teacher evaluations in the context of performance-based approaches to identifying teacher quality. Nationally, VAM and other performance-based policies are being implemented quickly, but with little regard for the current understanding of the effectiveness and limitations of those policies; this report fails to represent the current state of research on VAM accurately and depends on research and think-tank advocacy (for example, from the National Council on Teacher Quality [NCTQ]) that distorts the importance of teacher quality and the effectiveness of identifying teacher quality based on measurable student outcomes. At the very least, VAM must be field tested in order to identify its effectiveness; however, I remain skeptical that even field testing is a waste of precious time and funding—especially if issues of equity and opportunity in society and schools are not addressed.

While the LWVSC report remains supportive of performance-based policy recommendations, including teacher evaluations implementing VAM data at rates as high as 40%, it does identify cautions about test-based teacher evaluations, while also encouraging multiple measures in reformed teacher evaluation formulas and including teachers in the creation of a new evaluation system. Two failures, however, of the LWVSC report's endorsement of VAM and/or performance-based teacher evaluation systems include couching that endorsement in the distorted claims about teacher quality's impact on measurable student outcomes and relying on reports and policy recommendations made by NCTQ and the Bill and Melinda Gates Foundation. (For review evaluations of NCTQ and

Gates see the following: (a) NCTQ: Baker, 2010d; Baker, 2010c; Baker, 2010b; Benner, 2012; Ingersoll & Merrill, 2010; Schneider, 2013 [see additional parts to the review also]; and (b) Gates: Baker, 2010a; Baker, 2011; Libby, 2012; [Gates MET Project] Baker, 2013; Gabriel & Allington, 2012; Glass, 2013; Rothstein & Mathis, 2013; Rubinstein, 2013a; Rubinstein, 2013b.)

To better understand the teacher quality debate, and the recurring flaws of claims about teacher quality and teacher evaluation, the current knowledge base regarding VAM must be acknowledged as a complex, incomplete, and experimental process. What, then, are the current patterns from the research on VAM and performance-based models and how should those patterns shape policy? (For comprehensive examinations of research on VAM, see Di Carlo, 2012a; Di Carlo, 2012c [validity]; Di Carlo, 2012d [reliability]; Baker, 2012a [misrepresentations of VAM]; Baker et al., 2010; Ewing, 2011. For recent concerns about legal action and VAM-based teacher evaluation, see Baker, Oluwole, & Green, 2013; Pullin, 2013.)

VAM and test-based evaluations for teachers remain both misleading about teacher quality and misrepresented by think-tank reports, the media, and political leadership. Numerous researchers have detailed that teachers identified as high-quality or weak one year are identified *differently* in subsequent years: Numerous factors beyond the control of teachers remain reflected in test scores more powerfully than the individual impact of any specified teacher. The debate over teacher quality and measuring that quality, then, is highly distorted, as Di Carlo (2012a) explained: "Whether or not we use these measures in teacher evaluations is an important decision, but the attention it gets seems *way overblown*." Most advocates of VAM make that mistake.

VAM and performance-based teacher evaluations in high-stakes settings distort teaching and learning by narrowing the focus of both teaching and learning to teaching to the test and test scores. VAM and test-based data are potentially valuable as one metric (and only if not in a high-stakes environment) for big picture patterns and in-school or in-district decision-making regarding teacher assignment (see Peske & Haycock, 2006, in terms of the need to insure marginalized students with high-quality teachers), but high-stakes VAM and performance-based evaluations of *individual teachers* remain inaccurate and inappropriate for evaluation, pay, or retention.

In states where poverty and state budget concerns burden the state and the public school system, VAM and performance-based systems that rely on extensive retooling of standards, testing, and teacher evaluation systems are simply not cost-effective (Bausell, 2013): "VAM is not reliable or valid, and VAM-based polices are not cost-effective for the purpose of raising student achievement and increasing earnings by terminating large numbers of low-performing teachers" (Yeh, 2014). And further, rejecting VAM and using significant percentages of student test scores to evaluate and retain teachers is not rejecting teacher accountability, but confronting the misuse of data. Ewing (2011) clarified that VAM is flawed math and thus invalid as a tool in teacher evaluation:

> Of course we should hold teachers accountable, but this does not mean we have to pretend that mathematical models can do something they cannot. Of course we should rid our schools of incompetent teachers, but value-added models are an exceedingly blunt tool for this purpose. In any case, we ought to expect more from our teachers than what value-added attempts to measure. (p. 672)

If any district or state chooses to reform teacher evaluation—which remains a project far less urgent than other problems being ignored, as I discuss below—reform would be guided better by Gabriel and Allington (2012), who have analyzed and challenged the Gates Foundation's MET Project, which has prompted misguided and hasty implementation of VAM-style teacher evaluation reform:

> Although we don't question the utility of using evidence of student learning to inform teacher development, we suggest that a better question would not assume that value-added scores are the only existing knowledge about effectiveness in teaching. Rather, a good question would build on existing research and investigate how to increase the amount and intensity of effective instruction.

Instead, Gabriel and Allington (2012) recommended five questions to guide teacher evaluation reform, instead of VAM or other student-outcome-based initiatives:

> Do evaluation tools inspire responsive teaching or defensive conformity?
> Do evaluation tools reflect our goals for public education?
> Do evaluation tools encourage teachers to use text in meaningful ways?
> Do evaluation tools spark meaningful conversations with teachers?
> Do evaluation tools promote education experiences? (p. 46)

Again, these guidelines are evidence-based alternatives to discredited and experimental commitments to the misrepresented evidence in the report from LWVSC, but states across the U.S. remain overburdened by issues related to equity and opportunity that outweigh the need to reform teacher evaluation at this time, suggesting that debates about teacher quality and teacher evaluation are primarily both misguided and ill-timed.

On balance, the LWVSC report is *representative of calls for policy reform focusing on teacher quality* because the report misrepresents teacher quality and overstates the need and ability to identify high-quality teachers using VAM and other performance-based policies. The flaws in this report grow from an over-reliance on misguided and misrepresented research and advocacy while ignoring the rich and detailed evidence from the full body of research on teacher quality. Ultimately, the report encourages spending valuable time and resources on policies that are dwarfed by more pressing needs facing states and public schools—a failure of education reform leadership replicated in the perpetual retooling of education standards, such as adopting Common Core State Standards (Thomas, 2012b) and high-stakes testing based on revised standards while ignoring social and educational inequity (Thomas, 2012a). In short, states across the U.S. have a number of social and educational challenges that need addressing before committing to experiments with revising teacher evaluation and retention policies, including the following:

- Identify how better to allocate state resources to address childhood and family poverty, childhood food security, children and family access to high-quality health care, and stable, well-paying work for families.
- Replace current education policies based on accountability, standards, and testing with policies that address equity and opportunity for all students.
- Address immediately the greatest teacher quality issue facing public schools—inequitable distribution of teacher quality among students in greatest need (high-poverty children, children of color, ELL, and students with special needs).
- Address immediately the *conditions of teaching and learning* in the schools, including issues of student/teacher ratios, building conditions and material availability, administrative and community support of teachers, equitable school funding and teacher salaries, teacher job security and academic freedom in right-to-work states, and school safety.

Any policy changes that further entrench the culture of testing as a mechanism for evaluating students, teachers, and schools *perpetuate the burden of inequity in society and schools*. In fact, schools do not need new standards, new tests, or new teacher evaluation systems. All of these practices have been implemented in different versions with high-stakes attached for the past 30 years—with the current result being the same identified failures with public schools that were the basis of these policies. Leaders and the public need to come to terms with identifying problems before seeking solutions. The problems are ones of equity and opportunity, and no current teacher evaluation plan is facing those realities. As Flanagan (2013) confronted, however, teacher quality remains an important concern. Next, then, I consider how the teacher quality debate is also about the misaligned priorities of reform.

TEACHER QUALITY MANIA: BACKWARD BY DESIGN[4]

To help clarify how the debate over teacher quality is also distorted by overemphasizing the importance of addressing teacher quality as a first and primary reform need, I want to consider the allegory of the river (2011), slightly revised to fit the education reform debate.

Throughout the Land, people discovered babies floating in the river. A few were chosen to save those babies. While many babies were saved, too many babies continued to perish.

Technocrats, Economists, and Statisticians gathered all the Data that they could and discovered that at least 60% of the reason the babies survived or perished in the river was due to babies being tossed in the river; about 10–15% of the reason babies survived or perished was due to the quality of those trying to save babies in the river.

So the Leaders of the Land decided to focus exclusively on increasing the quality of those trying to save the babies floating in the river, saying, "There is nothing we can do about babies being tossed in the river, and there are no excuses for not saving these babies!"

While this revised allegory may appear to be far-fetched, I suggest this is exactly how the teacher-quality debate has skewed *when* reform should address teacher quality (not *if* teacher quality should be addressed). The altered tale above reads like a dystopian allegory, but it is a fair and accurate portrayal of the current mania to address teacher quality—a mania that simply has the entire reform process backward.

First, as discussed above, the body of research shows a clear statistical pattern about the array of factors influencing measurable student outcomes (Di Carlo, 2012e). When educators and education researchers note that teacher quality is dwarfed by other factors, primarily out-of-school factors associated with affluence and poverty, Corporate and "No Excuses" Reformers respond with the straw-man argument that quoting statistical facts is somehow saying teachers *cannot* have an impact on students or that quoting the data is simply an excuse for not trying to educate all students. (See Ferlazzo, 2013, and Cody, 2013, for examples of this phenomenon in the debate over teacher quality.)

Ultimately, however, the problem is not that teacher quality doesn't matter or that teachers do not want to be evaluated or held accountable. The problem is that addressing teacher quality in a single-minded way is self-defeating since (as the altered allegory above shows) it has the *priorities of reform backward*. Teacher quality reform must occur (Flanagan, 2013), but it must come *after* the primary factors impacting learning and teaching conditions are addressed, thus making it possible to make valid and reliable evaluations of teacher quality. That process must include:

(1) *First, and directly,* address the inequity of opportunity in the lives of children to create the conditions within which schools/teachers can succeed, and thus school and teacher quality can be better evaluated and supported. As stated in a recent review of misleading "no excuses" and "miracle" school claims: "Addressing out-of-school factors is primary and fundamental to resolving education inequality" (Paige, 2013).

(2) Next, address equity and opportunity within schools. Teaching conditions must be equitable in *all* school and for *all* students. Currently, affluent and successful students have the most experienced certified teachers and also sit in AP and IB classes with low student/teacher ratios, while poor and struggling students have new and un-/under-certified teachers, sitting in high-student/teacher-ratio classes that are primarily test-prep. *Inequitable teaching/learning conditions actually mask our ability to identify quality teachers.*

(3) Then, once out-of-school equity and in-school equity are addressed, focusing on teaching and learning conditions, teachers must be afforded *autonomy*; and finally, we can gather credible evidence to begin identifying valid teacher quality metrics to inform evaluating, supporting, and retaining teachers.

The first and second priorities can be implemented simultaneously and immediately, with the third priority delayed until conditions are equitable enough to make authentic assessments of teacher impact on student learning. (And regardless, everyone involved in teaching and learning can and must continue to teach as well as possible; that is a given.) Current arguments that only teacher quality matters are neither statistically accurate nor an effective reform priority; rather, they are a frantic effort to save the babies floating in the river while ignoring the real crisis of babies being thrown in the river in the first place.

WHAT'S REALLY WRONG WITH TEACHER QUALITY AND TEACHER EDUCATION?

Writing in *Mother Jones*, Drum (2013) reached a fatalistic conclusion about high standards and student achievement, after a study revealed that yet another reform has failed:

> My cynicism about the ed reform community grows by leaps and bounds every time I read a story like this. And that's pretty often. Here's my advice for what you should do whenever you read an article about a school that's shown miraculous results by applying some reform or another (or by hiring a miracle worker of some stripe or another):
>
> 1. Don't believe it if it's based on a single school or other small sample.
> 2. Don't believe it if most of the evidence comes from the school itself.
> 3. Don't believe it if the reform in question was put in place only a few years ago.
> 4. Don't believe it if it hasn't been replicated elsewhere.
> 5. Don't believe it unless it's been rigorously tested by academics who didn't already support the idea in the first place.
> 6. And even if it passes all those tests, don't believe it anyway.

This nexus of education reform, educational research, and the media led Di Carlo (2013) to make an equally disturbing statement: "Nobody wins these particular battles. Everyone is firing blanks."

The teacher quality reform debate sits squarely in the midst of a failed debate paradigm, as the discussion above reveals. Teacher quality and our ability to identify teacher quality are overstated and misrepresented, while policies connected to teacher quality are implemented far too quickly and carelessly. On balance, however, I agree with Flanagan (2013) that teacher quality must matter, and it must be addressed—but without high-stakes and not before addressing the overwhelming issues of social and educational inequity burdening our students, teachers, and schools.

Let's turn, then, to the final question: What's really wrong with teacher quality and teacher education?

The central teacher quality issue that can be addressed without delay remains the inequity of teacher assignment among classes and races of students. Experienced and certified teachers are assigned to affluent and white students, disproportionately, while high-needs students are assigned inexperienced and un-/under-certified teachers (including more and more TFA recruits). While this teacher problem is not easy to overcome, it is based on evidence and likely a reform that would significantly impact the quality of education high-needs students receive.

Another urgent teacher quality need is better preparing pre-service teachers and better supporting in-service teachers in their expertise and experience with working with the most time- and financial-intensive populations of students—children of color, children living in poverty, bi-/multi-lingual learners, and students with special needs. This teacher quality issue must be aimed at supporting and improving the current workforce, and not about labeling, ranking, and dismissing teachers.

School policy and practices could address both of these teacher quality problems and the outcomes would be positive if we also abandon our singular focus on measurable student outcomes (test data) and our silver-bullet mentality about change happening immediately. Student outcomes and teacher quality should be much more than test data, and change takes much more time than political and public sentiments allow.

Broadly speaking, *teacher quality should be reformed as a mechanism for insuring high- quality and well-supported teachers in equitable teaching and learning conditions for all students in all schools.* This is in direct contrast to the high-accountability paradigm being promoted currently that appears more concerned about dismissing teachers and making schools more cost effective (regardless of outcomes).

Next, what are the problems with teacher education?

My short answer is to first say, it's not what the National Council on Teacher Quality (NCTQ) is claiming. Part of the problem with teacher education is that the political and public discourse about teacher education has been historically condescending and, in the past few years, further eroded by the essential failure of teacher education: the technocratic and bureaucratic nature of certification.

While the NCTQ has fostered both an influential and compelling presence in the teacher education debate, we must acknowledge that think-tank advocacy and reports are often agenda-driven and not well suited for education reform (Welner, Hinchey, Molnar, & Weltzman, 2010). Further, Diane Ravitch (2012) has challenged the NCTQ's agenda, a review of the NCTQ's first report has highlighted the flaws in the NCTQ's methods and conclusions (Benner, 2012), and Cody (2012) and Hassard (2012) have further questioned the NCTQ's credibility. Political, public, and media failure to consider think-tank credibility (see Yettick, 2009, and Molnar, 2001), as well as what educational problems we are seeking to solve, remain corrosive dynamics in the teacher education debate.

Beyond these direct challenges to the NCTQ as a representative but powerful force in the policy directed at teacher education, however, lie the broader failures of teacher education—our repeated faith in standards, measurement, and certification. Teacher education, and teacher quality, must be reformed *away from* the certification process and *toward* building education as a challenging discipline and raising teachers to the level of both master teachers and autonomous scholars. Hewitt opened a volume on reinvigorating the study of philosophy in education by lamenting: "I never thought that I would ever have to justify the moral importance of social foundations courses—particularly philosophy of education courses—in Ph.D. and Ed.D. programs to a committee of colleagues, all holding Ph.D.s" (Kincheloe & Hewitt, 2011, p. ix). But the reality of education degrees throughout undergraduate and graduate education is that issues of certification and accreditation, along with market forces, have eroded the content of education degrees and supplanted that content with bureaucracy; for example, departments and colleges of education focus heavily on documenting compliance with accreditation and certification mandates that supplant their academic autonomy and the quality of coursework offered to students.

I, for example, am one of those people in education with a string of education degrees—an undergraduate and two graduate degrees in education. Without hesitation, based on my experiences as a student and my more recent decade as a teacher educator, the certification and accreditation requirements (identifying and meeting prescribed standards, for example) do more to inhibit than help the growth of educators and scholars, but every course and experience related to teacher education *not linked to certification* was invaluable to me.

This may sound simpler than I intend, but *the central reform that teacher education needs is not more or different standards and accountability for those standards, but a renaissance of expertise and scholarship in the field of education*—both for those professors and scholars of education and the undergraduate and graduate students seeking to be teachers and scholars. Professors in fields outside of education—English, political science, biology, for example—do not spend their professional time conforming to and addressing standards mandated by think tanks or the government. The agency and accountability for expertise rests within the professor. Yet, professors of education and K-12 teachers spend inordinate amounts of time and energy on bureaucratic compliance to issues related to standards, certification, and accreditation—time spent away from teaching, learning, and scholarship.

For both improved teacher quality and teacher education, then, we must set aside our historical and current commitments to technocratic bureaucracy. Instead, we must seek equity of access to quality teachers and schools for all students, and we must build teacher professionalism by focusing on teacher expertise and autonomy instead of standards and accountability.

Quintero (2012) explained how teacher commitment is impacted by misguided attempts to hold teachers accountable as an avenue to increased teacher quality:

> Furthermore, the evidence suggests that emphasis on performance and accountability "have effects that are substantially greater than overwork and stress." That is, when teachers feel that they are operating "under a disciplinary regime," negative emotions such as fear, anger and disaffection begin to take hold—and fester.

Teacher quality and teacher education matter, but our current misguided discourse and policies guarantee only to further ruin the promise of universal public education driven by teachers as scholars and leaders.

*

The assault on teachers and teachers unions includes inaccurate crisis discourse about "bad" teachers, the need to immediately reform teacher education and evaluation, and related reforms that indirectly address teacher quality such as the hiring of TFA recruits and growing commitment to charter schools. All of these reforms are misguided.

Becoming and being a teacher (Thomas, 2013a) is a complex and evolutionary state of being that is devalued, de-professionalized, and marginalized by purely technocratic discourse and policies. The great irony of the current focus on teacher quality is that virtually all of the policies are certain to actually lower expectations and erode quality.

As a final example, the charter school movement is a stark and disturbing intersection of calls for broadly reforming teacher quality and education. Charter schools, for example, have proven to worsen teacher churn (teachers leaving schools at high rates creating a concurrent influx of new teachers each year), a situation that significantly and negatively impacts students with high needs:

Using multi-nomial logistic regression, we found the odds of a charter schoolteacher leaving the profession versus staying in the same school are 132% greater than those of a traditional public school teacher. The odds of a charter schoolteacher moving schools are 76% greater. (Stuit & Smith, 2009)

Just as TFA recruits perpetuate the inequity of opportunity for students with high needs—a key problem within current public schools that must be reformed—charter schools also embody the same problems we must reform in our current system. As evidence such as this becomes more common, educators must raise a voice against education reform that doesn't address clear needs and often increases the problems.

But that raised voice must also keep a steady message that educators are seeking our professional autonomy in order to have higher expectations for each other as well as for all the children who enter our classrooms. In the end, teacher quality matters, but not in the ways the current teacher narratives suggest. Our job as a society is to make sure babies are not thrown in the river in the first place.

NOTES

1   Adapted from P. L. Thomas (2012). What's really wrong with teacher quality and teacher education? AlterNet. Retrieved from http://www.dailykos.com/story/2012/03/16/1074948/-Charter-Schools-Not-the-Answer-Especially-If-We-Fail-to-Identify-the-Question#

2   Adapted from P. L. Thomas (2013, January 3). Review [UPDATED]: "How to evaluate and retain effective teachers." Retrieved from http://radicalscholarship.wordpress.com/2013/01/03/review-how-to-evaluate-and-retain-effective-teachers-league-of-women-voters-of-south-carolina/

3   For additional examinations of out-of-school factors compared to teacher quality and in-school factors see Berliner, 2009, 2014; Hirsch, 2007; Rothstein, 2010; Traub, 2000.

4   Adapted from P. L. Thomas (2013, January 14), "Teacher quality mania: Backward by design" [Blog]. Retrieved from http://radicalscholarship.wordpress.com/2013/01/14/teacher-quality-mania-backward-by-design/

REFERENCES

Arkansas Children's Trust Fund for the Prevention of Child Abuse & Neglect. (2011, January). The allegory of the river. Retrieved from http://arkansasctf.weebly.com/uploads/3/6/6/8/3668913/allegory_of_the_river.pdf

Baker, B. (2010a, December 13). A few comments on the Gates/Kane value-added study. [Blog post]. Retrieved from http://schoolfinance101.wordpress.com/2010/12/13/a-few-comments-on-the-gateskane-value-added-study/

Baker, B. (2010b, December 4). The curious duplicity of NCTQ. [Blog post]. Retrieved from http://schoolfinance101.wordpress.com/2010/12/04/the-bizarre-hypocrisy-of-nctq/

Baker, B. (2010c, October 8). NCTQ: We're sure it will work! Even if research says it doesn't! [Blog post]. Retrieved from http://schoolfinance101.wordpress.com/2010/10/08/nctq-were-sure-it-will-work-even-if-research-says-it-doesnt/

Baker, B. (2010d, January 29). NCTQ teacher policy ratings: Where's the quality [Blog post]. Retrieved from http://schoolfinance101.wordpress.com/2010/01/29/nctq-teacher-policy-ratings-wheres-the-quality/

Baker, B. (2011, March 2). Smart guy (Gates) makes my list of "dumbest stuff I've ever read!" [Blog post]. Retrieved from http://schoolfinance101.wordpress.com/2011/03/02/smart-guy-gates-makes-my-list-of-dumbest-stuff-ive-ever-read/

Baker, B. (2012a, May 28). Two persistent reform misrepresentations regarding VAM estimates [Blog post]. Retrieved from http://schoolfinance101.wordpress.com/2012/05/28/two-persistent-reformy-misrepresentations-regarding-vam-estimates/

Baker, B. (2012b, January 7). Fire first, ask questions later? Comments on recent teacher effectiveness studies [Blog post]. Retrieved from http://schoolfinance101.wordpress.com/2012/01/07/fire-first-ask-questions-later-comments-on-recent-teacher-effectiveness-studies/

Baker, B. (2013, January 9). Gates still doesn't get it! Trapped in a world of circular reasoning & flawed frameworks [Blog post]. Retrieved from http://schoolfinance101.wordpress.com/2013/01/09/gates-still-doesn't-get-it-trapped-in-a-world-of-circular-reasoning-flawed-frameworks/

Baker, B. D., Oluwole, J., & Green, P. C. (2013). The legal consequences of mandating high stakes decisions based on low quality information: Teacher evaluation in the race-to-the-top era. *Education Policy Analysis Archives, 21*(5). Retrieved from http://epaa.asu.edu/ojs/article/view/1298

Baker, E., Barton, P. E., Darling-Hammond, L., Haertel, E., Ladd, H. F., Linn, R. L.,…Shepard, L. A. (2010, August 29). *Problems with the use of student test scores to evaluate teachers* (EPI Briefing Paper #278). Retrieved from Economic Policy Institute website: http://www.epi.org/publication/bp278/

Bausell, R. B. (2013, January 15). Probing the science of value-added evaluation. *Education Week, 32*(17), 22–23, 25. Retrieved from http://www.edweek.org/ew/articles/2013/01/16/17bausell.h32.html

Benner, S. M. (2012, January 10). *Quality in student teaching: Flawed research leads to unsound recommendations.* Retrieved from National Education Policy Center website: http://nepc.colorado.edu/thinktank/review-student-teaching

Berliner, D. C. (2009). *Poverty and potential: Out-of-school factors and school success.* Retrieved from National Education Policy Center website: http://nepc.colorado.edu/publication/poverty-and-potential

Berliner, D. C. (2014). Effects of inequality and poverty vs. teachers and schooling on America's youth. *Teachers College Record, 116*(1). Retrieved from http://www.tcrecord.org/content.asp?contentid=16889

Bessie, A. (2010a, December 29). To fix education: Fire human teachers, hire holograms. *Daily Censored.* Retrieved from http://www.dailycensored.com/to-fix-education-fire-human-teachers-hire-holograms/

Bessie, A. (2010b, October 15). The myth of the bad teacher. *Truthout.* Retrieved from http://www.truth-out.org/the-myth-bad-teacher64223

Bessie, A. (2011, January 22). Let's not "reform" public education. *Truthout.* Retrieved from http://www.truth-out.org/lets-not-reform-public-education67006

Bracey, G. W. (2003). April foolishness: The 20th anniversary of *A Nation at Risk. Phi Delta Kappan, 84*(8), 616–621.

Casey, L. (2013a, April 18). America's union suppression movement (and its apologists), part two [Blog post]. Retrieved from http://shankerblog.org/?p=8177

Casey, L. (2013b, April 17). America's union suppression movement (and its apologists), part one [Blog post]. Retrieved from http://shankerblog.org/?p=8174

Cody, A. (2012, May 25). Payola policy: NCTQ prepares its hit on schools of education [Blog post]. Retrieved from http://blogs.edweek.org/teachers/living-in-dialogue/2012/05/payola_policy_nctq_prepares_it.html

Cody, A. (2013, January 11). Hopes for the new year: Begone ghosts of reform past! [Blog post]. Retrieved from http://blogs.edweek.org/teachers/living-in-dialogue/2013/01/hopes_for_the_new_year_begone_.html

Di Carlo, M. (2010, July 14). Teachers matter, but so do words [Blog post]. Retrieved from http://shankerblog.org/?p=74

Di Carlo, M. (2011a, April 27). The new layoff formula project [Blog post]. Retrieved from http://shankerblog.org/?p=2377

Di Carlo, M. (2011b, March 31). The nonsense behind the "X consecutive teachers" argument [Blog post]. Retrieved from http://www.washingtonpost.com/blogs/answer-sheet/post/the-nonsense-behind-the-x-consecutive-teachers-argument/2011/03/29/AFlU345B_blog.html

Di Carlo, M. (2011c, February 18). Value-added: Theory versus practice [Blog post]. Retrieved from http://shankerblog.org/?p=1928

Di Carlo, M. (2012a, November 13). Value-added, for the record [Blog post]. Retrieved from http://shankerblog.org/?p=7179

Di Carlo, M. (2012b, July 30). The irreconcilables [Blog post]. Retrieved from http://shankerblog.org/?p=6372

Di Carlo, M. (2012c, April 18). Value-added versus observations, part two: Validity [Blog post]. Retrieved from http://shankerblog.org/?p=5670

Di Carlo, M. (2012d, April 12). Value-added versus observations, part one: Reliability [Blog post]. Retrieved from http://shankerblog.org/?p=5621

Di Carlo, M. (2012e, January 8). The persistence of both teacher effects and misinterpretations of research about them [Blog post]. Retrieved from http://shankerblog.org/?p=4708

Di Carlo, M. (2013, February 4). Why nobody wins the education "research wars" [Blog post]. Retrieved from http://shankerblog.org/?p=7586

Drum, K. (2013, January 28). Big surprise: Yet another ed reform turns out to be bogus [Blog post]. Retrieved from http://www.motherjones.com/kevin-drum/2013/01/big-surprise-yet-another-ed-reform-turns-out-be-bogus

Ewing, J. (2011, May). Mathematical intimidation: Driven by the data. *Notices of the American Mathematical Society, 58*(5), 667–673. Retrieved from http://www.ams.org/notices/201105/rtx110500667p.pdf

Ferlazzo, L. (2013, January 13). Do teachers undercut our "relevance" by pointing out other factors that affect student achievement? [Blog post]. Retrieved from http://larryferlazzo.edublogs.org/2013/01/13/do-teachers-undercut-our-relevance-by-pointing-out-other-factors-that-affect-student-achievement/

Flanagan, N. (2013, February 1). "About those bar exams for teachers…" [Blog post]. Retrieved from http://blogs.edweek.org/teachers/teacher_in_a_strange_land/2013/02/about_those_bar_exams_for_teachers.html

Gabriel, R., & Allington, R. (2012, November). The MET Project: The wrong 45 million dollar question. *Educational Leadership, 70*(3), 44–49. Retrieved from http://216.78.200.159/RandD/

Educational%20Leadership/MET%20Project%20-%20Wrong%2045%20Millon%20Question%20-%20Gabriel.pdf

Glass, G. V. (2013, January 14). Gates Foundation wastes more money pushing VAM [Blog post]. Retrieved from http://ed2worlds.blogspot.com/2013/01/gates-foundation-wastes-more-money.html?

Goldhaber, D. D., Brewer, D. J., & Anderson, D. J. (1999). A three-way error components analysis of educational productivity. *Education Economics, 7*(3), 199–203.

Hanushek, E. (2010, December). *The economic value of higher teacher quality* (Working Paper 56). Washington, DC: Calder, The Urban Institute.

Hanushek, E. A., Kain, J. F., & Rivkin, S. G. (1998, August). *Teachers, schools, and academic achievement. NBER Working Paper Series* (Working Paper 6691). Retrieved from National Bureau of Economic Research website:

Hassard, J. (2012, May 30). NCTQ study of assessment in teacher preparation courses flunks. *The Art of Teaching Science.* Retrieved from http://www.artofteachingscience.org/2012/05/30/nctq-study-teacher-preparation-sham/

Heilig, J.V. (2013, April 18). Top ten list: Why "choice" demonstrates money matters. [Web log]. Retrieved from http://cloakinginequity.com/2013/04/18/top-ten-list-why-choice-demonstrates-that-money-matters/

Hirsch, D. (2007, September). *Experiences of poverty and educational disadvantage.* Retrieved from Joseph Rowntree Foundation website: http://www.jrf.org.uk/knowledge/findings/socialpolicy/2123.asp

Holton, G. (2003, April 25). An insider's view of "A Nation at Risk" and why it still matters. *The Chronicle Review, 49*(33), B13.

Ingersoll, R., & Merrill, L. (2010). [Review of the brief *Teacher layoffs: Rethinking 'Last hired, first fired' policies* by the National Council on Teacher Quality]. Retrieved from National Education Policy Center website: http://nepc.colorado.edu/thinktank/review-teacher-layoffs

Jersey Jazzman. (2013, April 7). "X months of learning" is a phony metric [Blog post].Retrieved from http://jerseyjazzman.blogspot.com/2013/04/x-months-of-learning-is-phony-metric.html

Kincheloe, J. L., & Hewitt, R., (Eds.). (2011). *Regenerating the philosophy of education: What happened to soul?* New York, NY: Peter Lang.

League of Women Voters of South Carolina. (2011–2013). *How to Evaluate and Retain Effective Teachers: Study by the League of Women Voters of South Carolina, 2011–2013.* Retrieved from http://www.lwvsc.org/teacherretention.html

Libby, K. (2012, March 2). A look at the education programs of the Gates Foundation [Blog post]. Retrieved from http://shankerblog.org/?p=5234

Molnar, A. (2001, April 11). *The media and educational research: What we know vs. what the public hears.* Paper presented at the 2001 AERA Annual Meeting, Seattle, Washington. Retrieved from http://epsl.asu.edu/epru/documents/cerai-01-14.htm

Nye, B., Konstantopoulos, S., & Hedges, L. V. (2004, Fall). How large are teacher effects? *Education Evaluation and Policy Analysis, 26*(3), 237–257. Retrieved from http://steinhardt.nyu.edu/scmsAdmin/uploads/002/834/127%20-%20Nye%20B%20%20Hedges%20L%20%20V%20%20%20Konstantopoulos%20S%20%20(2004).pdf

Paige, M. (2013, January). [Review of the report *Failure is not an option* by Public Agenda]. Retrieved from the National Education Policy Center website: http://www.greatlakescenter.org/docs/Think_Twice/TT_Paige_PublicAgenda.pdf

Pecheone, R. L., & Wei, R. C. (2009). [Review of the report *The widget effect: Our national failure to acknowledge and act on teacher differences* by The New Teacher Project]. Retrieved from http://epicpolicy.org/thinktank/review-Widget-Effect

Peske, H. G., & Haycock, K. (2006, June). Teaching inequality: How poor and minority students are shortchanged on teacher quality. Washington, DC: The Education Trust. Retrieved from http://www.edtrust.org/sites/edtrust.org/files/publications/files/TQReportJune2006.pdf

Pullin, D. (2013). Legal issues in the use of student test scores and value-added models (VAM) to determine educational quality. *Education Policy Analysis Archives, 21*(6). Retrieved from http://epaa.asu.edu/ojs/article/view/1160

Quintero, E. (2012, June 5). Teachers: Pressing the right buttons. Retrieved from http://shankerblog.org/?p=5990

Ravitch, D. (2010). *The death and life of the great American school system: How testing and choice are undermining education.* New York, NY: Basic Books.

Ravitch, D. (2012, May 24). Ravitch: What is NCTQ? (and why you should know) [Blog post]. Retrieved from http://www.washingtonpost.com/blogs/answer-sheet/post/ravitch-what-is-nctq-and-why-you-should-know/2012/05/23/gJQAg7CrlU_blog.html

Rockoff, J. E. (2004). The impact of individual teachers on student achievement: Evidence from panel data. *American Economic Review, 94*, 247–252.

Rothstein, J., & Mathis, W. J. (2013, January). Review of two culminating reports from the MET Project. Retrieved from the National Education Policy Center website. http://nepc.colorado.edu/thinktank/review-MET-final-2013

Rothstein, R. (2010, October 14). *How to fix our schools* (Issue Brief No. 286). Washington, DC: Economic Policy Institute. Retrieved from http://www.epi.org/publications/entry/ib286

Rowan, B., Correnti, R., & Miller, R. J. (2002, November). *What large-scale, survey research tells us about teacher effects on student achievement: Insights from the* Prospects *study of Elementary schools* (CPRE Research Report Series RR-051). Retrieved from the Consortium for Policy Research in Education website http://www.cpre.org/images/stories/cpre_pdfs/rr51.pdf

Rubinstein, G. (2013a, January 13). $50 million. 3 years. No clue [Blog post]. Retrieved from http://garyrubinstein.teachforus.org/2013/01/13/50-million-3-years-no-clue/

Rubinstein, G. (2013b, January 9). The 50 million dollar lie [Blog post]. Retrieved from http://garyrubinstein.teachforus.org/2013/01/09/the-50-million-dollar-lie/

Sanchez, C. (2013, January 29). Union backs "bar exam" for teachers [Blog post]. Retrieved from http://www.npr.org/2013/01/29/170579245/union-backs-bar-exam-for-teachers

Schneider, M. (2013, January 26). NCTQ letter grades and the reformer agenda—part I [Blog post]. Retrieved from http://deutsch29.wordpress.com/2013/01/26/nctq-letter-grades-and-the-reformer-agenda-part-i/

Stuit, D. A., & Smith, T. M. (2009). *Teacher turnover in charter schools.* Retrieved from the National Center on School Choice website: http://www.vanderbilt.edu/schoolchoice/search/publication.php?id=62

Thomas, P. L. (2011, December). Teacher quality and accountability: A failed debate [Blog post]. Retrieved from http://www.dailycensored.com/teacher-quality-and-accountability-a-failed-debate/

Thomas, P. L. (2012a, December 26). Tests fail South's legacy of inequity [Blog post]. Retrieved from http://www.dailykos.com/story/2012/12/26/1173910/-Tests-Fail-South-s-Legacy-of-Inequity

Thomas, P. L. (2012b, December 2). The CCSS stampede: Trampling why, what, how we teach [Blog post]. Retrieved from http://www.dailykos.com/story/2012/12/02/1166605/-The-CCSS-Stampede-Trampling-Why-What-How-We-Teach

Thomas, P. L. (2012c, August 23). Educators have no political party [Blog post]. Retrieved from http://www.dailykos.com/story/2012/08/23/1123277/-Educators-Have-No-Political-Party

Thomas, P. L. (2012d, March 16). Charter schools not the answer, especially if we fail to identify the question [Blog post]. Retrieved from http://www.dailykos.com/story/2012/03/16/1074948/-Charter-Schools-Not-the-Answer-Especially-if-We-Fail-to-Identify-the-Question#

Thomas, P. L., (Ed.). (2013a). *Becoming and being a teacher: Confronting traditional norms to create new democratic realities.* New York, NY: Peter Lang.

Thomas, P. L. (2013b, January 30). Schools can't do it alone: Why "doubly disadvantaged" kids continue to struggle academically [Blog post]. Retrieved from http://www.alternet.org/education/schools-cant-do-it-alone-why-doubly-disadvantaged-kids-continue-struggle-academically

Traub, J. (2000, January 16). What no school can do. *New York Times Magazine.* Retrieved from http://local.provplan.org/pp170/materials/what%20no%20school%20can%20do.htm

Welner, K. G., Hinchey, P. H., Molnar, A., & Weltzman, D. (Eds.). (2010). *Think tank research quality: Lessons for policy makers, the media, and the public.* Charlotte, NC: Information Age.

Yeh, S. S. (2014). A reanalysis of the effects of teacher replacement using value-added modeling. *Teachers College Record, 116*(1). Retrieved from http://www.tcrecord.org/Content.asp?ContentId=16934

Yettick, H. (2009). *The research that reaches the public: Who produces the educational research mentioned in the news media?* Retrieved from the National Education Policy Center website: http://epicpolicy.org/publication/research-that-reaches

CHAPTER FOUR

Teach For America, THE Neoliberal Alternative TO Teacher Professionalism

T. JAMESON BREWER AND ANTHONY CODY

INTRODUCTION

The biggest threat to teacher professionalism and the traditional dispositions associated therein is the neoliberal paradigm currently shaping the discourse of education reform in the United States and globally. Accordingly, the proponents of pro-market reforms seek to subvert teacher professionalism, commoditize teaching and learning for profit, and de-skill teaching in order to replace traditional colleges of education with fast-entry alternative training programs. In order to accomplish this, education reformers are attempting to manipulate the public's (and teachers') disposition towards education into a more quantifiable and thus accountable practice. This requires teachers and other stakeholders in public education to understand teaching as a standardized hard service rather than a more individualistic and reflexive practice. Boyles (2011) made this point by addressing the dualism of hard versus soft services, noting that

> [w]hat makes the service "hard" is really the *ease* [original emphasis] of measurement of the topic or process. Differently, "soft" services in schools include counseling and teaching. They are traditionally seen as "soft" because they have not been as easy to quantify. This distinction between the ease of accountancy associated with "hard" versus "soft" services gives us one indication of the larger purpose of privatization: to de-skill teaching and learning such that the traditional "soft" services become subsumed under the behavioristic, scientific, economistic logics of "hard" services. A form of reductionism, the ideology of

> privatization calls for breaking down complex relationships into their most component
> parts for ease of accountancy. (p. 359)

This positivist disposition towards education and teaching attempts to reduce teaching into segments of "best practices" that can then be duplicated en masse with quality control and measurement as both the means and ends of teaching. This disposition supports the assumption that anyone can be a teacher if they simply have the recipe of "good practices" and focus strictly on the measurable outcomes of testing rather on the "soft" services that teachers provide. Operating under such illusions, neoliberalism and its proponents—if allowed to continue shaping education policy—will subvert the traditional dispositions that teachers ought to enter the field with (e.g., caring, collaboration, quality-centered pedagogy over quantity, etc.) by replacing them with dispositions of standardization, replication, indoctrination, meritocracy, and the promotion of the self over the collective good. Yet, the only way that this shift in dispositions is possible is if teachers are kept away from the institutions that instill proper methodologies and ways of thinking by replacing them with private training, wherein corporations shape the discourse, control the rhetoric, and ultimately instill neoliberal dispositions into its teachers. We argue that this goal of de-skilling teachers via privatization of training and reductionist dispositions is best characterized by the alternative teacher training program Teach For America (TFA).

TFA was officially founded in 1990, and was the brainchild of Wendy Kopp's 1989 bachelor's thesis at Princeton University. Likening what she termed the "Teacher Corps" to the Peace Corps, Kopp argued for the creation and growth of a privately trained teaching force to aid in the then-present teacher shortage.

Kopp (1989) set the foundations for her organization on the first page of her thesis, where she described a conversation she had with a group of college business students at a convention. During this meeting, she and the other students posited that one of the three "major problems in our schools" is the "lack of qualified teachers" (p. i). Further, Kopp recalled that the dialogue about the improvement of schools "took a new direction" as they "began thinking about the phenomenal amount of interest that the conference participants were showing in teaching" (p. i). And, according to her perspective,

> [t]hese students were certainly the 'best and brightest' [because] they were nominated by
> their deans of their universities as the top students on campus and were then selected from
> a large pool of applicants on the basis of extracurricular activities and essays. (p. i)

Kopp (1989) went on to note that after hearing a few business speakers at the convention "speak of the state of our schools and the dire need for academically able teachers, many of these students had indicated a desire to spend a few years teaching" (p. i).

From those not-so-humble beginnings to now, TFA has grown into one of the largest recipients, among many, of federal and private philanthropy in education reform (deMarrais, 2012; Saltman, 2010) as it continues to have an impact on students nationally. In fact, according to TFA, the 2012 corps members will "reach 750,000 students in 46 regions across 36 states and the District of Columbia" (Teach For America, 2012b) in addition to growing to 25 countries internationally through its spinoff organization of Teach for All (Teach For All, 2012). However, despite the rapid growth of, and support received by, the alternative and privatized teacher training organization, many have grown skeptical of TFA's methods of recruiting, training, placement, and claims of effectiveness in recent years (Brewer, in press-a; Darling-Hammond, Holtzman, Gatlin, & Heilig, 2005; Heilig & Jez, 2010; Kovacs, 2011). This chapter seeks to examine: (1) neoliberalism's war on teacher professionalism, (2) neoliberalism's goals for education, (3) how TFA is situated within the larger neoliberal education reform movement, and finally (4) conclusions focused on how we can win the fight against neoliberalism with professional dispositions.

NEOLIBERALISM AND TEACHER PROFESSIONALISM

Peters (2011) asserted that neoliberalism is a struggle between "opposing and highly charged ideological metaphors of 'individualism' and 'community'" (p. 1). More to the point, Giroux (2004) posited that "[w]edded to the belief that the market should be the organizing principle for all political, social, and economic decisions, neoliberalism wages an incessant attack on democracy, public goods, and noncommodified values" (p. xiii). It is through this understanding of the world that neoliberalism seeks to undermine teacher professionalism. For those interested in shaping educational policy, traditional teacher training and traditional teachers are seen as a noncommodified value, whereas a privately trained and privately controlled group of teachers constitutes a commodified value. This reinforces the conflict between the individual and the community. Dispositions towards education are then characterized by what is best for the individual rather than the collective good.

But, despite being targeted for deprofessionalization, teaching has experienced instability with respect to its reputation as a profession. To a great extent, this is a result of the historical feminization of teaching (Urban & Wagoner, 2009). For numerous reasons, questions about the validity of teaching as a profession have been asked for decades (Ginsburg & Megahed, 2011). Presently, however, proponents of neoliberalism are actively seeking to deprofessionalize teaching by deskilling as part of the attempt to manipulate education into a commodity (Weiner, 2011). Arguing that neoliberalism has eroded professionalism as it seeks to centralize control and rewards within the managerial hierarchy, Ted Purinton (2012) noted that, an autonomous profession proves its worth to society—within markets or political system—as a result of the perceived value of its trademark skill, developed through *intense training* [emphasis added]. De-skilling, then, is the natural consequence of neoliberalism, which seeks occupational deregulation in favor of flexible employment. A profession controls employment through training, *credentialing* [emphasis added], and performance monitoring and then obtains certification granting rights from the state. Flexible employment markets allow for quicker introduction into a field, as well as simpler firings by managers and fewer certification constraints from the state. (p. 30)

As will be discussed later, TFA's training mechanisms do not match the traditionally accepted descriptions of what constitutes *intense training* or *credentialing*, but they do align with the neoliberal tenet of *quicker introduction into a field*. If entry into the teaching profession becomes easier, the rewards associated with teaching need not be great (Davis & Moore, 2008). In fact, Marion Brady (2011) argued that if teaching is thought to be so simple that almost anyone can do it, then it's hard "to make a case for having schools and teachers at all" (p. 211). Recently, the Louisiana State Board of Elementary and Secondary Education has been pushing to eliminate the need for teachers to be certified at all (Barnett, 2013). This ideology, and related attempts at deprofessionalization, may deter otherwise fully committed teachers from entering or staying in the classroom. What is more, there is growing evidence that school districts, operating under legal contract with TFA, are displacing traditionally certified and veteran teachers to accommodate teaching positions for corps members (see, for example, Cancino, 2010; Christmas, 2006; and Takahashi, 2012).

NEOLIBERALISM'S GOALS FOR EDUCATION

Part of the neoliberal goal is to deprofessionalize the role of teachers so that they are seen as interchangeable cogs whose craft can, according to neoliberal philosophy, be quantified into student test outcomes and comparatively measured. This is accomplished on the foundation of two myths: (1) schools have systematically failed students and therefore the nation; and (2) the best possible way to address this constructed myth is with competition, privatization, and standardization (Gorlewski & Gorlewski, 2013). What is more, neoliberal ideology seeks to replace tenure and salary schedules linked to advanced degrees and years of service with merit pay (Ahlquist, 2011). These goals are manifesting as philanthropists infuse more money into education reform.

However, juxtaposed with the philanthropists of centuries past, modern venture philanthropists who give large sums of money to education reform organizations seek to steer policy decisions and pedagogical practices (Saltman, 2010). Such practices are not covert in nature; rather, they are overt by design. For example,

Allan Golston of the Gates Foundation stated that "school-level investments aren't enough to drive systemic changes… [t]he importance of advocacy has gotten clearer and clearer" as the foundation plans to spend 15% of its education budget on advocacy (Dillon, 2011). Included in the policy ideologies are specific notions about teacher professionalism and worth. In fact, the Gates Foundation,

> views teachers as a group to be controlled rather than consulted. In Chicago, in response to a question of whether teachers would be part of a Gates-funded board that now governed the public schools, a Gates Foundation representative declared that teachers could not be part of the board because that would be a conflict of interest, "like having the workers running the factory." (Hursh, 2011, p. 46)

It would seem that the ideology characterized by the Gates Foundation, which has given between $10,000,000 and $24,999,999 to TFA (Teach For America, 2012a), seeks to remove teachers (compared to factory workers) from control of the profession. This would be consistent with the neoliberal push to replace traditionally trained teachers, who may protest such actions, with novice teachers who are financially backed by corporations (Saltman, 2010). Moreover, neoliberals want to replace traditionally trained teachers, who often develop unique teaching philosophies, with those who have been corporately trained into one philosophy and who take pride in donning a corporate brand. The neoliberal philosophy of education is focused on student outcomes that relate to increased teacher accountability. Teachers—not students, parents, or circumstances—are seen as the primary contributor to student success or failure. In fact, TFA advocates claim that a student's lack of access to healthcare, housing, food, or parental educational attainment has little or no bearing on student predispositions or outcomes—despite evidence to the contrary found in decades of research (Coleman et al., 1966; Sacks, 2007; Willis, 1977; Wrigley, 2011). The Gates Foundation has responded to accusations of misguided reforms that do not focus on the systemic causes of poverty, noting,

> [w]e know there is a lot of work to be done outside of the school building [focusing on eliminating poverty] as well, but again, we have to focus our resources. Inside the school, no one will have a greater impact on student achievement than the teacher in the classroom. And we intend to do everything we can to help that teacher succeed. (Williams, 2012, para. 8)

And, while the Gates Foundation is correct in their assertion that the teacher is the most important in-school factor in the equation of student success, this stance raises a few concerns. The Gates Foundation has asserted that it doesn't "have the resources" to focus on addressing systemic causes of poverty while also focusing on improving teacher quality (Williams, 2012). This assertion comes despite the knowledge that out-of-school factors impact two thirds of student outcomes whereas in-school factors (e.g., teacher quality, school resources, etc.) constitute only one third (Rothstein, 2010). What, then, is the message that the Gates Foundation sends to the teaching profession when it sends so much money into programs such as TFA? The willingness of the Gates Foundation to overtly ignore the real underlying causes of the achievement gap—more appropriately referred to as an opportunity gap (Milner, 2010)—by investing into an organization that undermines teacher professionalism and teacher quality is a manifestation of the chasm that divides those who seek to protect teacher professionalism and those who seek to fund its destruction. While the Gates Foundation is correct that teachers are the largest in-school variable affecting student outcomes, this statement is really a half-truth, because in-school variables all told are dwarfed by out-of-school variables, most of which are linked to poverty (Rothstein, 2010). The Gates Foundation has stated that it lacks the resources to address these factors, and chooses instead to focus on teacher quality (Williams, 2012). However Teach For America, which undermines teacher professionalism, is an unwise vehicle to promote this objective.

While the negative effects of poverty and segregation have been well documented, neoliberals have insisted that considering how these factors impact student achievement constitutes making excuses (Thernstrom & Thernstrom, 2003). This has led to the prevalence of teacher accountability and testing. Many K-12 teachers have been stripped of their professional capacity to collaborate as they are pitted against one another to produce better test scores. The professional disposition of collaboration has mutated into a culture of competition, motivated by profit rather than the quality of educative experiences. And, as some students underperform, despite the best efforts of a teacher, it is the neoliberal practice to blame the teacher. TFA's focus on "fixing" teachers derives from Kopp's (1989) assertion that, "teachers have traditionally come from among the least academically able of Americans" (p. 14). And, as Wendy Kopp penned in 1989, our nation is now focused more on fixing teachers rather than the circumstances that cause educational inequality.

TFA, THE NEOLIBERAL ALTERNATIVE TO TEACHER PROFESSIONALISM

The neoliberal insistence on increased teacher accountability saturates TFA. Corps members are immersed in this ideology as they begin to develop a personal philosophy of education. A required reading for all incoming corps members is Steven Farr's (2010) *Teaching as Leadership*. In the very first chapter, Farr (who serves as TFA's Chief Knowledge Officer) asserted that the Coleman Report (1966) "fostered a perspective absolving teachers and schools from responsibility for students' success or failure, encouraging a disempowering tendency to look 'outside their own sphere of influence' for reasons why students are not succeeding" (p. 5).

This approach to pedagogy supports TFA's Academic Impact Model, which informs corps members that if students fail academically, there is only one person to blame—the teacher (Brewer, in press-a). This myopic framework is consistent with the genesis of the organization as well as the broader neoliberal ideology. In contrast, an important aspect of professionalism is an educator's responsibility for the integrity of what is taught as well as the methods and strategies selected. Teachers learn to treat students as active learners within democratic spaces (Beane & Apple, 1995; Levine & Munsch, 2011), not empty receptacles for knowledge deposits and withdrawals (Freire, 1970/1992). This has led many teachers to question the overemphasis on test scores as the central goal for our work. A Declaration of Professional Conscience for Teachers, authored by Ken and Yetta Goodman two decades ago, states in part,

> [w]e will accept the responsibility of evaluating our pupils' growth. We will make no long- or short-range decisions that affect the future education of our pupils on the basis of a single examination no matter what the legal status of the examination. We will evaluate through ongoing monitoring of our pupils during our interactions with them. We will strive to know each pupil personally, using all available professional tools to increase our understanding of each and every one. (Cody, 2010)

In contrast to this stance, TFA corps members are expected to accept, without question, the use of test scores as the means of measuring student learning and evaluating teacher effectiveness (Kopp & Roekel, 2011). This short-sighted disposition towards teaching and learning informs corps members' approach to teaching, which negatively impacts students, as "[i]t is quite clear from research that teacher dispositions influence the impact teachers have on student learning and development" (Dottin, 2011, p. 405). These dispositions towards teaching and learning not only hurt students, but also undermine the teaching profession by considering the teacher as mechanistic and cold rather than intentional and caring. Yet, this approach—and its negative impacts—is a staple within TFA, as Crawford-Garrett (2013) pointed out that corps members' "socialization into the profession positions them as passive recipients of knowledge and engenders deficit ideologies of students, families and communities" (p. 12).

TFA places itself in a meritocratic framework; corps members represent individual exemplars of academic success. Their goal is to transmit that success to students, through motivating them to achieve high marks on tests of all kinds. The classrooms of TFA corps members often feature posters that declare "Our Big Goal: 80% Mastery." Student performance on quizzes and tests is closely tracked by corps members and uploaded to TFA's district and national offices, while the primary role of the TFA Manager of Teacher Leadership and Development (MTLD, formerly termed a Program Director or PD) is to meet with corps members once a month to review their test data. Teachers whose students are performing poorly on tests are given strategies to boost test performance. Student performance is charted on wall displays, with stars to indicate successes. MTLDs are responsible for collecting data on the performance of corps members' students as they are evaluated on ratios of successful versus unsuccessful corps members in relation to student test scores. In effect, TFA's narrow and mechanistic disposition towards teaching and learning approaches pedagogy as a mindless activity of number crunching rather than approaching teaching as a response to student interests and needs. Converse to this de-skilled approach to teaching, Dottin (2011) argued that "[p]edagogues' dispositions are, therefore, habits of pedagogical mindfulness and thoughtfulness (reflective capacity) that render their professional actions and conduct more intelligent" (p. 406).

TFA's focus on raising test scores is indoctrinated into corps members during their Institute training. Prior to teaching students who are attending summer school due to failure on state standardized tests, corps members distribute standardized pre-tests mirroring state tests to establish a baseline of student test performance. Upon review of the initial data, corps members divide up standards associated with low test score areas; develop lesson plans utilizing test questions and answers provided by the Institute Student Achievement Toolkit (ISAT); teach students specific content, test-taking strategies; and then administer the pre-test at the end of 4 weeks of test-prep instruction. If students memorized content long enough to increase the overall test score, corps members were deemed successful. Classrooms are decorated with propaganda surrounding increased test scores while "growth" on tests is celebrated with students as a manifestation that an educative experience has transpired.

Upon successful completion of the hiring process (in fact, corps members are not hired by TFA and are never employees for the organization—corps members are employees of the school districts in which they work) corps members receive Pre-Institute work consisting of readings (including Farr's text) and workbooks. This material lays the foundation for the belief that testing is the best way to measure student learning. Additionally, such a belief caters to poor pedagogical practices characterized by teaching to the test.

In early summer, TFA Summer Inductions and Summer Institutes begin on staggered dates and last for 6 weeks as dictated by the adjacent school districts fall start date. During Induction, corps members spend a week engaging in ice-breakers, community volunteer service (a feature only recently implemented in Atlanta during the 2011 Induction), teambuilding, and sessions centered around talk of how corps members are participants in the *civil rights movement of our time*. Holding Institute training sessions away from a final placement site is problematic, given that each region has its own pedagogical challenges. TFA's use of combined regions for Institute suggests a belief that students throughout the nation learn the same way.

Because neoliberal supporters are opposed to unions and formal credentialing, and in favor of a *quicker introduction into a field* (Purinton, 2012, p. 30), TFA is successfully operating within, and furthering, the neoliberal agenda. The quick introduction into the field of education and acting as the teacher of record follows soon at the end of the recruiting phase for each corps member. In fact, corps members receive only 18 hours of lead teaching time in an environment very different to the realities of the classrooms they find themselves in once the school semester begins (Brewer, 2013). Corps members team teach (in groups of two at the high school level and groups of four at the elementary and middle school level) a class of approximately 10–15 students under the supervision of a veteran teacher (the Faculty Advisor or FA) and a Corps Member Advisor (CMA). When corps members are not teaching, they attend sessions taught by TFA staff members who themselves have little teaching experience (Brewer, in press-a). Others have pointed out, tongue-in-cheek, how ludicrous it is to assert to corps members, school districts, parents, and funders that 18 hours of teaching practice equals or surpasses a full semester of student teaching within a realistic classroom following a 4-year education degree or a 4-year degree in a content area followed by a master's degree in teaching or other state-sanctioned credentialing program. For example, Barbara Veltri (2010) pointed out the naïveté of TFA's brazen claims, wondering if corps members "consider[ed] that in other professions, such as cosmetology, licensure requires a 9-month program of study to be operating legally" (p. 34). Despite the obvious contradiction that TFA's training plays into notions of teacher professionalism, school districts are hiring corps members in spades, often at the expense of otherwise fully certified and/or veteran teachers (Takahashi, 2012).

Upon completion of Institute, corps members make their way back to their assigned regional placement and begin employment with a hiring school district based on a predetermined brokered agreement on hiring (Christmas, 2006). Corps members are issued emergency teaching licenses, with many teaching subjects outside of their baccalaureate studies—most surprisingly, many are placed into special education positions. In the state of Georgia, emergency or provisional teaching certificates are good for a period of 3 years. During that time, the educator is expected to enroll in a master's program with the goal of obtaining a clear and renewable teaching license. However, most corps members teach only for the 2 years of their TFA/AmeriCorps contract, and there is no oversight of their pedagogical training; as a result, many corps members enter and leave their classrooms with only their TFA training.

High teacher turnover within TFA not only undermines the teaching profession, it has been shown to be highly detrimental to the very students TFA claims to help. Research has shown that only 10 to 15% of TFA corps members are still in their placements after 4 years (Heilig & Jez, 2010). Additionally, this high turnover rate is beneficial to charter schools who partner with TFA, as corps members can be worked to the bone, to the point of suffering burnout, but then replaced by an endless supply of new blood (Horn, 2011) who possess a business-minded disposition that working 7 days a week with little attention to personal needs such as sleep and food is what is best for students (Brewer, in press-a). Clearly, the use of TFA novices who do not embody the dispositions of professional educators contributes to instability in our most challenging schools. Further, teacher turnover has been shown to be highly detrimental to the very students TFA aims to "save." Research shows that teacher retention is beneficial to students, while high teacher turnover negatively affects student outcomes, namely in schools serving more low-achieving and Black students. In fact, "an increase in teacher turnover by 1 standard deviation corresponded with a decrease in math achievement of 2% of a standard deviation" (Sawchuk, 2012, citing Ronfeldt, Loeb, & Wyckoff, 2013). Further, Gene Glass (2008) noted that there "is a positive correlation between a secondary school's drop out rate and its percentage of new teacher hires; the drop out rate is negatively correlated with the average level of teaching experience of the school" (p. 186, citing Felter, 1997).

We argue that professional behavior among colleagues is among the professional dispositions that all teachers should embrace. And while one of the core values of TFA includes "Respect & Humility," TFA struggles to rein in an overtly arrogant attitude towards non-TFA teachers. In fact, on many occasions, corps members have publicly and privately insisted that corps members are better than traditionally trained educators, noting that "[corps members] wouldn't have to be here doing this job if traditionally trained educators did it right" (Brewer, in press-a). Certainly, this type of professional disposition can contribute to a toxic working environment.

With that said, a vital aspect of professional behavior within education is collaboration. Teachers should be afforded the opportunity to engage one another with questions, suggestions, and provided resources and insights as needed. The need for novice teachers to seek out experienced expertise and the need for veteran teachers to share that knowledge is paramount to teachers' professional dispositions. If most TFA corps members are entering our schools with negative attitudes about how traditional teachers do the work of educating students, then it seems plausible that such negative dispositions will undermine collaboration among veteran and novice corps members. What follows, then, is the reinforcement of a narrow view of education because "epistemological beliefs, that is, beliefs about knowledge and cognitive dispositions, such as willingness to consider alternative points of view, are positively correlated" (Dottin, 2011, pp. 405–406).

Additionally, corps members' negative disposition towards traditionally certified teachers, in addition to the revolving door that characterizes corps members' entrance and exit of schools, does not incentivize veteran teachers to actively reach out and collaborate with corps members that (1) do not want help from traditionally trained veteran teachers; and (2) who are likely already counting the days until they leave. In fact, the majority of corps members enter teaching with the intention of only staying for 2 years or less, while research suggests that those who do stay likely had traditional pedagogical training prior to entering TFA (Cody, 2012; Donaldson & Johnson, 2011). In short, these characteristics of corps members dramatically undermine a culture of collaboration, which is one of the most powerful dispositions that teachers should embrace.

CONCLUSIONS AND DISCUSSION

We have argued that a fundamental goal of neoliberalism is the systematic deprofessionalization of teaching as it seeks to commoditize education for profit, and that quick entry programs such as TFA aid in such goals. Historic battles to gain professional status for teaching have been set back by TFA's exaltation of the superiority of their novices, because this undermines the need for training and expertise. TFA reinforces the emphasis on test scores as the ultimate measure of both student learning and teacher quality. This reduces the complex world of the classroom into a simple set of measurable outcomes, and enables teachers to be replaced if their scores do not improve. TFA contributes to harmful instability at low-income schools. TFA novices, whose path is paved with loose credentialing requirements and school district agreements stipulating the hiring of corps members, are replacing traditionally trained and more-veteran teachers at an alarming rate.

TFA, in many ways, has called attention to our nation's achievement gap and educational inequities. TFA has undoubtedly brought in some individuals who have developed into good teachers—perhaps due to their embodiment of traditional dispositions associated with the teaching profession. And, as pointed out, many TFA alumni who stay in the classroom following the 2-year commitment may be individuals with traditional pedagogical training prior to TFA who were seeking an avenue towards employment in a school district. However, the assertion that TFA corps members represent the "best and brightest" reinforces a missionary model, where students from middle-class backgrounds are sent to rescue hapless denizens of the inner city. And, as TFA ramps up plans to funnel alumni into leadership positions through its principal pipeline and into policy positions through its political arm, Leadership for Educational Equity, teachers must take a united stand against present and future attempts to deprofessionalize teaching. Teaching is an art form that cannot be learned in 18 hours. As a nation, we must attend to the ailments of our schools. However, an organization that promulgates a message that teachers are broken and can, or rather should, be replaced with novices who have no pedagogical training will not improve schools. Brokering deals with superintendents and state licensing officials undermines the credibility of the teaching profession. It is ironic that an organization created to remedy a lack of qualified teachers has become a major supplier of them.

Efforts to strengthen the professional status of educators are best pursued in the context of strengthening educational opportunities for our most vulnerable students. Educators following this path insist that teachers should be well-trained before being given the awesome responsibility of leading classroom instruction for a year. We also seek to establish a greater degree of autonomy for teachers, rather than subject them to constant pressure to raise test scores. We seek to stabilize and strengthen struggling schools, and that means we must turn them into places where highly trained educators can make their careers. Professional educators, who take the educational endeavor as being more than successful performance in terms of standardized measures, not high turnover missionaries, are the key to lasting change.

REFERENCES

Ahlquist, R. (2011). Whose schools are these anyway—American dream or nightmare?: Countering the corporate takeover of schools in California. In P. R. Carr & B. J. Porfilio (Eds.), *The phenomenon of Obama and the agenda for education: Can hope audaciously trump neoliberalism?* (pp. 147–167). Charlotte, NC: Information Age.

Barnett, K. (2013, January 28). Board discusses eliminating certification for teachers. *St. Charles Herald Guide.* Retrieved February 8, 2013, from http://www.heraldguide.com/details. php?id=12014

Beane, J. A., & Apple, M. W. (1995). The case for democratic schools. In M. W. Apple & J. A. Beane (Eds.), *Democratic schools* (pp. 1–25). Alexandria, VA: Association for Supervision and Curriculum Development.

Boyles, D. (2011). "Public" schools, privatization, and the public/private distinction. In S. Tozer, B. P. Gallegos, A. M. Henry, M. B. Greiner & P. G. Price (Eds.), *Handbook of research in the social foundations of education* (pp. 358–366). New York, NY: Routledge.

Brady, M. (2011). Why current education reform efforts will fail. In P. E. Kovacs (Ed.), *The Gates Foundation and the future of U.S. "public" schools* (pp. 203–219). New York, NY: Routledge.

Brewer, T. J. (in press). Accelerated burnout: How Teach For America's "academic impact model" and theoretical culture of hyper-accountability can foster disillusionment among its corps members. *Educational Studies.*

Brewer, T. J., (2013) From the trenches: A Teach For America's corps member's perspective. *Critical Education, 4*(12), 1-17.

Cancino, A. (2010). Teach For America supplies charter schools: Partnership brings 25 teachers to fill openings. Retrieved from http://articles.chicagotribune.com/2010-09-27/news/ct-met-charter-teachers-20100927_1_charter-schools-teacher-certification-city-teachers-union

Christmas, T. (2006). Memorandum of understanding with Teach For America, Inc,. *Oakland Unified School District.* Retrieved from http://legistar.granicus.com/ousd/attachments/ax/9e/9e5e301f-0597-4880-b1a3-d2e867dbd382.pdf

Cody, A. (2010). A declaration of professional conscience for teachers: Now, more than ever. *Education Week: Living in Dialogue*. Retrieved from http://blogs.edweek.org/teachers/living-in-dialogue/2010/10/a_declaration_of_professional.html

Cody, A. (2012). TFA says 8 year claim is an estimate, "not really appropriate for publicizing." *Education Week: Living in Dialogue*. Retrieved from http://blogs.edweek.org/teachers/living-in-dialogue/2012/12/tfa_says_8_year_claim_is_an_es.html

Coleman, J. S., Campbell, E. Q., Hobson, C. J., McPartland, J., Mood, A. M., Weinfeld, F. D., & York, R. L. (1966). Equality of educational opportunity. Washington, DC: U.S. Department of Health, Education, and Welfare.

Crawford-Garrett, K. (2013). *Teach For America and the struggle for urban school reform: Searching for agency in an era of standardization*. New York, NY: Peter Lang.

Darling-Hammond, L., Holtzman, D. J., Gatlin, S. J., & Heilig, J. V. (2005). Does teacher preparation matter? Evidence about teacher certification, Teach For America, and teacher effectiveness. *Education Policy Analysis Archives, 13*(42).

Davis, K., & Moore, W. E. (2008). Some principles of stratification. In D. B. Grusky (Ed.), *Social social stratification: Class, race, and gender in sociological perspective* (pp. 30–33). Boulder, CO: Westview Press.

deMarrais, K. (2012). Asking critical questions of philanthropy and its impact on U.S. educational policy: Tracking the money in school reform. In S. R. Steinberg & G. S. Cannella (Eds.), *Critical qualitative research reader* (Vol. 2, pp. 276–294). New York, NY: Peter Lang.

Dillon, S. (2011, May 21). Behind grass-roots school advocacy, Bill Gates. *The New York Times*. Retrieved from http://www.nytimes.com/2011/05/22/education/22gates.html?pagewanted=all&_r=2&

Donaldson, M. L., & Johnson, S. M. (2011). TFA teachers: How long do they teach? Why do they leave? Retrieved from http://www.edweek.org/ew/articles/2011/10/04/kappan_donaldson.html

Dottin, E. S. (2011). Social foundations and the professional preparation of teacher educators. In S. Tozer, B. P. Gallegos, A. M. Henry, M. B. Greiner, & P. G. Price (Eds.), *Handbook of research in the social foundations of education* (pp. 399–409). New York, NY: Routledge.

Farr, S. (2010). *Teaching as leadership: The highly effective teacher's guide to closing the achievement gap*. San Francisco, CA: Jossey-Bass.

Felter, M. (1997). Staffing up and dropping out: Unintended consequences of high demand for teachers. *Education Policy Analysis Archives, 5*(16).

Freire, P. (1970/1992). *Pedagogy of the oppressed*. New York, NY: The Continuum Publishing Company.

Ginsburg, M., & Megahed, N. M. (2011). Comparative perspectives on teachers and professionalism. In S. Tozer, B. P. Gallegos, A. M. Henry, M. B. Greiner, & P. G. Price (Eds.), *Handbook of research in the social foundations of education* (pp. 662–671). New York, NY: Routledge.

Giroux, H. A. (2004). *The terror of neoliberalism: Authoritarianism and the eclipse of democracy*. Aurora, Canada: Garamond Press.

Glass, G. V. (2008). *Fertilizers, pills, and magnet strips: The fate of public education in America*. Charlotte, NC: Information Age.

Gorlewski, J. A., & Gorlewski, D. A. (2013). Too late for public education? Becoming a teacher in a neoliberal era. In P. L. Thomas (Ed.), *Becoming and being a teacher: Confronting traditional norms to create new democratic realities* (pp. 119–134). New York, NY: Peter Lang.

Heilig, J. V., & Jez, S. J. (2010). Teach For America: A review of the evidence. East Lansing, MI: The Great Lakes Center for Education Research and Practice. Retrieved from http://www.greatlakescenter.org/docs/Policy_Briefs/Heilig_TeachForAmerica.pdf

Horn, J. (2011). Corporatism, KIPP, and cultural eugenics. In P. E. Kovacs (Ed.), *The Gates Foundation and the future of U.S. "public" schools* (pp. 80–103). New York, NY: Routledge.

Hursh, D. (2011). The Gates Foundation's interventions into education, health, and food policies: Technology, power, and the privatization of polical problems. In P. E. Kovacs (Ed.), *The Gates Foundation and the future of U.S. "public" schools* (pp. 39–52). New York, NY: Routledge.

Kopp, W. (1989). *An argument and plan for the creation of the teacher corps.* (bachelor's thesis). Princeton, St. Louis, MO.

Kopp, W., & Roekel, D. V. (2011, December 20). Column: 3 ways to improve the USA's teachers. *USA Today.* Retrieved from http://usatoday30.usatoday.com/news/opinion/forum/story/2011-12-20/teachers-education-public-schools/52121868/1

Kovacs, P. (2011). Philip Kovacs: Huntsville takes a closer look at Teach For America's "research" [Blog post]. Retrieved from http://blogs.edweek.org/teachers/living-in-dialogue/2011/12/huntsvilles_research-based_com.html

Levine, L. E., & Munsch, J. (2011). *Child development: An active learning approach.* Thousand Oaks, CA: Sage.

Milner, H. R. (2010). *Understanding diversity, opportunity gaps, and teaching in today's classrooms: Start where you are, but don't stay there.* Cambridge, MA: Harvard Education Press.

Peters, M. A. (2011). *Neoliberalism and after? Education, social policy, and the crisis of Western capitalism.* New York, NY: Peter Lang.

Purinton, T. (2012). Teachers as professionals: Owning instructional means and negotiating curricular ends. In J. A. Gorlewski, B. J. Porfilio, & D. A. Gorlewski (Eds.), *Using standards and high-stakes testing for students: Exploiting power with critical pedagogy* (pp. 27–44). New York, NY: Peter Lang.

Ronfeldt, M., Loeb, S., & Wyckoff, J. (2013). How teacher turnover harms student achievement. *American Educational Research Journal, 50*(1), 4–36.

Rothstein, R. (2010, October 17). Rothstein: Why teacher quality can't be only centerpiece of reform. *The Washington Post.* Retrieved from http://voices.washingtonpost.com/answer-sheet/school-turnaroundsreform/rothstein-on-the-manifestos-ma.html

Sacks, P. (2007). *Tearing down the gates: Confronting the class divide in American education.* Los Angeles, CA: University of California Press.

Saltman, K. J. (2010). *The gift of education: Public education and venture philanthropy.* New York, NY: Palgrave Macmillan.

Sawchuk, S. (2012). Teacher turnover affects all students' achievement, study indicates [Blog post]. Retrieved from http://blogs.edweek.org/edweek/teacherbeat/2012/03/when_teachers_leave_schools_ov.html

Takahashi, P. (2012, June 22). Despite mass layoffs, board hires 50 from Teach For America. *Las Vegas Sun.* Retrieved from http://www.lasvegassun.com/news/2012/jun/22/despite-layoffs-board-oks-hiring-50-teach-america-/

Teach For All. (2012). Locations & programs. Retrieved from http://www.teachforall.org/network_locations.html

Teach For America. (2012a). Donors: Lifetime donors (foundations and individuals). Retrieved from http://www.teachforamerica.org/support-us/donors

Teach For America. (2012b). Teach For America announces the schools contributing the most graduates to its 2012 teaching corps. Retrieved from http://www.teachforamerica.org/sites/default/files/20120905_Press.Release_Top.Contributers.pdf

Thernstrom, A., & Thernstrom, S. (2003). *No excuses: Closing the racial gap in learning.* New York, NY: Simon & Schuster.

Urban, W. J., & Wagoner, J. L. (2009). *American education: A history* (4th ed.). New York, NY: Routledge.

Veltri, B. T. (2010). *Learning on other people's kids: Becoming a Teach For America teacher.* Charlotte, NC: Information Age.

Weiner, L. (2011). Neoliberalism's global reconstruction of schooling, teachers' work, and teacher education. In S. Tozer, B. P. Gallegos, A. M. Henry, M. B. Greiner, & P. G. Price (Eds.), *Handbook of research in the social foundations of education* (pp. 308–318). New York, NY: Routledge.

Williams, C. (2012). The Gates Foundation responds: Poverty does matter—but it is not destiny [Blog post]. Retrieved from http://blogs.edweek.org/teachers/living-in-dialogue/2012/08/the_gates_foundation_responds_.html

Willis, P. (1977). *Learning to labor: How working class kids get working class jobs.* New York, NY: Columbia University Press.

Wrigley, T. (2011). Culture, class, and curriculum: A reflective essay. In P. E. Jones (Ed.), *Marxism and education: Renewing the dialogue, pedagogy, and culture* (pp. 11–38). New York, NY: Palgrave Macmillan.

Imagination, Joy, AND Wisdom

CHAPTER FIVE

The Joy OF Educating

JED HOPKINS

EDUCATION'S JOY

One of the disturbing features of modern life is that we live in times in which it is no longer possible to know what to expect of the future based on what we now know of the past. All we can be sure of is that the future will not be much like the past we have known, and because historical time is constantly accelerating, it is a future that will arrive ever more quickly. The disorientation this causes, the disorientation that comes from living modernity's form of life, can become so intense and perplexing that we find it hard to contain our anxieties. We panic.

It is time to initiate a public discussion on what it means to be human, and how reflection on this question can guide us in determining what kind of futures we want for ourselves.

(KOMPRIDIS, 2009, P. 23)

"Experience leads, to that openness to experience that is set free by experience itself."

(GADAMER, 1989, P. 339)

The new beginning inherent in birth can make itself felt in the world only because the newcomer possesses the capacity of beginning something anew, that is, of acting.

(ARENDT, 1958, P. 9)

"THE JOY OF COOKING," "THE JOY OF SEX," "THE JOY OF GARDENING;" "THE JOY OF EDUCATING"?

The early 1970s saw a number of popular how-to books that used the rubric "Joy of..." in their title. Thinking about these original "Joy of..." books made me wonder how nice it was to hear the word "joy" being used in relation to these common practices and apparently being taken seriously. Of course there is something very comforting about the word itself—we wish our lives to be joyous—and using it in the title of a book helps to project the idea that the book might be more than just another technical manual or how-to guide. It was like saying that these books will embody a certain kind of *orientation* connecting us to what is really the whole point, core, or essence of the practice: namely, its joy. Did the authors and publishers back then recognize that the technical know-how and advice they contained might not, in itself, be enough to sell the book? Perhaps it was recognized that there is more to a human practice than skill and competency, especially if these are understood in isolation from the human good of joy. I'd like to think so, and I'd like to think that this wasn't a feature restricted only to practices construed as leisure pursuits.

Doubtless, the motive for the title was partly a marketing ploy, and perhaps they were still only manuals and how-to books after all. Nevertheless, the promise of their title sends us an important message worth reflecting upon. By implying that the featured practice would be treated in ways other than the merely technical, the books were also suggesting that it *ought* to be so treated. We ought to treat the practice of "X" as an opportunity not only to consider and hone our competency and skill but also, and perhaps especially, as an opportunity to locate its joy. How refreshing. How hopeful. How educational?

But let's be honest, a title such as "The Joy of Educating" doesn't sound very serious and professional to our ears even if we are sympathetic to the idea that without the promise of joy, just about any fundamental human practice would suffer over the long term. To resolve this, "joy" will have to be given some philosophical teeth, so to speak, as well as showing how it has concrete and practical application for the work we do as educators. In particular, it will have to be shown why a human practice is more than a mere assemblage of tasks and procedures— even if carried out effectively—and ultimately why teacher education might be best seen as the struggle to locate refreshing and hopeful ways of thinking about practices. I wish to focus on the "philosophical teeth," mindful that this kind of discussion has tended to be marginalized and is difficult to bring to the media's attention—especially at a time when educational mainstream public discourse, which I shall refer to as EMPD (pronounced "empty"), seems mostly to be concerned with measurable competence and its achievement as the regulative ideal of education, without even a look-in for some notion of deep fulfillment.

Educational Perfectionism

This is an ambitious undertaking to do in one chapter and, needless to say, I will be relying on the promising avenues others have already carved out in critical theory, existential phenomenology, and feminism. What these different intellectual traditions of thinking have in common, and what I believe is so lacking in EMPD, is a concern for what I take to be of central importance in *any* thinking about the meaning of education: attention to that which gets educated—that is, human *beings*, and that means human *being*. It may sound trivial to point out that it is human beings who get educated (what else would?) but, to say at least this much is already to suggest that thinking about the meaning of education involves thinking about that which *makes us* human beings; it is to underline the requirement that we need to consider human beings' distinctive predicament or condition if we are to do any wise educational thinking. In making this the focus, we are proceeding in an existentially sensitive way that will explain, amongst other things, that education cannot simply be taken as the instrument for effective learning, or some set of performance indicators, or even some less-determinate notion of "excellence," if these are thought to be understandable in isolation from what they could mean for the human condition. Insofar as education has something to do with the promise of wisdom and joy, an existential understanding emphasizes a non-reductionist and non-instrumental way with human being, reminding us that education is essentially about the perfectability of being human, that it is the endeavor with the overriding concern with what we could become based on what we are.[1] We have to ask, then, three things: (1) what *are* we?; (2) how might what we are play out for our greatest flourishing?; and (3) what are the kinds of conditions, skills, or dispositions that best appropriate this flourishing, making education *educational* as it were?

In his account of the meaning of education, the philosopher Iain Thomson (2005) similarly utilized a perfectionist framework with a distinctively existential phenomenological twist. As Thomson[2] explained, the lineage of philosophical perfectionism derives mainly from Aristotle, who, in the *Nicomachean Ethics*, defined its framework in terms of three interrelated aspects: an ontological thesis, an ethical thesis, and a principle linking the two. The ontological thesis defines what is importantly distinctive about the form of life human beings embody, setting us apart from (and, typically, above) other kinds of entities; the ethical thesis maintains that our greatest fulfillment, or flourishing, follows from the cultivation and development of what makes us distinct; and, finally, the linking principle, which characterizes the connection between the ontological thesis and the ethical thesis by "specifying the link between the relevant ontological skills or capacities that distinguish us and our greatest possible ethical fulfillment or perfection" (Thomson, 2004, p. 441). Hence, the framework addresses three interrelated questions:

what are human beings? (the ontological thesis); what is human life at its best? (the ethical thesis); and, how is this to be actually and concretely realized in education? (the linking principle). Aristotle's own application of this framework has been very influential in the Western tradition. For him, human beings are distinctive in terms of their active intellect and ability to reason (the ontological thesis) and are most fulfilled by striving to maximize this (the ethical thesis) by cultivating ways to understand and reason (the linking principle). One can see that the liberal view of education, with its cognitive and intellectual bias, is a form of this particular perfectionism.[3] But, the existential perfectionism that Thomson proposed, and the one I wish to pursue in this chapter, is different to this in some crucial ways. For reasons that will become clear, we will refer to this form of perfectionism as ontological education. This is basically a view of education that restores its ontological dimension.

Ontological education basically employs a philosophical perfectionist framework but adds one more crucial question to the ones listed above: namely, what *is it* to understand humans—or more accurately, human *being*? In other words, an ontological understanding of education will require us to consider what is at stake with understanding itself when human being is at stake. The reason for this is related to the peculiar ontological status of human being. To begin to explain this we first need to understand the difference between everyday understanding and theoretical understanding.

Understanding Human Being/s

One important feature of an everyday understanding can be seen in the way our daily comportment through the world presupposes that what we experience and what we do is largely intelligible. Though there are occasions when we get truly perplexed, typically, we see familiar things, where everything is largely encountered "as" something. Even problems, or disruptions to this normal state of affairs, are encountered as certain *kinds* of problems or disruptions—and so, we're rarely in utter perplexity, as it were. Insofar as this constitutes the default and most common way of existing, we might say that we exist *understandingly*. As such, we don't usually worry about "understanding" things and human beings per se: we operate *already* with an understanding (which is not to say that misinterpretation isn't still possible). In other words, our daily comportments usually don't require the development of a theoretical understanding of things and each other, and much of it can be characterized in terms of practical know-how rather than theoretical definition (or what we'll call "know-that" activities). For example, I understand how to ride a bicycle, and this means that I have the requisite know-how even in the absence of access to a valid theory of what is involved in being able to do this. Similarly, one doesn't have to be a theoretician of language, such as a linguist, in order to be a very effective user of language. All of this suggests that useful and important though theoretical understanding is, it is not the most pervasive way we understand, and may not even be the most fundamental. Nevertheless, with its emphasis on propositional content—that is, with its commitment to articulating what is taken "to be the case" by representing some aspect of the world—theoretical understanding does seem to hold a higher status over everyday understanding. But, high status or not, to return to the original question—What is it to understand human being?—We need to ask how appropriate theoretical understanding is for getting at what it means to be human (the ontological thesis).

An important feature of theoretical understanding, and no doubt an important reason for its high status, is its privileging of the epistemological concern with legitimacy. In particular, it requires that understanding be expressible in language or propositions that are connected to, or emerge out of, formal practices or fields of inquiry. Such fields define what counts as content in ways that try to honor and maintain validity as they go about the business of defining the nature or essence of things. Since there are many things to understand, not surprisingly, there has evolved a diversity of fields such as biology, sociology, psychology, history, mathematics, and so forth. It might seem natural, then, to turn to one or more of such fields as part of seeking a theoretical understanding of human being. However, as we shall see, there is a problem with doing this. Namely, that the epistemological bias of theoretical understanding ignores a particular "feature" that is peculiar to what it means to be a human being. To really appreciate this, we have to see what is both gained and lost with any theoretical understanding.

Let us start by noting an important general feature of theoretical understanding. Astronomers inquire about stars and *what* they are but never *that* they are—that is, what it means for them to be or exist. In other words, astronomy is epistemologically rather than ontologically biased and, in this, it is like many theoretical fields: well-suited for investigating things where the phenomenon under investigation has no relationship to its own being. Though a field's object of inquiry, such as stars, numbers, unicorns, cells, and rocks *are* (or exist) in different ways, none of them is in a position to choose how they are.[4] They present aspects that we can categorize and/or measure, but the question of their ontological status is largely irrelevant. In fact, it is the categorizing that is part of a field's explanatory work in discerning and accounting for the nature of things. Theoretical understanding is essentially a matter of investigating phenomena in terms of the properties that they *have*, within a category, that makes them distinct. In other words, theoretical understanding has a categorical way with understanding. But, if we exclusively apply such a categorical way with understanding to human being, and think of humans only in terms of the properties they *have*, we are likely to miss a distinctiveness that is born out of the way they *are*.[5] Why is this?

Unlike the entities that science and mathematics study, human being is not "thing-like." To say this is, crucially, to say that human beings are not indifferent to their own being and, consequently, that they are not merely a certain type of object. Even though a biologist may want to distinguish me from other biological entities by claiming that I am, say, a sample of *homo sapien*, and go on to describe various biological traits that I typify as the particular kind of mammal I am, and all this would be true, none of it gets close to what I am in essence: Jed, a Brit, a professor of education, a husband and father of two boys. Importantly, these "characteristics" are not properties of me in the way that entities have categorizable and objective features such as density, weight, or other measurable features. *Being* British, *being* a father, *being* a husband, and other facets of my identity, are not just facts that can be *given in a here and now* (such as my current body's density, weight, and blood pressure). They are part of my past and also my future, since they open up the possible ways for me to be in the world. I am able to think and feel as a Brit, husband, father, and professor. Whenever I realize one of these possibilities, I am choosing to be someone—I am interpreting who I am.[6] Furthermore, the question of who I am, is always "an issue" for me (though not necessarily in the sense that I am consciously reflecting on it); and I am always assigned the task of being someone, whether I like it or not.

To sum up, then, theoretical understanding misses this existential dimension of human life because theoretical fields operate with some ontological assumption concerning what things are without, normally, reflecting on this assumption. In doing this, fields focus on what there is—beings or entities in all their multiplicity—and not that they *are*—the existing of those entities[7]: their being. But, crucially, in the case of human being, missing the ontological is here to *miss the entity*. Human being, unlike things such as stars, cells, and (say) the biologically measurable processes that constitute and sustain our biological life, is ontological.

So now we can complete our answer to the question—What is at stake with understanding when we understand human being? What is at stake is that we are ontological beings and that requires an ontological understanding that attends to being—an alternative to understanding humans categorically or theoretically. It is precisely such a non-theoretical, non-categorical way with understanding that provided Martin Heidegger (1962) with his suggestively phenomenologically existential insight that humans are the being (the entity) whose way of being is to be concerned about their Being.[8] Notice that this approach to understanding—a phenomenological understanding—rests on a distinction between beings (and the properties or characteristics they have) and Being (that which gives rise to what they are). This important distinction enables a non-reductive concept of the person as a being for whom things matter, and matter in a peculiarly human way. As such, it displaces "consciousness" as the key criterion for personal identity, as a theoretical psychological theory might tempt us to do, making it no longer easy to assimilate human beings to living cognitive machines, to things that think. Firstly, we are not things, and, as we shall see in more detail, consciousness is not the primary, or, more accurately, primordial thing about us.

So, let us now start to unpack a philosophical perfectionism that is based on this ontologically biased view of the meaning of human being—a focus on *how* humans *are* rather than *what* they *have*. What understanding of education will this provide us with?

The Ontological Thesis

The ontological thesis amounts to saying that humans are the being (the entity) whose way of being is to be concerned about, or more accurately to take a stand on, their being. It is to say that care is definitive of who we are. One implication of this is that the very way reality shows up for us is filtered through and circumscribed by the stands we take on ourselves, the embodied life-projects that organize our practical activities and so shape the intelligibility of our worlds.[9] It is easy to miss the radical nature of this last way of putting it, for we are used to thinking that things are intelligible as a result of the account we can give of them. Along such lines, we are tempted to believe that the more refined our categorical scheme, the more intelligible things will be. So, for example, by applying a suitable categorical scheme we can see that the fluffy moving shape over there is *really* an animal, better still a mammal, a cat, a Persian cat, a female Persian cat, a female Persian cat in heat, and so forth. We might be tempted to think that a theoretical understanding commands the most fundamental relation between the human individual and the beings in her surrounding world (including herself). But, when we appreciate the special ontological dimension of human being, theoretical knowledge is put in its place, as it were, as representing only one kind of intentional behavior. This is just a consequence of our existing understandingly (our way of being); theoretical knowledge is founded on more fundamental modes of behavior, modes of practical engagement with the surrounding world, rather than *being their ultimate foundation*.

Notice that this turns on its head the classic account given by the mid-17th-century philosopher René Descartes referred to as the *Cogito* and often summarized in the thesis, "I think therefore I am," where a realm of essentially meaningless substantive matter is opposed to an insubstantial realm of meaning-conferring thinking. But, in contrast to this dualistic Cartesian philosophy, an entity is the entity it is insofar as it "shows up" within a context of practical engagement, not because it has certain inherent properties ascertainable by disinterested categorization and contemplation. Using Heidegger's (1962) famous example for illustration, this means that a hammer is a hammer not because it has certain hammer-like properties that a thinking subject can ascertain, but because it is used for hammering. That is, it is a piece of equipment that is the thing it is only because it belongs to a holistically integrated functional system of other things (such as nails, wood, carpenters, houses, and so forth.) Heidegger called such a context a "world," which roughly has the same meaning as the word "discourse" if understood as more than a purely linguistic phenomenon, or "human practice" (think of teaching, business, parenting, and so forth), or even "culture," if taken as not necessarily pertaining to ethnicity.

This notion that humans are worlded creatures, rather than self-sufficient minds, is at the heart of a phenomenological existential understanding of human being. Human beings are embodied beings who act in the world and get their identity by so doing because the world coordinates how things show up as the things they are. Hence, in the world of basketball, a suspended net is the thing to aim the ball at; in the world of shop-keeping, the people coming through the door are potential customers; and so forth. In short, the world is the transparent background that informs what is the meaningful thing to do or not do—the context that "tells" us, for example, if it's appropriate to eat with one's hands, or with a knife and fork, or with chopsticks—along with what purposes, values, and distinctions are the operable ones. In sum, all this has very important implications for what it means and doesn't mean to be a human being. In particular, it suggests that a human being is not essentially a particular kind of organism, or even a mind in a body, or consciousness, but a being-in-a-world who cares about their own being.

The Ethical Thesis

So much for the ontological thesis, then. What about the ethical thesis and the connecting principle? In other words, given this ontologically biased understanding of the human, what counts as flourishing *as* such beings? (the ethical thesis); and, what will this specifically look like when or if it can be realized (the connecting thesis)? I will complete this section by answering the first of these and reserve the second question for the second section, "Education's Space." There are two aspects to consider when answering the ethical question and both of these follow from taking seriously the "worlded" structure of human being that was just discussed: I will call them the assimilative and the existential and, take them in that order.

As we've seen, things and actions are meaningful insofar as they belong to a holistically integrated functional system. As such, it must be the case that worlds exist prior to the activity of any given person. Hence, learning, generally speaking, has the conservative aspect of being a matter of learning how to be "one of us" by moving into the system of assignments that define how we are supposed to act with what things in which situations. Ultimately, the hammer or the basketball is to be *circumspectively* seen—that is, *not* to be seen and reflected upon, *not* to be thematized, but used—and understood as a hammer or basketball, and this normatively central "seeing-as" is always already articulated prior to the human action.[10] In other words, carpenters and basketball players do not have to invent their practices (they are given, so to speak), and understanding is to engage with the world as something that is largely transparent. As Dreyfus (1980, cited in Stern, 2000, p. 12) put it, understanding is therefore more like coming to understand another culture where you come to share "its know-how and discriminations rather than arriving at agreement concerning which assumptions and beliefs are true."

> And he goes on to point out that this, coordination comes about not by making a translation, or cracking a code, but by prolonged everyday interaction; the result is not a commensuration of theories but what Heidegger calls "finding a footing" and Wittgenstein refers to as "finding one's way about." (ibid. p. 12)

Given the worlded "nature" of human beings, understanding, then, is radically praxitical—it is something we do "in" the world rather than a "purely" cognitive process.[11] This assimilative, socializing, finding-one's-way-about understanding of understanding has enormous implications for what it means to teach and the meaning of curriculum, which will be explored in the next section. But, it is still an incomplete phenomenology of human being without the existential aspect, which we will now turn to.

As we've discussed, human beings' way of being is to be concerned about their own being. This ontological characteristic was the main reason why an exclusively theoretical approach to understanding human being was thought to be inadequate. In light of what has been said about the praxitical nature of understanding, it shouldn't be surprising that this concern with Being, which is at the heart of human being, is not *fundamentally* cognitive. How I am Jed the Brit, the father, the researcher, the husband, the student, and so forth, is realized in what I do and how I go about being these things. Of course, at times, we do agonize and consciously reflect on who we are, but most of our living is spent in a non-reflective, or better still, pre-reflective coping. In sum, human existence is characterized in how we practice our everyday comporting more than the theoretical understandings we may also sometimes indulge in. Important though these latter activities are, they are derivative. That is, they occur against the background of the non-theoretical. In fact, one could say that our existence is decided in praxitical understanding.

In other words, we live our lives with each other and around things that are meaningful to us largely in terms of their use in certain contexts, and these are defined by social norms. This is important, for without this fixation of meaning life would be ruined in understanding. Living understandingly means that in it the abundance of meanings that find themselves in a continuous dissemination are controlled in favor of certain interpretations. Thus, prejudice plays a necessary and positive role. This shouldn't be hard to see when we consider that though we make frequent individual and, seemingly, autonomous judgments, such as what clothes to wear today, we rarely have to decide things such as what counts as appropriate clothes, or whether or not to wear clothes in the first place, or whether to wear our own clothes rather than somebody else's. Nor do we need to think up a procedure for determining what counts as clothes belonging to one person rather than another, or define what is meant by the concept of possession, and so forth. These things, and many other such things that we are not even conscious of, have already been "decided," as it were, in the world or culture. Without this, living life intelligibly would be inconceivable.

On the other hand, life would also be ruined should fixations or norms have the final word, and there are certainly times when we experience their sheer contingency, sensing or desiring that things could mean something other than they do, or that the way we do things is founded on nothing essential or logically necessary. *How I am* a Brit, a father, a teacher, a student, a husband, and so on, is never resolved or finalized. This is the case even if I were to take an active interest in the theoretical literature that may be associated with any of these areas. Doing so may tempt me to say something of the form that I subscribe to doing "X" because "research has shown...," but the ways of being who I am in the doing of "X" nevertheless opens up possibilities that, ultimately, are mine. Theoretical research may influence me, but it doesn't get me off the existential hook, as it were, as it would still be me doing the appropriating. Unlike out of time theory, how I am my roles is always ahead of me as future time possibility.

I didn't invent the institution of fatherhood, the meaning of teaching and learning, or marriage itself; how I live through these institutions, what possibilities I allow myself to become open to (and what possibilities are consequently closed off) is the constrained freedom I have as a human being. Of course, I can deny such freedom and be content to simply do, think, feel, and perform in terms of what others, or society, would have me do, think, feel, and perform. For much of the time, that is doubtless what I and others tend to do—living life in total acquiescence with the expectations of the myriad social roles we inhabit—but, if that is all I do, I would be denying the possibility of being more fully human, more authentically the person I am, for I would be these roles rather than facing my possibilities for being. From this it can be seen that our ethical or moral lives involve a practical relation to ourselves amounting not only to asking ourselves questions such as—Who am I and what do I truly want for myself?—but also, as Kompridis (2006) put it, more troubling questions, such as—"Am I the author of my life? Are these words I use to describe myself my own? Do my actions originate from me or from something alien to me?" (p. 53). There is an important political implication that follows from this, and that education has a stake in. Put simply, it is this: though it is not hard to accept that a necessary condition of democracy is that everyone has a voice, an existential understanding of human being would also suggest that it is equally important to have a voice of one's own.

The assimilative and the existential, then, are together, but in creative tension when we face our own being. That is, when we are at our best as human beings. The assimilative thesis, the idea that our practical concerns and issues enable a differentiated world to show up, has to be combined with the existential thesis, namely that care is definitive of being human by taking a stand on our own being. Hence, our ultimate for-the-sake-of-ourselves gives us a world in which what shows up not only matters for everyday coping, but can (to use Charles Taylor's terms) be worthy or unworthy. Crucially, then, this notion of care is not equivalent to what we might call something like pragmatic concern because, as Dreyfus explained:

> [a]nimals have concern—they can distinguish the central from the peripheral experiences—but not *care*. [But,] when the meaning of one's being is at stake, a world opens in which things are not only salient [as they would be for animals] but *have significance* [emphasis added]. (cited in Guignon, 2000, p. 320)

To be the authentic student, teacher, father, sister, wife, husband, researcher, etc., we have to somehow face the prospect that for us humans, there is no access to "the Truth"—something final and incontrovertible—about how to go about doing the things that really matter to us, such as justice, the self, each other, reality, or even the "moral law." All we can do is find ways of authentically facing up to this and embrace our finitude. There is no final word on what it means to be the beings we are. The ethical thesis, which can be taken as education's specific role or aim, is to help us deal with this predicament of predicaments.

From what has been said, I hope it can be seen that such a "dealing" cannot amount to definitively answering the question "what is life at its best?" but that that in itself doesn't mean that it shouldn't be asked. For one thing, it is perhaps *the* most human of all questions we could ask and, in line with ontological and existentialist perfectionism, we can think of education as perhaps *the* site where it needs to be continually kept in view (accompanied, of course, by a sufficiently rich ontological understanding of understanding and human being). As we've already mentioned, it is human beings that get educated, and any educational discourse that loses sight of what this means, ontologically, is bound to be misguided.

So, let us pause here and consolidate where we've been in terms of the title of this chapter. What is the joy of educating and where is it located? A quick way with the question might now be to say that joy is being human and is located in the responsibility an individual can take for the possible way of being who they are that opens further possibilities. Notice in that last sentence that the word "possibility" was used twice: the kind of possibility that is at stake here is the kind that begets further possibility: it is the possibility that promises a sequel. Joy has this organic quality and education's space is the kind of space where this stands more than a mere chance of getting realized.

The Disclosure of Possibility

Since humans are profoundly connected to each other and practices—they are beings-in-a-world—the joy of educating is going to involve inviting students into worlds or practices. But, since we've also seen that humans are capable of owning who they are in the face of the historical and contingent nature of where they find themselves with the "hand they have been dealt," so to speak, the invitation is one that plays on possibility. To reiterate, humans are creatures of ontological possibility, rather than natural things, and education educates for *this*. In doing so, what is called for cannot simply be the sorts of practices that we might develop when we are dealing with natural things—that is, practices that seek to predict, control, and manage—but instead practices that allow for what we called the assimilative aspect of human being to take off in order that the existential—the willingness to own what we can be and do in distinction to living only the default position of acquiescing with what others would want us to be and do—can occur. All this can be summarized by saying that as an educator, my educational wish is for my students to stick with things (recall the assimilative aspect) but not get stuck with them (our existential predicament).[12]

To stick with things but not get stuck with them is not the same as wishing students to realize their (natural) potential as we often hear in educational circles (especially amongst elementary teachers).[13] As existential beings, we are not like the acorn, which has the full-blown oak tree pre-programmed in its DNA, resulting, if all goes well and it gets the right kind of nurturing, in the full-blown product. The possibility of the acorn is biologically predetermined, while the possibilities that are being opened by being the being I am, are not. Of course this is not to deny that humans don't have bodies that also happen to have biologically determined trajectories; we all get old, after all. But, like Mick Jagger, we have the option of owning what this means. An acorn is indifferent to its way of being, while, to reiterate, human beings' way of being is precisely for being to be an issue. This can be a source of anxiety—based on the fact that our ways of organizing the world are contingent—but it's also the source of our greatest dignity as the beings we are. As Mark Wrathall (2005) put it:

> We can change how we relate to the things around us. In the process, we can change the significance those things hold. The way we understand ourselves is always open to question, our being is always an issue yet to be resolved. To flee from anxiety over the world—to try to deceive ourselves about the contingency of our lives by affirming our social norms as if they somehow reveal the final, ultimate truth about how one should live—is to fail to

realize what is unique about us—our ability to be authentic, to discover the world in our own way. (p. 61)

We could say that the acorn merely requires the right kind of nurturing or gardening, but ontologically concern-full human beings are another matter. So, what do they "need"?

Another popular candidate, perhaps getting closer to what's really at stake here, might be to point out that humans need joy, and therefore that educating comes down to something like the joy of discovery, the joy of coming to know something that one didn't know before, by one's own efforts. Like "realizing potential," this too has roots in certain Romantic traditions of the ideal of the self; and certainly, such talk of "discovery learning" is still a respected idea being promoted in elementary circles. But, to invoke the anti-Cartesian thinking being supported here, this can only get us partially there if this idea is still associated with a self-sufficient mind. To think in such a way is consistent with teaching practices where it is thought sufficient to give children total free reign to "do their own thing" as though discoveries occur through an act of creative genius: the pedagogical equivalent of a creation ex nihilo.[14] Of course, "discovery" *needn't* be thought of in such a Cartesian flavored way and attention may equally be given to the importance of helping students understand social context and the possible roles and discriminations it affords. But, the existential point that needs to be kept in view is that the joy of discovery, coming to know something that you didn't know before, is the joy it is insofar as it *discloses possibilities for the self and for the world*. There is no joy in knowledge for knowledge's sake without this existential dimension—a dimension that speaks to the worlded "nature" of human beings and the stake they have in being.

EDUCATION'S SPACE

In more concrete terms then, what might the joy of educating, the particular human flourishing that we'd want to associate with the educational endeavor, look like? Whatever it is, in contrast to EMPD, I hope we can see that it cannot be *sufficiently* characterized in terms of mere learning or even the demonstration of competency. Imagine a student who learns that mathematics is, at best, boring, and, at worst, intimidating. Such a student has almost certainly narrowed their own possible ways of being where mathematics playing a role in their life is concerned (the only role it will play is likely to be something to be avoided). Alternatively, imagine a student who learns that mathematics is an intriguing and, perhaps, an ultimately mysterious phenomenon. Such a student is likely to live with it, or through it, as a realm of possibility. And, of course, for such a person, there is then the possibility of "mastery," but, importantly, mastery understood as less an endpoint, or even something like the *willful* control of the phenomenon, and more as an openness and sensitivity to what *it affords*, what future possibilities it opens up. Even for the master, or especially for the master, mathematics continues to be enchanting and unfathomable. Notice that what is at stake in these two examples of ways with mathematics is first and foremost ontological rather than epistemological: that is, it revolves around questions of personal identity (being a mathematician) and what the phenomenon *is* (the possibilities of mathematics) rather than simply issues of valid procedures and representing that "one knows." To further bring this out, notice the conceivability of the first student having enough mathematical skill to do "well enough" on a math test (which, of course, typically doesn't test for such things as imaginative dispositions) and the latter student doing poorly, perhaps because she has decided to ignore the planned curriculum and forged, in "auto-didactical style," a path that, by chance, didn't overlap with the tested content. It isn't that competency is not important, it's just that teachers and curriculum designers would benefit from a more existentially rich interpretation of what is really at stake *educationally*: in particular, the conditions that best make for an openness to possibility.

All this focus on human possibility in the context of education might sound strange given how accustomed we are to equating education with the more familiar concept of learning and competence. But a little bit of reflection will make it apparent that just to think in these more familiar terms and to assume that this is education's essential point is inadequate. As the example with the reluctant math student makes clear, we ought not to say that his experience, despite learning enough mathematics for "getting through" the program, amounted to an *education* in mathematics. The reason for this is not because learning didn't occur but because what and how the phenomenon of mathematics was learned diminished or squelched, rather than opened up, avenues of possibility involving mathematics. To see the relationship between education and learning and do justice to the existential aspect of human being, then, we have to insist that the learning must be of a quality involving the disclosure not just of content but of possibility. Of course, teachers are all too familiar with the phenomenon of students deliberately resisting or restricting what they learn,[15] but they should be equally worried by missing educational opportunity as when learning is done in a way that is non-receptive to the disclosive possibilities that might be opened up by what is learned. If the so-called good student practices an existentially weak, albeit pragmatic, stance to learning, and this becomes the norm, resulting in the continual failure for the disclosing of a practice's disclosive potential, in the terms of educational perfectionism, education has here failed to get off the ground. This doesn't mean that students have, in some sense, failed if they are not enchanted by every academic field presented to them. It does mean, however, that everything that one experiences in school will not be educational. But, more to the point, I concur with Nel Noddings's (1992) view that it is unrealistic and unreasonable to expect everyone to be equally called to every academic field they are exposed to, and therefore it is perverse if a system is premised on just such an assumption. In fact, the view of philosophical perfectionism that is being described here is also consistent with Noddings's view that one of the functions of school should be to help students find what fields and subjects can bring out the best in them and how that best can be nurtured.

Of course, if this is right, lots of implications follow. Not least, it means that we shouldn't automatically equate the institutional arrangements, collectively called schooling, with education, as such, and we shouldn't think of education as *essentially* demonstrating competence as merely the correct application of rules— of course EMPD tends to do both of these things. In contrast, we are saying that it is the disclosing of a practice's disclosive potential that is really at stake. And that's where the joy lies.

EDUCATION AND THE NEW

As a way of concluding this work, I would like to draw out some implications concerning the contribution of ontological education to some of the conditions of our present time—a time that feels like unprecedented uncertainty and change. The Nikolas Kompridis (2009) quote at the beginning of this chapter beautifully describes the situation we are in and begs the question: What precisely should be the educational take on the new? Borrowing from Kompridis' reconstruction of critical theory in his book *Critique and Disclosure: Critical Theory between Past and Future* (2006), and his paper on technology (2009), I would like to lay out three candidates for how we can understand the new in order to see what view has the most resonance with ontological education. In a way, this might be taken as a test for the worthwhileness of thinking through the possible meaning of education being sketched in this chapter. How important is it to think in terms of the joy of educating in the light it sheds on how to handle the new?

The New As Frantic Mood

A pervasive idea of the new is one that would see it as an end in itself. That is, a view that the new is good simply by being new and that embracing the new promises a way to legitimacy. For example, we hear adolescents making the accusation of "oh that's so 'X'" where "X" is some thing, idea, or past trend that is now to be regarded as hopelessly passé. We are also often reminded that we live in an age where new knowledge is accelerating at an exponential rate and that we therefore need to keep up with it: perhaps by embracing new technologies of information retrieval and storage. Of course, this "keeping up" with the new often takes the form of getting on board with yet another new program or initiative before we've hardly had time to digest the last one, and where our failure to do so might be seen as a sign of inflexibility or even some form of Luddism. In such a frantic world of newness, it is not uncommon to hear people, usually older people, lament, "the more things change, the more things stay the same."

It isn't hard to argue how this frantic view of the new might have a largely negative impact on education proliferating the idea that education is chiefly a matter of information management, though it might also be seen as spawning the more legitimate concern that the curriculum needs to be current and relevant—often expressed generally as "relevant to the 21st century." But outside this generality, it's hard to see how education could make anything of such an idea until some principle for embracing the new is developed *other than that it is new.*

The New As Enlightenment Project of Progress

A second candidate for the meaning of the new that might seem much more relevant to education is the idea that the new is that which gets us beyond the everyday and ordinary understandings we might have of things and closer to a realm of undistorted truth and reliability. Perhaps this is the basic promise behind the Enlightenment's idea, or ideal, of progress. The new here is not good because it is new, but because it is more expert, more objective, more useful, more powerful, more encompassing, more specialized, and so forth. As such, it is validated by procedures correctly applied by expert others, a professional community that has access to a scientific realm of methods and accountability mechanisms. Where the first conception of the new despises the old and seeks to reject it, this progressivist ideal seeks to improve upon it. Where the first conception values less and less the ordinary and everydayness of our experiences, this progressivist ideal seeks to transcend these. The upshot of all this is that there is not a realm that cannot be improved by a cadre of experts.

Perhaps this enlightenment view of the new seems promising for education because of its emphasis on methods of reason and inquiry as a means for getting us towards a more undistorted representation of how things are. This seems to be a truth-driven ideal and, on the face of it, falls in easily with a view of education that would similarly value critical thinking and reasoning. Indeed, it would seem reasonable that an account of what is at stake with a liberal education ought to refer to the necessity of equipping students with forms of disciplinary understanding[16] in order to ensure success in developing such things as "a sense of social responsibility, as well as strong and transferable intellectual and practical skills such as communication, analytical and problem-solving skills, and a demonstrated ability to apply knowledge and skills in real-world settings" (AACU website, 21st Century Liberal Education).

Perhaps the strongest bond between the enlightenment progressivist view of the new and such an understanding of education is that both see the need to concern themselves with accountable procedures for validating the truth of things and how we go about finding the truth of things. This naturally leads to an objectivist approach to schooling, where forming objectives seems reasonable and where learning can be operationalized, that is, defined in a way that can be measured or expressed quantitatively or unambiguously as part of ensuring that students are learning the correct procedures. From this perspective, the curriculum is basically a set of specific objectives, and assessment is done in such a way as to minimize subjective interpretation of a student's performance. Does this sound familiar?[17]

But, from the perspective of ontological education, I hope it can be seen how reductionist a view this is. Perhaps a concern with legitimacy and accountability is necessary *in some way*, but the way Enlightenment thinking has worked this particular vein has been too singular, owing to its view of human understanding. As we have seen, the joy of educating is dwelling in the work of enlarging the scope of what is possible for humans. What is missing from the Enlightenment view is a rich enough understanding of the role possibility plays in human life. It is as though a concern with a rationalistic view of correctness and accountability has over-shadowed the disclosive power of disclosivity. Is there, then, a third candidate in how to think of the new that education, in the perfectionist terms supported in this chapter, can take seriously?

The New As Disclosing Possibility

From a perspective of the new as that which discloses possibilities, the new would not be for the purpose of replacing the past with an improved knowing, nor would it be to transcend the everyday and the ordinary. In fact, here, the new is envisioned as necessarily in dialogue with the past and anchored in the everyday insofar as the new arises out of genuine need. Like the Enlightenment perspective on the new, this perspective is consistent with the idea of professional communities and experts who have access to specialized techniques of accountability. But, there is an important difference: here, there is a healthy suspicion of the search for a grounding in distortion-free procedures, and more of an interest in the dynamics of the human practices in which they operate and, even more, an interest in the conditions optimal for their *disclosive work.*

As we discussed earlier, the joy of disclosure is not just the joy of discovery, of knowing something that you didn't know before for example, but more essentially the joy of a new possibility. And that means it is the joy that there is a sequel. The sequel carries us forward so, in a sense, there is the intimation of progress, but unlike the Enlightenment ideal of progress, we, *in all our existential fragility*, are coming along for the ride. Unlike the Enlightenment ideal, there can be no hands-off idea of progress here, as when we say it is science that progresses. From this perspective, all are implicated.

At stake here are the educational conditions of disclosivity. Certainly, science can be thought of as disclosing new understandings of the universe. In a sense, the Enlightenment view "runs" with this potential. But, a better way of doing science is to *disclose science as it discloses* new understandings of the universe. For example, when *what we are with the planet earth* is ignored or bracketed—for example, when we disclose genetic mechanisms enabling us to manipulate species in new ways—it is done at our peril. But, when we take disclosing disclosivity seriously, we can see that science is only one way of disclosing and that there might be something worthwhile in the way indigenous cultures live with the earth, for example. We might call this education's ecological way with the new, which understands that there is a danger not with science, per se, but with an acquiescence with a totalizing view of science as when we assume that it is the only legitimate way to the truth, the only way of understanding. Ontological education can help us guard against this danger, where progress doesn't have to be taken as a matter of sacrificing or filtering out our subjectivity in the name of undistorted or disinterested truth, but also to disclose ourselves and our practices as we disclose new possibilities through our practices. If the existential perfectionist thesis is right, the space for authentic joy is also the space where we are invited to be the beings who care about being. Perhaps it is not too much to suggest that an ontological understanding of education may well be the antidote that will save the planet from social and ecological disaster.

At the beginning of this chapter I referenced the "Joy of…" books. But I'd like to end now with another reference to a series of books, the title rubric of which seems to imply a very different concern and ontological orientation. I am speaking of the "'X' for Dummies" books. Useful though these books doubtless are, their title is rather revealing of where we stand currently, especially as we understand, or fail to understand, the praxitical and existentially fragile nature of understanding. Too often, our present times' concern for practices no longer reside in the challenge of being open to their joy and existential possibility so much as a concern with the deficiency of individuals in need of being "fixed." Is it not the case that the way teachers in the U.S. are now customarily treated by officials and much of the media, along with the concomitant policies and so-called reforms that are being tried on them, essentially amounts to an urge to fix the system and to fix them—an "Education for Dummies" rather than an acquiescence in education's joy? For behind this is an instrumentalist thinking operating with a technological understanding of being. As such, it fails to consider how to help teachers focus on the work of making the curriculum an occasion for opening up possibilities for who we are, and where attention to an ethos respecting receptivity is understood at the heart of the educational work we need to do.

NOTES

1 Please note that by "perfectability," I don't mean anything like a psychological "perfectionism," a neurotic inability to bring anything to a satisfactory completion.

2 For Thomson's most detailed explanation of philosophical perfectionism, see his 2005 book, *Heidegger on Ontotheology: Technology and the Politics of Education*, especially Chapter 4.

3 The classical view justifies a liberal education for the sake of a liberal education by first asserting that the mind's proper function or nature is realized in the pursuit of knowledge. Pursuing knowledge is, therefore, at the same time, pursuing mind. Secondly, it is taken that knowledge, based on the right use of reason, can get us to the essential nature of things, and this turns out to be that which is non-changing (immutable), beyond mere appearance, opinion, or belief—pure being or, in its Platonic version, Form. In this way, the "liberal" part of liberal education is meant to signal the idea that an education, based on the right use of reason, would free the mind to function according to its true nature—freeing it from error and illusion. Much enlightenment thinking is similarly motivated: rationality becomes the proper end of what a human being is. For a contemporary attempt to reinvigorate this line of thinking, see the work of Paul Hirst (1974) who attempted to work out the nature and meaning of curriculum when it is assumed that the human capacity for understanding is essentially an epistemic one.

4 It might be objected that unicorns simply don't exist, and that numbers are insubstantial, so their existence is questionable too. But this is to beg the question of what it means for something to be. Certainly, unicorns are mythical creatures and are different, in that regard, to horses. Similarly, numbers are insubstantial in that they are purely conceptual. Nevertheless, both unicorns and numbers can become objects of serious inquiry despite not having substantiality and extension.

5 For example, with Aristotle, we could say that in the category of "animal," humans have rationality and that this makes them distinct from other animals. This highly influential categorical understanding of human perfection would therefore view humans as essentially rational animals, the possessors of rationality.

6 In saying that "I am choosing to be someone" it is important not to hear "choice" as equivalent to "an act of decision" as though our identity could be willed. The existential notion of "choice" here must be heard to include openness and receptiveness and the suspension of the will as much as its deployment. Similarly, in saying "I am interpreting who I am" it is important to resist assuming that interpretation must be a conscious process.

7 The distinction between being (ontic entity) and Being (ontological) is sometimes referred to by Heidegger (1962) as the ontological difference. As he put it in *Being and Time*, Being is: "that which determines entities as entities, that on the basis of which entities are already understood.... The Being of entities 'is' not itself an entity" (pp. 25–26).

8 This formulation isn't quite technically accurate, as Heidegger (1962) employed the German neologism "Dasein" in order to emphasize, amongst other things, that he wasn't talking about humans as an objective entity—a thing—so much as the site of a disclosive space of meaning. Heidegger wrote that Dasein is "an entity which does not just occur among other entities. Rather it is ontically [i.e., factually] distinguished [from other entities] by the fact that, in its very Being, that Being is an issue for it" (p. 32). Also, notice the use of the capitalized "being" to distinguish it from the entity (a being) as opposed to the way of existing of an entity. Importantly, Heidegger wanted to propose that a way of Being is not itself a being.

9 It is an insight such as this that forms the foundation for the "caring schools" vision that the educational philosopher Nel Noddings (1992) supports.

10 Though I'm trying to keep philosophical jargon down to a minimum in the body of the chapter, the phrase "circumspectively seeing" seems important to say, rather than just leaving it as "seeing," which normally comes with theoretical connotations.

11 The word "nature" has quotation marks because the essence of human being isn't its nature, such as its biology, but its relationship to Being. The word "in" has quotation marks to remind us that the "in" here is to be heard existentially rather than spatially. It is to denote that we are not, say, physical objects in an environment, but self-interpreting beings. The word "purely" has quotation marks around it because there cannot be a purely cognitive anything. This is the anti-Cartesian existential phenomenological thesis: we are not purely minds or consciousness but beings-in-a-world.

12 I owe this way of putting it to a saying by John Haugeland that was reported in the documentary *Being in the World* (Raspoli, 2010). It's also worth mentioning that this overall view of education has resonances with the political philosopher Hannah Arendt's (1958) views. There is a lot to explore here but, as I understand her, Arendt wanted to point out that teachers should be responsible for preserving the world against children—who, being new, have yet to appreciate it—as well as preserving natality—which I take as children's refreshing re-appropriation of traditions—in order to guard against banalization.

13 Such thinking can no doubt be traced back to the educational philosophy of Rousseau and the "scientific" elaborations his work spawned in developmentalists such as Piaget.

14 I take this to be behind the main criticism someone such as Lisa Delpit in her 1995 book *Other People's Children* brought against process-oriented as opposed to skills-oriented writing instruction. A more linguistically nuanced critique has been articulated by adherents of the "Sydney School" and followers of the linguist M. A. K. Halliday. Halliday coined the phrase "benevolent inertia" to describe what he took to be the biggest weakness of progressivist and constructivist Anglo-American approaches to literacy (Rose & Martin, 2012).

15 See, for example, Herbert Cole's (1995) *I Won't Lean from You* for a discussion of authentic sources.

16 This is essentially the view of a liberal philosopher of education such as Paul Hirst (1974).

17 Clearly, a whole lot more can be said about the philosophical underpinnings of an Enlightenment view of progress that probably had its most articulate origin with the thinking of Immanuel Kant and his more modern heirs, such as Jürgen Habermas in the field of critical theory and John Rawls in the field of justice. For an insightful discussion of this, see Kompridis (2006, 2009). Also, a lot more could be said about conceptions of liberal education and the role the disciplines play in providing frameworks of legitimacy.

REFERENCES

Arendt, H. (1958). *The human condition.* Chicago, IL: University of Chicago Press.

Blattner, W. D. (2006). *Heidegger's being and time.* New York, NY: Continuum.

Bonnett, M. (1983). Education in a destitute time. *Journal of Philosophy of Education, 17*(1), 21–33.

Canavesio, G. (Producer), & Ruspoli, T. (Director). (2010). *Being in the world* [Motion picture]. USA: Mangusta Productions.

Delpit, L. (1995). Other people's children: Cultural conflict in the classroom. New York, NY: The New Press.

Dewey, J. (1930/1981). *Construction and criticism: Later works, Vol. 5: 1929–1930.* Carbondale, IL: Southern Illinois University Press.

Donnelly, J. F. (1999). Schooling Heidegger: On being in teaching. *Teaching and Teacher Education, 15*(8), 933.

Dreyfus, H. (1980). Holism and Hermeneutics. *Review of Metaphysics,* 34(7).

Dreyfus, H. (1999). *Being-in-the-world.* Cambridge, MA: MIT.

Gadamer, H.-G. (1989). *Truth and method.* New York, NY: Continuum.

Guignon, C. (2000). Philosophy and authenticity: Heidegger's search for a ground for philosophizing. In M. A. Wrathall & J. Malpass (Eds.), *Heidegger, authenticity, and modernity.* Cambridge, MA: MIT Press.

Habermas, J. (1981). *The theory of communicative action* (Vol. 1). Boston, MA: Beacon Press.

Halliday, M. A. K., & Martin, J. R. (Eds.). (1993). Writing science: Literacy and discursive power. Pittsburgh, PA: University of Pittsburgh Press.

Heidegger, M. (1962). *Being and time* (J. Macquarrie, Trans.). Bloomington, IN: Indiana University Press.

Heidegger, M. (1977). The question concerning technology (W. Lovitt, Trans.). In *The question concerning technology and other essays.* New York, NY: Harper & Row.

Hirst, P. (1974). Liberal education and the nature of knowledge. In P. Hirst (Ed.), *Knowledge and the curriculum.* London, England: Routledge.

Hirst, P. (1974). *Knowledge and the curriculum.* London, England: Routledge and Keegan Paul.

Hopkins, J. (2011). Education as authentic dialogue or resolute attunement. *Journal of Russian and East European Psychology, 49*(2), 50–55.

Kohl, H. (1995). *I won't learn from you.* New York, NY: New Press.

Kompridis, N. (2006). *Critique and disclosure.* Cambridge, MA: MIT.

Kompridis, N. (Ed.). (2006). *Philosophical romanticism.* New York, NY: Routledge.

Kompridis, N. (2009). Technology's challenge to democracy: What of the human? *Parrhesia, 8,* 20–33.

Lave, J., & Wenger, E. (1991). *Situated learning: Legitimate peripheral participation.* Cambridge, England: Cambridge University Press.

Matusov, E. (2009). *Journey into dialogic pedagogy.* New York, NY: Nova Science.

Noddings, N. (1984). *Caring: A feminine approach to ethics and moral education.* Los Angeles, CA: University of California Press.

Noddings, N. (1992). *The challenge to care in schools: An alternative approach to education.* New York, NY: Teachers College Press.

Okshevsky, W. C. (1992). Epistemological and hermeneutic conceptions of the nature of understanding: The cases of Paul H. Hirst and Martin Heidegger. *Educational Theory, 42*(1), 5–23.

Rawls, J. (1971). *A theory of justice.* Cambridge, MA: Belknap Press.

Rose, D., & Martin, J. R. (2012). *Learning to write, reading to learn: Genre, knowledge and pedagogy in the Sydney school.* Sheffield, England: Equinox.

Solomon, R. C. (2000). Trusting. In M. A. Wrathall & J. Malpass (Eds.), *Heidegger, coping and cognitive science.* Cambridge, MA: MIT Press.

Stern, D. (2000). Practices, Practical Holism, and Background Practices. In M. A. Wrathall & J. Malpass (Eds.), *Heidegger, coping and sognitive science.* Cambridge, MA: MIT Press.

Taylor, C. (1992). *The ethics of authenticity.* Cambridge, MA: Harvard University Press.

Thomson, I. (2004). Heidegger's perfectionist philosophy of education in being and time. *Continental Philosophy Review, 37,* 439–467.

Thomson, I. (2005). *Heidegger on ontotheology: Technology and the politics of education.* Cambridge, England: Cambridge University Press.

Wrathall, M. A. (2005). *How to read Heidegger.* New York, NY: W. W. Norton and Company.

CHAPTER SIX

Seeking THE Authentic

Inquiry and Dispositions, Teacher Candidates, and Ourselves

BY PAMELA J. HICKEY AND MARY H. SAWYER

The end result does not have to be perfect but the progression of the students' work is the real thing.—Jackie,[1] teacher candidate, reflection journal, October

INTRODUCTION

In this chapter, we share discoveries from a semester in our on-going efforts to support the development of "inquiry" dispositions with future teachers even as we strive to grow in our own understandings and implementations of inquiry and teacher candidate support. As one of our students, Jackie, reminds us, the real learning is in the work itself. To achieve the end is to stop learning. As Berghoff, Blackwell, and Wisehart (2011) noted, inquiry is a cyclical process that "spirals, with each iteration laying the groundwork for the next" (p. 26). While we acknowledge the evidence of success that we saw in our students' work across the semester-long inquiry cycle we engaged in, we also strive to be honest. Our successes are mediated and informed by our challenges, doubts, and mistakes as we worked alongside our teacher candidates to grow as professionals and to find a pedagogically sound balance in the tensions between the lofty ideal of maximizing student success in the hypothetical classroom and the messiness and joy of being human.

INQUIRY DISPOSITIONS

In an educational culture where evidence of successful teaching and learning is increasingly being funneled into numbers, abstractions, and individual teacher accountability, we argue that as teacher educators it is our responsibility now, more than ever, to support teacher candidates to both look beyond the numbers and to create collaborative relationships with their greatest professional resources—their colleagues—within the context of an intentional learning community. We have sought to do this through our co-taught student teaching seminar for teacher candidates in secondary English education, by constructing the course around the development of the practices and dispositions that support social learning through a semester-long project known as the Instructional Study. The Instructional Study is designed to help candidates focus on the impact of their instruction on student learning.

Research points to the natural tendency of teacher candidates and teacher novices to focus on themselves, rather than on their students and their students' learning (Athanases, 2013; Kagan, 1992). However, Athanases found that structured inquiry and mentoring was successful in scaffolding teacher candidates and novice teachers to focus on student learning, as evidenced through student work. Our goal in seminar was also to focus candidates on the "intellectual quality" (Newmann & Associates, 1996) of their assignments and the resulting student work. We hoped this would combat the pressures candidates would likely face to frame their curricula in narrow ways because of wide-scale "backwash"—which Hughes (2003, p. 53) described as "the effect tests have on learning and teaching"—from standardized assessments. Furthermore, given the often isolated work of teaching (Hadar & Brody, 2010), we wanted our teacher candidates to discover the resources of their peers and colleagues in order to be open and ready to develop collaborative and reflective support systems in their future schools.

Specifically, we sought to develop that which we term "inquiry dispositions," which support a reflective, critically questioning stance around teaching and around the evidence provided by student responses and student work. Friesen (2009) asserted that inquiry "is a disposition that is cultivated," and that this disposition includes bringing experience, adding information to that experience, and creating knowledge. Given the research around inquiry as well as the literature on dispositions, we prepared for our work with our teacher candidates by identifying dispositions essential to inquiry. As noted by Taylor and Wasicsko (2000), dispositions may include "attitudes, beliefs, interests, appreciations, values, and modes of adjustment" (p. 2). They also asserted that "it is important for teacher educators to know and understand the dispositions of effective teachers, so as to design experiences that will help to develop these characteristics in students" (p. 2). Given that the seminar was designed to support their professional development during their student teaching experience, we focused our syllabus on the semester-long project of the Instructional Study with the intention of supporting it through regular in-class study groups. The Instructional Study assignment is an analysis of candidates' own teaching, as evidenced through the work of their students; it is intended to support them in beginning to focus on the impact of their instruction. We designed each class session around study group meetings in order to create the space for collaborative inquiry. Our goals for the explicitly collaborative inquiry were not only to support each teacher candidate's Instructional Study project but also to explicitly demonstrate the social learning possibilities of working with one's peers in a mutual exploratory process.

Our understandings around inquiry draw upon the work of Cochran-Smith and Lytle (2009) and Fecho, Price, and Read (2004). Cochran-Smith and Lytle wrote of "inquiry as stance," noting,

> We see this as a worldview and a habit of mind—a way of knowing and being in the world of educational practice that carries across educational contexts and various points in one's professional career and that links individuals to larger groups and social movements intended to challenge the inequities perpetuated by the educational status quo. (p. viii)

Inquiry, therefore, is not an instructional activity, nor even a pedagogical approach. It is, in short, a way of being. Fecho (2011) wrote of a student who declared, "Trying to teach from an inquiry stance is like trying to achieve Buddha mind" (p. 1). Explaining himself, the student noted,

> The Buddha tells us that because there are many paths to enlightenment, no one can show you your way. They can only point in directions. That's inquiry…. You have to be engaged in a process and a journey that have no end. (p. 1)

Thus, as we have stated, while inquiry itself is unending, it may also be cyclical and recursive, as we turn back to our original assumptions and interpretations with new understandings and wonderings. As Gallagher (1996) wrote, "questions and answers will be continually rethought, refelt, and reconstructed" (p. 42). We hoped that our Instructional Study assignment and the questionings, dialogues, and explorations around it would serve to seed an inquiry stance within our students, even as they were encountering their first experiences of classroom teaching. Indeed, given "that inquiry involves investigating questions arising from one's own life and teaching practice" (Meyer & Sawyer, 2006, p. 49), we expected their challenges in the classroom to feed the inquiry process, as they returned to the same questions but with the refocused lenses offered by the range of experiences they were acquiring daily.

Fecho (2011) urged us to "use the difficulty" (p. 45) to explicitly speak of and address the toughest issues that we might most like to remain unspoken and tucked away safely out of sight. One difficulty that we as teachers of the seminar discovered was in the essentially social aspect of the inquiry itself. Research on collective approaches to professional development and educational reform has demonstrated the benefits of approaching inquiry as a social, dialectical process involving multiple points of view and experiences to generate ideas and directions (Fecho, Price, & Read, 2004; Meyer & Sawyer, 2006). In order to be true to our inquiry stance, we had to be honest—both with our students and with each other. As we will demonstrate, this was one of the difficulties that we, professors and teacher candidates, were able to "use" to become more authentic inquirers. As Richards (2011) argued, "By taking a critical look at our shortcomings, beliefs, curriculum, and pedagogy, we can bring about changes surrounding our own and our education majors' dispositions" (p. 69). Our inquiry stance creates the space and context for us to reflect upon our instruction and dispositions even as we ask our students to do the same.

In constructing our syllabus and in revising the Instructional Study assignment from previous semesters, we revisited the literature on dispositions and inquiry, and, through an analysis of the course goals to support teacher candidates in connecting their classroom learning to their first foray into classroom teaching, we identified what we call "inquiry dispositions," that is, beliefs that support the ongoing process of inquiry. Embarking on our journey, we also made a pact that we ourselves would be part of the inquiry process. Given our approach to inquiry as a way of being, let alone as a way of teaching or planning a student teaching seminar, we resolved to be honest with candidates regarding our own inquiry process. We also hoped that the nested nature of our inquiry—professors engaging in inquiry around the teacher candidates' inquiry dispositions—would enable us to "walk our talk" and further our ongoing learning.

Thinking logistically about the upcoming semester, we intended that our own inquiry stance would serve as a model for our students, provide a broadened opportunity for dialogue and collaborative reflection beyond the teacher candidates' experiences in their schools and in their study groups, and that our own dialogue would be facilitated by the "conversational distance" between our respective offices. Fecho (2011) wrote, "If we want inquiry, critique, and dialogue to exist in our classrooms, we must bring them there with intent and dogged insistence" (p. 25). As we have noted, we committed ourselves to a nested inquiry around our candidates and their inquiry into their students' learning. We drafted our syllabus and the Instructional Study assignment, and delving into the research literature we teased out the following dispositions as being most essential in supporting the development of an inquiry stance within our teacher candidates:

- The belief that colleagues and peers will be a source of relevant and meaningful ideas, insights, and resources discovered through dialogue and conversation (Berghoff, Blackwell, & Wisehart, 2011; Fecho, 2011; Meyer, 2002).

- The belief that we will be able to raise important questions about instruction and student learning in the dialogue (Fecho, 2011; Waff, 2009).
- The belief that we will be able to design and implement instruction that is authentic, meaningful, and intellectually rigorous and to analyze the student work produced via instruction through the lenses of these criteria (Bowne, Cutler, DeBates, Gilkerson, & Stremmel, 2010; Newmann & Associates, 1996; Richards, 2011).
- The belief that we are able to use our own mistakes as opportunities for learning (Butler & Schnellert, 2012; Richards, 2011).
- The belief that we are able to approach teaching as a complex process of inquiry (Butler & Schnellert, 2012; Fecho, Price, & Read, 2009).

Having identified these dispositions, we revisited the seminar syllabus to refine its focus on these inquiry dispositions, engaging in a backwards-design process as we re-worked the "Instructional Study" assignment, the "Dispositions Self-Assessment," and the "Protocol for Analyzing Student Work" that guided study group discussions of the work that the teacher candidates would bring from their placements to share with their colleagues.

THE CONTEXT OF STUDENT TEACHING SEMINAR

The inquiry cycle we are unpacking centers on the Secondary Education student teaching seminar we co-teach at a middle-sized state university in the Northeast. The teacher candidates whom we refer to are studying to be secondary English teachers. The program is accredited by the National Council of Accreditation of Teacher Education (NCATE). All undergraduate students are English majors (42–43 credits), who take an integrated education curriculum plan that includes 100 hours of pre-student teaching fieldwork, typically involving experience in two distinct districts. Graduate students enrolled in the class are seeking their MA in Teaching degree, hold BA degrees in English, and take an additional 12 credits in graduate English coursework alongside their integrated education program. Undoubtedly, many readers will be aware of the various assessments required by NCATE accreditation: The Instructional Study is a project designed to assess "candidate effect on student learning" (NCATE Required assessment #6) while supporting the development of professional dispositions. These professional dispositions, identified in our college's "conceptual framework" and (self) assessed at the beginning, middle, and end points in the students' program include: intellectual curiosity; engagement in one's own learning and self-directed learning; self-reflection and actively using feedback from others; demonstrating the need to develop professionally and make plans for improvement; exhibiting caring and collegial relations; believing in the capacity and desire of all students to learn and reflecting on personal biases; and commitment to educational equity and social justice (SUNY New Paltz Conceptual Framework).

The student teaching seminar is designed to support teacher candidates who are in the culminating semester of their English education program and are now engaged in fulltime student teaching. The student teaching seminar is a one-credit course (taken satisfactory/fail) alongside fulltime student teaching. The seminar meets eight times over the course of the semester—about every other week. Due to the rural character of our location and its dispersed population, over half of our candidates have long commutes (1 hour each way) to their placements, so frequent in-person seminar meetings are not possible. The semester of this study, the seminar included nine graduate students and 12 undergraduates for a total of 21 teacher candidates (nine males and 12 females). These teacher candidates were working with 12 different college supervisors who were encouraged to participate in the seminar and facilitate study group sessions by managing time and clarifying roles. Because the study groups are designed to develop candidates' professional voices, supervisors were encouraged to listen rather than talk.

THE INSTRUCTIONAL STUDY

The primary assignment for the course is the Instructional Study, and seminar meetings are designed to support students in completing the assignment's requirements. A version of this assignment has been part of the program for over 10 years and serves to evidence "assessment of candidate effect of student learning." The original assignment name reflected its roots in Japanese "lesson study" (Lewis, Perry, Hurd, & O'Connell, 2006); however, we changed the name due to candidate confusion. A "lesson" conjured up a single day's instruction, whereas the assignment is designed to examine the impact of at least 3 days of connected instruction. The rubric for assessing the Instructional Study is a common rubric developed during our NCATE accreditation process and is used by all programs offered by our institution, including candidates in elementary, communication disorders, art education, and educational administration. The process of developing the Instructional Study is designed to support the professional dispositions that we define as "inquiry dispositions."

The assignment asks candidates to "write a report that describes your instruction and analyzes its impact on student learning." Candidates are directed to "provide explicit evidence from student work in the analysis, and to discuss the 'intellectual quality' of students' final products and the extent to which it reflects students' 'college and career readiness.'" To provide candidates with an analytic frame for examining the quality of their assignments and student work, we introduce them to Fred Newmann's research on authentic achievement through two short readings, "Authentic Intellectual Achievement in Writing" (Sisserson, Manning, Knepler, & Jolliffe, 2002), which serves as a core text, and "Standards for Authentic Achievement and Pedagogy" (Newmann & Wehlage, 1993), from which we derive criteria of "authentic intellectual achievement." These texts define student authentic intellectual achievement as "intellectual accomplishments that are worthwhile, significant, and meaningful" (Newmann & Wehlage, p. 23) and that can be identified through three criteria: construction of knowledge (as opposed to reproduction of knowledge); disciplined inquiry or evidence-based reasoning (as opposed to superficial understandings); and having value beyond school and relevance to students' lives (as opposed to assignments that function merely to earn grades or prove competence). We also encourage candidates to use the Common Core Learning Standards' (CCLS) analytic lens of "college and career readiness" when examining their instruction, which serves to focus candidates on the "big picture" of their instruction, giving more room for a critical perspective on both the CCLS and their own instruction rather than a myopic focus on meeting various individual learning standards.

INQUIRY ON INQUIRY

Given that we undertook to investigate our teaching and learning, as well as the impact of our instruction on our teacher candidates' teaching and learning, as demonstrated through evidence of their secondary English students' learning, the data that informs our analysis is drawn from both our work and our teacher candidates' work. We include in our data the teaching journals of both Mary and Pamela, as well as our emails, anecdotal records from the seminar itself, and notes and memos written informally by each of us throughout the focal semester. Data from our teacher candidates include their inquiry dispositions and self-assessments, which they addressed at the beginning of the semester in September, and at the end in December; reflection journals that they completed at the end of each study group session, held at each of the first six meetings (of eight total); and the narratives of their instructional studies, which they completed at the end of the semester.

Although we will refer to the class as a whole in our own reflections upon it, in order to provide a stronger focus on, and a richer analysis around, the experiences of the teacher candidates, we have selected the data of one study group rather than watering down our analysis by attempting to address the self-assessments, reflection journals, and Instructional Study narratives of all of the teacher candidates in the class. We have selected the study group of Van, George, Ivan, Jackie, and Misty because they were a group that we had an opportunity to observe and facilitate frequently. As we have noted, many of the student teaching supervisors also attended the seminar. They generally helped to facilitate study groups in which one or more of their particular teacher candidates were working.

"Homework" for each seminar meeting was for each teacher candidate to bring an artifact of student work from his or her current placement. Each teacher candidate completed two placements, one in a middle school, and one in a secondary school, one of which was designated as a "high needs" school identified as having a large number of students coming from low socioeconomic backgrounds. We scaffolded the discussion of the study group in two ways: at the first meeting of the study group at the beginning of each placement, the emphasis on student work focused simply on using it through guiding questions to provide information about the school and instructional context to all members of the study group. For every other meeting of the study group, we provided a structured study group protocol that outlined the steps of analysis and offered sentence frames as a foundation for discussion. At the end of each study group, students responded in written reflection about their experiences in that evening's session, addressing questions about what they had contributed to, and learned from, the dialogue around student work. After the class had ended, we returned to our offices and wrote our teaching journals.

What Did We Learn?

We analyzed our data separately through a recursive process of coding guided by the inquiry dispositions that we had identified at the beginning of the semester. Initially, we found that we were not in agreement with our interpretation of some of the data, and discovered that the "difficulty," and thus the extra push to insight, of collaborative data analysis is the dialogue that arises from respectful disagreement. The work and interpretations we share here are a snapshot of a particular place in the ongoing process of inquiry. One of our early findings was that we learned not only from what the data had to share, but also from our conversations as we each provided evidence for our individual points of view as seminar co-instructors and inquiry co-researchers and worked to come to a place of agreement, learning much from each other along the way. We find this to be part of the beauty and the messiness of inquiry work, and we will continue to hold this dialogue and to dig deeper into the data we plan to gather long after this particular inquiry cycle. In this writing, we share the following themes that have arisen from our analysis, organizing our findings in light of the inquiry dispositions we sought to support.

Discovery through dialogue

As we have noted, one of our early findings was the way that the challenges of collaborative inquiry pushed us to further our understandings and build upon our individual interpretations. Given the dialogical nature of inquiry, we were delighted to watch this play out in the focal study group across the course of the semester even as we were experiencing it ourselves.

> *I observed a few study group discussions, most of which included lots of appreciative, thoughtful, and complimentary comments on the work being done by their colleagues.* (Pamela, teaching journal, November)

Both Pamela and Mary's observation that this study group was appreciating and benefitting from the mutual exchange of ideas is revealed through comments from the teacher candidates' reflection journals:

> *I enjoy hearing my colleagues' experiences and see their assignments and the designs behind them. I think that hearing all of their experiences shows me that teaching is a different experience based on many factors.* (Ivan, reflection journal, October)

> *I got some really good ideas for an argument unit and other steps to take.* (Misty, reflection journal, November)

> *I was given a lot of advice which I used the very next day!* ☺ [smiley face included in the original] (Van, reflection journal, November)

> In November, George wrote in his reflection journal that he was able to provide a good suggestion to a conundrum that Van was striving to address.

Our teacher candidates' reflections consistently demonstrated both their celebration of their colleagues' insights and gratitude for the shared ideas.

Despite the supportive environment of their study group, the teacher candidates still seemed to feel very much on their own when they were off in their schools during the day. This comes through in Van's compelling description of his "first day of school":

> *The anticipation of trying out pedagogical strategies, activities, learning styles, and other things that you learn while in school was almost overwhelming. And then, I stood at the front of the classroom for the first time, and for the first time in my life, I went from complete confidence of the task at hand, to an almost fearful recognition that I had no clue what I was doing.* (Van, Instructional Study)

Although it offered a place for supportive dialogue where candidates could ask and answer questions about the student teaching experience, both the study group and the student teaching seminar were not sufficiently connected to the students' day-to-day experience to address the all-too-common feeling of being overwhelmed. Although we realized that this was one of the constraints of our seminar model, we hoped that the teacher candidates would find collaborative inquiry possibilities with their cooperating teachers at their school placements. We also hoped (and intended through our scaffolding) that the teacher candidates would see the professional and interpersonal benefit of collaborative inquiry and gain the confidence to instigate similar engagement with their future colleagues, although the limits of our current investigation preclude us from addressing that.

Raising important questions

In teasing out inquiry dispositions from the research literature on inquiry, we agreed that the belief that one will raise important questions to push the dialogue further is an essential part of the inquiry process. Although we did not see clear evidence that teacher candidates believed they were raising compelling questions in their reflections, we did see questions being raised in their Instructional Studies. However, the challenge of locating this as a disposition is not solely in whether or not it is being accomplished but also in the teacher candidate's awareness that he or she is doing this and that it is supporting the inquiry process.

As mentors of the inquiry process and pedagogical models, we found that we were also challenged in light of this disposition. We, as well as the supervisors, found ourselves fighting the tendency to make statements of opinion or fact to our teacher candidates rather than raising questions when we facilitated the study group sessions. As evidenced by Mary's journal, which reflects both of us, we have much to develop in this particular area:

> *I did exactly what I had told students and supervisors not to do—with judgments and advice giving.* (Mary, teaching journal, September)

As we have noted, while we identified evidence of compelling questions raised within the Instructional Study narratives, the teacher candidates did not identify this in their final self-assessments recorded in December. Van and Jackie both seemed to misunderstand the item. George noted that he had not engaged in questioning "to my memory…this year," and Misty left the item blank. The exception, Ivan, caught our attention with his clear-eyed assertion that:

> *I think I sometimes annoy my colleagues because I ask questions about instruction and student learning all the time during lunch [at my school placement].* (Ivan, self-assessment, December)

Whereas we could see Ivan grappling explicitly with this issue, part of our learning about our teaching is that we failed both in making this disposition explicit to our students, but also in scaffolding and in modeling what it meant to raise "important" questions.

Designing and implementing authentic and intellectually rigorous instruction

When we first sought to observe evidence of this developing disposition in our teachers, we were, to put it plainly, frustrated. However, in regards to this disposition, we were delighted to ultimately witness growth, both through our observations, and through the self-reported evidence provided by students. Our excitement in examining the teacher candidates' work as a whole as part of our inquiry was the clear movement noted in students' self-assessments and in our own teaching journals. For example, after observing a study group at work in September, Mary noted with evident irritation:

> *I wonder if they would rate this work as being high on the "intellectual achievement scale"???* *Is it? This is a good question, one I feel I could argue that this is just the kind of lower-order stupid stuff that alienates kids from school and English.* (Mary, teaching journal, September)

Our teacher candidates also recognized that this was an area with great potential for growth:

> *I want this to be a goal. I have already started to think what real world experience I can build into my class.* (George, self-assessment, September)

As we have noted, we used Sisserson et al. (2002) as a core text to provide a foundation for evaluating and identifying instructional assignments and the resulting student work as authentic and intellectually rigorous. After the seminar meeting that was the focus of Mary's comment above, we identified the need for explicit clarification and modeling, beginning the next seminar meeting with a think-aloud on how to analyze student work in light of our core text. Such scaffolding paid off, as students both appreciated and benefited from this explictness. Responding to the same item in his December self-assessment, George referred to the first author of the core text, using this name as an eponym for assignments that result in student work that is worthwhile, significant, and meaningful:

> *This is something I'm proud of; I often produce sufficiently Sissersonian work.* (George, self-assessment, December)

In her teaching journal that evening, Mary wrote about a culminating whole class discussion on authenticity:

> *Was really excited students seemed to appreciate the "authentic" Sisserson lenses.* (Mary, teaching journal, December)

Furthermore, in an email to Pamela after the end of the semester, Mary reported:

> *In re-reading our logs I noticed lots of disappointment in my journals in some of the student teachers' seminar performances, especially the initial session and also the last session. But examining their written final products, I really saw the glass half full.* (Mary, email to Pamela, February)

What we both found was that in the ongoing struggle to balance the tensions of students' personal needs regarding time and emotional support around their student teaching experiences with the need to provide effective pedagogy around the Instructional Study assignment, we had to continually remind and support each other to hold on to the inquiry stance when the day-to-day logistics of keeping up with our multiple work commitments got in the way. We found that one of our strategies for maintaining our inquiry stance was to always return to the student work. By going directly to the page, we could lose the filters of frustration, exhaustion, and busyness that could cloud our perspective. Unfortunately, this is a lesson learned only in the hindsight of this inquiry cycle, but fortunately, it is a lesson that we can share now.

Making mistakes and learning from them

In setting off on this journey, we acknowledged that in order to be authentic to the inquiry process, we would model this disposition in student teaching seminar. We also found that given our co-sharing of the responsibility for the class, our trust and respect for each other, and our commitment to the process of improvement led to an organic reflection of the successes and mistakes in each seminar class that we discussed as we cleaned up the room and carried our materials back to our offices in multiple trips. Realizing this, we made a habit of going back to our office and listing elements to be revised or addressed in planning for the following seminar session as well as making changes based on teacher candidate feedback.

Our explicit modeling of learning from the impact of our instruction was documented in the study group protocol, which we revised several times to streamline and clarify over the course of the student teaching seminar. Before transitioning into study groups, we would share the changes we had made and explain why we had tweaked the protocol, noting that we were also teachers engaged in an ongoing process of adjusting our instruction in light of student responses.

Early on, we noticed that the study group members were shy in sharing their personal experiences in the group setting, and in individual conversations with us they frequently shared their concerns that they were not being as successful as their peers. Meeting with the same study group and building trust over time seemed to address this issue, as noted by Jackie:

> *I also think just being able to reassure the other members of my group that I'm having the same issues/fears is helpful in general.* (Jackie, self-assessment, December)

The importance of making, recognizing, and addressing mistakes is addressed explicitly by Van:

Many of the lessons contained within this study only worked because of failure, and it is in that seed of failure where success dwells. (Van, Instructional Study, p. 3)

Given that mistakes help to nourish the inquiry cycle, we can also see how our teacher candidates' approach to mistakes informs our understanding of the role of our final inquiry disposition in their development.

Acknowledging and owning the complex process of inquiry

Perhaps it is this belief, that inquiry is an ongoing and frequently difficult, yet optimistic learning from the journey rather than a need to reach a hoped-for endpoint that most clearly links the work of inquiry to professional teacher dispositions. In order to live within an inquiry stance, one must dedicate oneself to critical questioning. Again, we turn to the work of Van:

I am confident that I will never be perfect. This acceptance that I will never be perfect allows me to constantly change, rework, and adapt to the ever changing, and ever diverse student population. (Van, Instructional Study, p. 15)

Van does not simply acknowledge his inability to achieve perfection, he celebrates it as a strength that will support him in his ongoing quest to improve his teaching and address the changing needs of his students. The first step in moving into an inquiry stance must be the epiphany that ongoing imperfection is what will help us to improve our practice and to be mutually supportive of our colleagues grappling with the same issues. We return to the work of Jackie, which opened this chapter and served as a mantra during our reflection and writing after the ending of our seminar course:

The end result does not have to be perfect but the progression of the students' work is the real thing. (Jackie, reflection journal, October)

LIMITATIONS AND TENSIONS

Given the nature of inquiry, what we identify as our limitations in this investigation also overlaps into our own learning from this particular inquiry cycle. Both the limits of our time with our students (one semester) and the limits of our teacher candidates' time with their students (8 weeks each at two placements) impacted the inquiry process by forcing questions and dialogue at a speed that felt inappropriate and inorganic. We discovered that given the risks of honesty demanded by collaborative inquiry, a level of trust among collaborators must be met in order for the inquiry process to truly begin. We saw this in self-reported discomfort of our teacher candidates as they worked to be honest with their colleagues, although keeping the study groups the same enabled students to gain a measure of trust and to take risks in discussion later in the semester.

The abbreviated nature of the time teacher candidates spent at their schools impacted their instructional studies by forcing them to design, implement, and evaluate instruction for students they were still in the process of getting to know. The students felt rushed, unsure, and pressured. This rushed process is evident in their narratives, and in conversations and emails to us where they requested more time to address the assignment because many of them only reached a point where they were beginning to implement unit plans at the end of the semester, having used the first 8-week placement as an opportunity, justly, to "find their feet in front of the classroom." This is a finding that has arisen from this inquiry process. Unfortunately, one of the challenges of teaching is in finding creative ways of working inside constraints over which we have little agency. We do not directly impact the design and length of the student teaching experience at our institution. However, given our findings, we can make a recommendation for change.

We also found that the constraints of our large class size and the limits of the student teaching seminar time made it impossible to fully address the range of important concerns and frustrations that teacher candidates brought to seminar regarding their individual student teaching placements. Many of them found that their school culture and the goals of their cooperating teachers limited the learning goals they could support through their instruction, especially in their efforts to implement authentic assignments in an environment constructed by the pressures around standardized tests. This is another issue that we do not have direct agency to address, but it is our hope that our continued writing about our inquiry work may shed light on the negative ways that accountability processes may impact student learning when assessment backwash—its impact on teaching and learning—becomes overwhelming to teachers and their students.

Furthermore, despite taking time during each seminar to do an explicit "check-in" with the teacher candidates and also offering individual advising sessions at each session, we still feel that we have not found the appropriate balance between supporting candidates' professional needs to begin to think about the impact of their instruction on students in concrete ways and their needs for socioemotional support around the multiple stresses of student teaching. A question that will continue to drive our inquiry process is: How can we support candidates' professional growth in ways that support and link to their humanity and life beyond school? Given that this is a question we asked our teacher candidates to consider at every seminar meeting and in their instructional studies, we only do justice to their answers by pursuing this question ourselves.

BEGINNINGS

Living the inquiry process alongside our teacher candidates reminded us sharply that despite its philosophical beauty, inquiry is difficult, messy, and sometimes frustrating because it is rooted in very human work characterized by very human difficulties, anxieties, needs, and challenges. As noted by Pamela, "It was never pretty" (personal memo, January). Despite our understanding of the challenging process of inquiry, we found ourselves fighting an unsatisfied desire to have our new understandings wrapped in a box and tied with golden ribbon. Instead, we experienced professional development as inquiry, which is "associated more with uncertainty than certainty, more with posing problems and dilemmas than with solving them, and more with recognition that inquiry both stems from and generates questions" (Cochran-Smith & Lytle, 2001, p. 56). Although we missed the "prettiness" of a nicely wrapped package, this investigation helped us appreciate the value of a vision of professional development and learning that is greater than the individual and that stretches out beyond a single semester into a life-long perspective. The triumph in this investigation is that we were reminded of the personal satisfaction, the positive implications for our teacher candidates, and the unexpected joys of the inquiry process by our students, whom we had intended to be the beneficiaries of our inquiry process. We thank our students for teaching us that our own learning, as professors, benefits from their honesty about their struggles. Their work will inspire us as we continue our inquiry journey.

We wish to share the immediate impact that the work documented here had on our journey as teachers and researchers. Immediate steps that we took included a revisiting of the seminar syllabus and work to simplify and streamline the course through a backwards design process to further scaffold the Instructional Study assignment. Given changing certification and assessment requirements, we anticipate that our syllabus will be altering drastically in the future. We are both eager to see the ways that inquiry dispositions will be influenced by these requirements, and we are equally determined to find ways to keep inquiry and authenticity at the forefront of our work and the work we ask of our candidates. We are concerned that in a culture of standardized assessment, professional teacher dispositions, including inquiry dispositions, will be neglected and considered irrelevant because of the difficulties of quantifying them and including them in current evaluations and measures of accountability.

We view the work shared in this chapter as the beginning of an ongoing collaboration as we continue to learn more about the process of inquiry and its necessary place in the student teaching experience and beyond. The process of examining our own beliefs and understandings are ongoing, as is our analyses of evidence from candidates on later semesters of the student teaching seminar. Additionally, we are delighted to now count some of the candidates from the semester we describe as allies in our inquiry journey. They have since graduated from the program, and we are delighted to be working with them as colleagues, co-learners, and co-researchers on this pilgrimage to insight on the world of teaching and learning in an age of high-stakes assessment. We look forward with hope and anticipation.

NOTES

1 All names, with the exception of the authors, are pseudonyms.

REFERENCES

Athanases, S. Z. (2013). Questioning and inquiry in mentoring new teachers of English: A focus on learners. *English Journal, 102*(3), 40–48.

Berghoff, B., Blackwell, S., & Wisehart, R. (2011). Using critical reflection to improve urban teacher preparation: A collaborative inquiry of three teacher educators. *Penn GSE Perspectives on Urban Education, 8*(2), 19–28.

Bowne, M., Cutler, K., DeBates, D., Gilkerson, D., & Stremmel, A. (2010). Pedagogical documentation and collaborative dialogue as tools of inquiry for pre-service teachers in early childhood education: An exploratory narrative. *Journal of the Scholarship of Teaching and Learning, 10*(2), 48–59.

Butler, D. L., & Schnellert, L. (2012). Collaborative inquiry in teacher professional development. *Teaching and Teacher Education: An International Journal of Research and Studies, 28*(8), 1206–120.

Cochran-Smith, M., & Lytle, S. L. (2001). Beyond certainty: Taking an inquiry stance on practice. In A. Lieberman & L. Miller (Eds.), *Teachers caught in the action: Professional development that matters* (pp. 45–58). New York, NY: Teachers College Press.

Cochran-Smith, M., & Lytle, S. L. (2009). *Inquiry as stance: Practitioner research for the next generation.* New York, NY: Teachers College Press.

Fecho, B. (2011). *Teaching for the students: Habits of heart, mind, and practice in the engaged classroom.* New York, NY: Teachers College Press.

Fecho, B., Price, K., & Read, C. (2004). From Tunanak to Beaufort: Taking a critical inquiry stance as a first year teacher. *English Education, 36*(4), 263–288.

Friesen, S. (2009, November 20). Inquiry as a disposition [Video file]. Retrieved from http://www.edtalks.org/video/inquiry-disposition#.UR6M_GdRGuQ

Gallagher, D. J. (1996). On becoming an interpretist: From knowing as a teacher to knowing as a researcher. In L. Heshusius and K. Ballard (Eds.), *From positivism to interpretivism and beyond: Tales of transformation in educational and social research* (pp. 93–99). New York, NY: Teachers College Press.

Hadar, L., & Brody, D. (2010). From isolation to symphonic harmony: Building a professional development community among teacher educators. *Teaching and Teacher Education: An International Journal of Research and Studies, 26*(8), 1641–1651.

Hughes, A. (2003). *Testing for language teachers* (2nd ed.). Cambridge, England: Cambridge University Press.

Kagan, D. M. (1992). Professional growth among preservice and beginning teachers. *Review of Educational Research, 62*(2), 129–169.

Lewis, C., Perry, R., Hurd, J., & O'Connell, M. P. (2006). Lesson study comes of age in North America. *Phi Delta Kappan, 88*(4), 273–281.

Meyer, T. (2002). Novice teacher learning communities: An alternative to 1-on-1 mentoring. *American Secondary Education 31*(1) 27–42.

Meyer, T., & Sawyer, M. (2006). Cultivating an inquiry stance in English education: Rethinking the student teaching seminar. *English Education, 39*(1), 46–71.

New York State Education Department. (2012, December 29). *New York State P-12 common core learning standards for English language arts and literacy.* Retrieved from http://www.engageny.org/sites/default/files/resource/attachments/nysp12cclsela.pdf

Newmann, F. M., & Associates. (1996). *Authentic achievement: Restructuring schools for intellectual quality.* San Francisco, CA: Jossey-Bass.

Newmann, F. M., & Wehlage, G. G. (1993). Five standards of authentic instruction. *Educational Leadership, 50*(7), 8–12.

Richards, J. (2011). Exploring two interventions to promote graduate education majors dispositions toward culturally responsive teaching: Taking action to address my shortcomings as a literacy teacher educator. *Reading Improvement, 48*(2), 59–80.

Sisserson, K., Manning, C. K., Knepler, A., & Jolliffe, D. A. (2002). Authentic intellectual achievement in writing. *English Journal, 91*(6), 63–69.

Taylor, R. L., & Wasicsco, M. M. (2000). The dispositions to teach. Retrieved from http://coehs.nku.edu/content/dam/coehs/docs/dispositions/resources/The_Dispositons_to_Teach.pdf

Waff, D. (2009). Coresearching and coreflecting: The power of teacher inquiry communities. In D. Goswani, C. Lewis, M. Rutherford, & D. Waff (Eds.), *Teacher inquiry: Approaches to language and literacy research* (pp. 69–89). New York, NY: Teachers College Press.

CHAPTER SEVEN

The Big "O"

Occupying against Reductionism in Education Using Small and Sustained Actions

BARBARA ROSE

INTRODUCTION

In the United States, we have seen many examples of mobilizing for change, including the formation of workers' unions and the battle for civil rights for many groups. The phrase "Occupy movements" became common vernacular in 2011 with Occupy Wall Street, which was inspired in part by the Arab Spring protests. The phrase has increasingly been applied to various protests against inequality around the world, generating a shared organizing concept for discussion and action. The website Occupy Together (www.occupytogether.org) is one example of a discussion forum for Occupy movements; it includes the goals to "resist," "restructure," and "remix" as a process for work to make fundamental changes in institutions and systems of inequity. The voices of scholars, politicians, and celebrities further demonstrate the robustness of Occupy movements as an organizing concept. Cornel West, for example, noted the connections between change process and democracy, calling the Occupy movement a "democratic awakening" (Quinn, 2012).

Education is a major institutional system in the United States, and is historically based on the idea of building citizens for a democratic society. While that idea raises questions such as "Who is allowed to participate in that democracy and who isn't?" there is very little doubt that increasingly the democracy of schools is no longer within the hands of teachers, students, families, or communities. Education is not neutral; rather, it reflects the dominant paradigms of the culture, as seen in 2010 when the Texas Board of Education made over 100 amendments to social studies curricula that focused on adding conservative ideology, and in 2012, when Arizona banned ethnic studies programs. The corporatization of schools is seen in the rise of for-profit standardized testing, influences of textbook companies, and the proliferation of for-profit schools, among others.

Despite numerous examples, the politicization and corporatization of education are often unknown, unacknowledged, ignored, trivialized, or disputed, in large part because of the complexity of education and the intersections of social, political, and economic forces that are largely invisible to most people. The public view of "education" is the human face of students, teachers, families, and communities, and the physical structures of school buildings. Education is personal. It is tangible. The human face of education as a collection of interacting people (children, teachers, families) is what is seen in the bustling school yards and classrooms, in the yellow buses on the roads in the early morning and afternoon, in the community pride of sporting events, and in the local newspapers reporting school activities and student achievements.

What is largely unseen by the public—state mandates, initiatives that reduce teacher autonomy and create cultures of compliance engendered through public school policies and practices—is a web of causes and effects of lessening emphasis on human relationships in schools, and increased emphasis on control by profit-generating corporations. The following brief example illustrates the interrelationships of mandates, initiatives, and cultures of compliance. The federal No Child Left Behind Act (NCLB) of 2002 ties "scientifically based" reading programs to federal funding; scripted programs that are intended to improve student test scores have been widely used to meet that standard (Ede, 2006). NCLB is the mandate that drives the development and sale of scripted curricula and the tests that measure student improvement by for-profit corporations; they are the initiatives that respond to the mandate. Reduction of teacher autonomy and increased expectations of compliance occur when "scripted" curricula are imposed on teachers. Student achievement, as measured by the test scores, is then used to evaluate teacher performance, thus putting teachers in positions where lack of compliance can have dire consequences.

Increasingly, constraints in higher education impact faculty and areas of study as well. Legal challenges from organizations such as the National Association of Scholars (NAS) (www.nas.org) and the Foundation for Individual Rights in Education (FIRE) (http://thefire.org) include accusations of liberal biases, challenges to cultural and ethnic studies programs, and calls (and action) to eliminate many anti-bias programs. The description of its history says that NAS was founded to "confront the rise of campus political correctness" (NAS, 2013). FIRE's mission includes pledging "to defend and sustain individual rights at America's colleges and universities. These rights include freedom of speech, legal equity, due process, religious liberty, and sanctity of conscience—the essential qualities of individual liberty and dignity" (FIRE, 2013). In practice, many of the FIRE cases, both current, and those documented in their case archive, involve university initiatives designed to protect the rights of minorities and oppressed groups, such as bias reporting programs, speech codes, and behaviors of campus organizations and individuals.

Teacher education programs are affected by compliance initiatives at state and national levels. State departments of education frequently define curricula for teacher education. What *must* be included often leaves little room for what *could* be included, resulting in standardization of programs within a state. The National Council on the Accreditation of Teacher Education (NCATE) accredits hundreds of programs in the United States, and sets standards for necessary "content, skills, and dispositions" of teacher candidates (www.ncate.org). NCATE and a second accrediting body, the Teacher Education Accreditation Council (TEAC), are currently being subsumed by a new organization, the Council for the Accreditation of Educator Practice (CAEP). Therefore, at the time of writing, the relationship between NCATE, TEAC, and CAEP is still evolving.

There are numerous benefits to applying the tenets of Occupy movements to education, both in public schools and in colleges and universities. First, there is a widespread recognition of the concept in general, and language that has emerged as part of it. A number—"99 percent"—is instantly recognizable by many as a concept and a synonym for inequity. Many websites and links have emerged using the phrase (e.g., www.wearethe99percent.tumblr.com, http://thinkprogress. org/progress-report/the-99-percent-movement/, www.wearethe99percent.us/). Second, the Occupy movement, while sharply focused on injustice, is highly elastic in its use as an organizing concept. Clearly, the variety of ways it has been deployed around the world illustrates robustness, ranging from protesting systemic issues (e.g., Wall Street) to the stories of individual people. The Tumblr, We Are the 99 Percent, for example, invites readers to tell their stories; in June 2013, it profiled an older man who is deaf, describing his daily life and its challenges. (www.wearethe99percent.tumblr.com, 2013). The purpose of another website, also entitled "We Are the 99 Percent," is stated as being to provide "facts, graphics, and reading about income inequality, wealth concentration, and our corrupt economic system" (www.wearethe99percent.us/, 2013). Third, the movement shows examples of impact that small groups can make to inspire big change, which then inspires others to take action.

In education, a recent example of the small group, big change potential is the group of Seattle teachers at Garfield High School who boycotted administering a required standardized test. The test, Measures of Academic Progress (MAP), which cost over four million dollars, was brought to Seattle by then superintendent

Maria Goodloe-Johnson, who did not disclose that she was on the board of the company that produced the test (Seattle's Teacher Uprising, 2013).

In the protest, the teachers prepared a thorough analysis of the reasons for their decision. They called a press conference and released a letter that noted that while standardized tests are appropriate for the uses for which they are designed (a point that is also clearly made by the companies that design the tests), the MAP test was not aligned with their curriculum, was used for purposes not intended (e.g., evaluating teachers), hurt ELL and special-education students, made computer labs inaccessible for academic work, and was not valid for a variety of other reasons (Hagopian, 2013; Seattle Education, 2013).

In an interview with Amy Goodman, Garfield High School teacher Jesse Hagopian noted that Jimi Hendrix and Quincy Jones were Garfield alumni, and said,

> We have a long tradition of teaching our kids to think creatively. And, you know, Quincy Jones ended up producing the album *Thriller*, so I'm so glad that he didn't have to be subjected to this MAP test and have his confidence killed and not produce one of the greatest albums of all time. (Seattle's Teacher Uprising, 2013)

The actions of the Seattle teachers spotlight an interesting conundrum. A challenge for teachers and teacher educators is how to continue a primary focus of creating environments that support student learning, while also being knowledgeable about, and responsive to, political forces. Most teachers do not enter teaching to become radicalized and push back against the system; rather, their focus is on their classrooms and students. The skill set for student-centered teaching does not always include predispositions for understanding "big picture" political, economic, and social impact, let alone questioning or challenging those systems. The Seattle teachers' message focused on the negative impact of standardized testing on their own students. The teachers were doing what they could do in their school, in their community, and with their students. The issues and their responses and direct actions were about people—their neighbors and their own families.

This chapter will propose an analytic framework for exploring educational issues using the concept of reductionism. A variety of examples of reductionism in curricula will be included, as well as how readers can explore examples from their own institutions. As importantly, the chapter will move beyond awareness to include examples of small and sustained strategies (e.g., questioning practices and policies; exploring the cost and impact of accreditation culture; demanding data and transparency to support decisions and policies; developing student-centered pedagogy for curricula; exploring benefits and limitations of decisions) that can disrupt the impact of reductionism in teacher education. By seeing how anti-reductionist thinking can become an integral part of a teacher education program we might better understand what is vital and promising about this form of critique.

DISPOSITIONS FOR CHANGE

So how, if at all, are professional dispositions related to responding to current political and economic issues in schools? Part of the answer is in the language for what is deemed "unacceptable," "acceptable," or "target" dispositions for accreditation compliance, which is a powerful driver of how hundreds of accredited teacher education programs define and measure dispositions. Three concepts are included across compliance levels in the current NCATE language: (a) professional dispositions delineated in professional, state, and institutional standards; (b) classroom behaviors that are consistent with the ideal of fairness and the belief that all students can learn; and (c) work with students, families, colleagues, and communities (NCATE, 2013). The target level also includes the following: "Candidates demonstrate classroom behaviors that create caring and supportive learning environments and encourage self-directed learning by all students. Candidates recognize when their own professional dispositions may need to be adjusted and are able to develop plans to do so" (NCATE, 2013).

There are several dimensions within the current NCATE language that *could* be used to support a broad definition of dispositions. Dispositions in support of fairness and a belief that all children can learn could include exploration of issues of conscious and unconscious bias, racial and ethnic differences, and poverty—both in and outside of the classroom. Work with students, families, and community could include strategies emphasizing authentic engagement and community building. Creating caring and supportive learning environments and encouraging self-directed learning could include identifying curricular practices that hinder those goals. The complexity of these issues is the likely reason they are not fully reflected in the standards, because the necessary task of measuring outcomes is also more complex; further, many educators do not have the background or motivation to address them.

What *could* be in dispositions is often not reflected in what *is intended*. The assumption that dispositions can be broadly defined to include issues of equity, social justice, and resistance is in sharp contrast to the standards of NCATE. NCATE's political nature (and connections to NAS and FIRE) was most notably exposed in 2006, when it removed "social justice" from the glossary of NCATE standards, under pressure from the Department of Education's politically appointed National Advisory Committee on Institutional Quality and Integrity. This action led to a firestorm of responses from the educational community, including the November/December 2007 issue of the *Journal of Teacher Education*, which was devoted to the controversy. The smack down of the social justice language sent a chilling message—not only did NCATE narrowly define dispositions, but it also did not defend broader interpretations and strategies. It is unknown at the time of writing whether CAEP will expand its view of dispositions. However, a review of the draft standards, which were tentatively approved in June 2013 and are expected to be fully approved by fall 2013, suggests that dispositions will likely continue to be defined narrowly (CAEP, 2013).

Even if more support existed for viewing dispositions broadly within CAEP, accreditation reporting processes and practices that privilege convergent thinking over divergent thinking discourage risky, "out of the box" responses. There is a lot at stake for institutions in their preparation of accreditation materials. For example, if evidence of professional dispositions toward families can be shown using descriptions of types of communication that are provided (e.g., parent teacher conferences, newsletters), why would an institution examine the inherent power relationships and one-sided nature of such correspondence, or any of the other messy complexities of school-family interactions? From a compliance standpoint, there is little benefit, and perhaps great real or perceived risk, to conceptualizing dispositions as a strategy for change. In interpreting the NCATE and CAEP standards broadly, the question of what the term "evidence" means and who decides is rarely discussed. It is likely that what is given to the accreditors is frequently a pragmatic (and reductive) decision based on replicating and using examples from "successful" institutions. The approach of "Let's give them what they want (or what has worked for others) with as minimal effort as possible and without venturing into uncharted territory, so we can get on with our real work" reflects a likely lack of trust in the accrediting process as a way to uncover new possibilities and ways to think.

REDUCTIONISM

What compliance-driven mandates and convergent thinking responses have in common is reductionism; each reduces complex issues to simple solutions. Reductionism that comes from the process of complex thinking (e.g., "less is more," attributed to architect Mies van der Rohe) can provide elegant and effective solutions, and is widely used in design and science. In education, however, reductionism driven by constraints and oversimplifications in mandated processes frequently bypasses critical thinking, multiple perspectives, individual experience and judgment, and transparency in favor of derivative and convenient solutions. While reductionism is the problem of distorting and oversimplifying the phenomenon, operationalization is the tendency to substitute something determinate and measurable for the phenomenon (e.g., human understanding becomes a test score; a disposition becomes a response on a survey tool). An assumption for this chapter is that effective teaching is holistic and includes divergent thinking that is not served well by reductionism. Teachers whose preparation includes identifying and questioning the impact of narrow ways of operationalizing will be better teachers and advocates for the children they serve.

Using Reductionism for Issue Identification and Strategies for Change

What could education look like without reductive processes? Examining policies and practices in teacher education with a "lens" of reductionism provides a seldom-used framework for analysis. Using reductionism as an authentic inquiry stance raises possibilities for social and political action.

There are many examples of how reductionism can be applied in public schools and teacher education as an organizing concept to identify and examine educational issues. Three examples are included in this chapter, representing a range of issues designed to illustrate how small actions and questions can be used to create transparency and advocate for change. Each example impacts teacher candidates and, consequently, the future of teaching. The model of discussion for each—identifying the issue and presenting examples of strategies—can be applied to explore *any* issue, event, policy, or practice.

A necessary presupposition of using reductionism to critique education is whether or not educators have an ethical responsibility to question and systematically explore challenges and issues in education. If the answer is yes, then identifying and exposing areas of reductionism can be an important tool for change.

Small and sustained actions can contribute to developing and implementing strategies for change; the following are infused throughout the examples. *Asking questions* can be a powerful tool to gather information, identify gaps in information, shine light on problematic practices or policies, and disrupt negatively impactful behaviors. *Breaking up big issues into smaller questions and answers* can be useful in avoiding burnout or feeling the system is just too big for change. *Vigilance* is necessary because information gathering and change can be slow, and patterns of inequity when left unchecked tend to seep into other areas. *Moving to strategies* is essential; without strategies for change, the identification and understanding of issues is just information.

Given that reductionism is about what is left after issues are distilled, part of exploring reductive processes is to identify what was there and is now gone. What fills the space of what "is" represents only part of an issue. Using the following examples, in admission policies, what fills the space are the reductive criteria that are used. For state standards, accrediting organizations, standardized testing, and curricula, what fills the space is what is included, or privileged, as valuable.

EXAMPLE 1: TEACHER EDUCATION ADMISSION PROCESSES

The Issue

The importance of admission and retention policies for students entering teacher education programs is clear. The potential length of a teaching career (30 or more years) means that the future teachers who are admitted to teacher education programs at any given point in time can influence generations of students. Admission policies are affected by student demand related to the job market, and institutional priorities such as seeing teacher candidates as important sources of revenue. So, the question "How can teacher education programs select the best candidates who will be excellent teachers?" may not be the primary consideration for admission. Even when it is, the definition of "excellence" is elusive. Is "excellence" defined as the highest academic achievers, as measured by standardized tests? Or is it defined as students with desired "professional dispositions" or other criteria? In recent years, standardized testing in the admission and retention of teacher education students has included widespread adoption of the Educational Testing Service (ETS) Praxis series. The Praxis I Pre-Professional Skills Tests (PPST) measures "basic skills in reading, writing and mathematics. In addition to licensure, these tests are often used to qualify candidates for entry into a teacher education program" (Educational Testing Service, 2013). In the State of Ohio (the home state of the author), for example, Praxis I is required for admission in most of the teacher education programs. In some cases, alternates are allowed, such as ACT or SAT scores, which are also standardized tests.

There are a number of unsubstantiated beliefs about Praxis I that support their use, including that they are linked to college success, becoming an effective teacher, or passing the Praxis II Subject Assessment tests, which measure content mastery in a variety of subject areas. However, those presumptions are not supported by independent research. Even the ETS, which produces the Praxis Series, does not make those claims.

So, how do current admission processes based on standardized tests reflect reductionist thinking? Privileging standardized tests as "the answer" or as a gatekeeper to teacher education programs ignores the value of other measures, or the importance of multiple criteria that evaluate different dimensions of prospective teacher candidates. Another example of both the derivative and unexamined dimensions of the widespread use of Praxis I can be seen through a brief and informal examination of the websites for teacher education programs in Ohio that was done by the author. In most cases, descriptions of the Praxis I admission test are taken verbatim (and without citation) from the ETS narrative; a similar review for other states requiring Praxis I would likely yield the same observation. Reporting the validity of "the test" in university "public face" materials such as bulletins and departmental websites is an example of how institutions represent themselves as professional, with mechanisms for policing and ensuring quality. Operationalizing quality using Praxis 1 also reduces workload in teacher education departments, but abdicates responsibility for thoroughly understanding the use of a particular measure in the institutional context. "Why do we use this test as a primary criterion for entry to teaching?" should be a question that has been considered in every teacher education program, because it affords the opportunity to make meaning about the educational endeavor rather than assume tradition or the "experts" have already settled this.

Strategies for Change

Question the context, assumptions, and impact of admission policies

Examining current practices using questions can be an effective strategy for increasing transparency and identifying assumptions. If an underlying assumption for admission to teacher education programs is that the criteria will yield excellent teachers, a number of questions examining admission policies and practices can be asked, including the following:

- What are the assumptions about admission criteria?
- Who benefits from the current criteria, and how do they benefit? Who doesn't?
- What are the correlations between admission criteria and desired outcomes?

Expect and demand transparency, research, and validity of admission criteria

If the core of validity is measuring what you intend to measure, then all admission criteria should be examined through that lens. The proliferation of the use of Praxis I as a valid admission criterion is problematic; it is the responsibility of ETS to be more transparent about why it is valid, and in what contexts. For example, if the Praxis I tests measure basic skills, do recent high school graduates score better on the test than older students returning to college? Further, programs considering adoption of Praxis I as an admission criterion should have responsibility to consider their own institutional contexts. Without independent research, it is difficult to determine the contexts for which the use of Praxis I is appropriate, and ones where its use could be problematic.

Track the impact of admission criteria on prospective and admitted students

Creating departmental and program level databases of who is admitted and who is not (and why), and achievement as students matriculate through college is necessary to thoroughly evaluate the impact of admission criteria, and to question the effectiveness of criteria. For example, when I was coordinating the Early Child-hood Education program in my institution at the height of demand for the pro-gram several years ago (typically 250+ applicants for fewer than 60–90 spots), an analysis of the relationship between admission criteria (Praxis I, university grade point average in general education classes, an essay, and an applicant statement of experiences with children), Praxis I was not significantly correlated with GPA of college courses, raising the question "Why are we using it?"

A more challenging question to answer by systematically tracking students is "Who do we lose as potential teachers with any given set of admission criteria?" While we may assume that if we privilege standardized tests, we will lose students who don't do well on standardized tests, what is meant by that loss is unknown. One strategy to minimize that kind of reductionism is to use multiple criteria, taking care to insure that the criteria actually measure different things.

Shift focus to include dispositions

One "different thing" is professional dispositions. Although CAEP currently de-fines professional practice as including "content, skills, and dispositions," criteria for dispositions are rarely addressed in admission criteria. The work of Martin Haberman (2013), founder of The Haberman Foundation, and Mark Wasicsko (2006), founder of the National Network for the Study of Educator Disposi-tions (NNSED), share the following important foundational assumptions: (a) appropriate professional dispositions of teachers are critical in student learning; (b) the extent to which professional dispositions can be learned is limited; and (c) admission criteria that include measures of dispositions can reduce the number of teachers with dispositional deficiencies that can adversely impact children and their learning.

Haberman (2013) and Wasicsko (2006) have different approaches to exploring dispositions in a systematic and thoughtful way. Haberman has developed instru-ments, including the Star Teacher Pre-Screener and the Star Administrator Ques-tionnaire, that can be used in admission criteria for teacher education programs and hiring decisions by school districts. The instruments include questions on catego-ries such as teacher persistence, response to authority, fallibility, and approach to at-risk students. Wasicsko's work is less well published, but has had impact through the organizational structure of the NNSED, including numerous professional con-ferences that bring together people exploring dispositions. His focus includes the importance of interviewing techniques and questions to explore dispositions based on perceptual psychology and the work of Arthur Combs (Wasicsko, 2006).

It is likely that teachers who exhibit student-centered dimensions of disposi-tions to the benefit of students in their classrooms (e.g., persistence, questioning authority when student interests are at stake) will also be predisposed to apply dispositional qualities to school policies and practices, and systemic social and political barriers in education. Including dispositions as a criterion in admission processes will increase the ability of teachers to create change.

EXAMPLE 2: TEACHER EDUCATION ACCREDITATION COMPLIANCE

The Issue

NCATE, the largest teacher education accreditation organization, currently includes six standards for teacher education programs: candidate knowledge, skills, and professional dispositions; assessment system and unit evaluation; field experiences and clinical practice; diversity; faculty qualifications, performance, and development; and unit governance and resources (NCATE, 2013). As mentioned earlier, at the time of writing, standards for the new umbrella accreditation council, CAEP, are being developed. Five draft standards were submitted for public comment in February 2013: content and pedagogical knowledge; clinical partnership and practice; candidate quality, recruitment, and selectivity; program impact; and provider quality, continuous improvement, and capacity (CAEP Commission on Standards and Performance Reporting, 2013).

Though it is still unclear as to what the final standards will be, the charge for the Commission on Standards gives a glimpse into the likely final product.

> The CAEP Commission on Standards and Performance Reporting will transform the preparation of teachers by creating a rigorous system of accreditation that demands excellence and produces teachers who raise student achievement. Specifically, the Commission will develop accreditation standards for all preparation programs that are based on evidence, continuous improvement, innovation, and clinical practice. Along with rigorous standards and evidence, the Commission will recommend transparent CAEP public accountability reporting with multiple measures, including those directly linked to student achievement. (CAEP Commission on Standards and Performance Reporting, 2013)

In theory, the current NCATE reporting parameters for compliance are broad and flexible for institution-specific needs. In practice, over the years the process has shifted to a reductive model with perceptions of increasingly narrower ways to do it "right." Interpretation of the standards is a key element here; institutions have shared culpability in the narrowing of interpretations and the shift to more reductive practice, and need to consider their role in that shift.

One factor that has led to reductive practices is related to what is and is not included as mandatory for inclusion, and the language for "unacceptable," "acceptable," and "target" ratings defines what schools include and, too often, value. It is likely that there is little discussion in institutions about what is missing (and why) because attention is paid instead to "studying for the test." Another factor is that reporting has become increasingly complex. For most colleges, gone are the days of faculty sitting around a table discussing the strengths and weaknesses of their programs, and describing them in reports that include the nuances and complexities of real issues in real programs. NCATE compliance has become a complicated labyrinth of requirements, with increasing demands on faculty and staff time. Again, institutional exploration of whether it has to be that way is rarely part of the process.

Increased reporting complexity has led to another factor that has dramatically shifted the process—the proliferation of full-time accreditation coordinators. The idea of a coordinating person has considerable merit. Ideally, a position (or portion of a position) dedicated to accreditation compliance can reduce faculty workload. The Coordinator can learn about programs to explain and guide the process for faculty for how best to communicate programs within the CAEP parameters, and how to use the assessment process in ways that encourage authentic program reflection. In practice, however, CAEP requirements may be presented by some Coordinators (accurately or inaccurately) as rigid and formulaic, with "right" answers that mandate how programs must comply.

There are elements in the current NCATE system that may inadvertently encourage that flawed approach. One is that accreditation is "unit-wide," not program-wide. Given the number of disparate programs (e.g., licensure grade levels, content areas) that are often included in Schools of Education, it is difficult to create "one size fits all" data-collection instruments, but since those data are more expedient to collect and easier to report, there are logistical benefits to doing so. Those logistical benefits may be outweighed, however, by the potential loss of usefulness for specific programs in aggregate data measuring whatever the common denominators are in diverse programs. Identifying generic questions that can be asked across disparate programs, rather than focusing on identifying questions that make sense to be answered, is problematic, leading to data that are the "road to nowhere." "Bad" data, generated for reasons that do not assist in program reflection or preparing teachers, also raise the ethical issue of expending faculty resources, class time, and student time in completing surveys and assessments and so on.

Guiding and leading the process of accreditation is a challenging task, with multiple competencies necessary. Examining current position descriptions for NCATE coordinators is illustrative in several ways. First, there are a lot of positions available at any given point in time, supporting the assumption that the type of position is increasing. In June 2012, 68 job postings for accreditation coordinator positions (full- and part-time) were listed on simplyhired.com. An examination of position descriptions on the same site in February 2013 showed that the structure and requirements of the positions vary. Positions are sometimes within departmental or divisional faculty or administrative (e.g., assistant or associate dean) positions, and sometimes at more of a staff level. This is an important distinction, and one that is also frequently connected to educational requirements (e.g., PhD/ university teaching experience versus BA, MA, or MEd, or K-12 school experience.)

Finally, "key assessments" that must be identified and included in program "benchmarks" can dramatically impact curriculum. Since every student must complete key assessments, there are curricular implications, including the following two. Since key assessments must be included in required courses, the pool of appropriate courses is more limited, and there is additional pressure on required courses to develop assessments that "fit." Course substitutions or waivers cannot be granted if the interpretation is that key assessments are required, even in cases where students have completed the appropriate coursework elsewhere, or need appropriate substitutions. With narrow interpretations, the overriding question shifts from "What do *students* need?" to "What does *the accreditation organization* need?"

Strategies for Change

Avoid dichotomizing accreditation organizations

Often, conversations about accreditation organizations and mandates are dichotomized into "good" and "evil" camps. Like any complex issue, there are multiple perspectives, and benefits and limitations of each. Conversations that divide people or perspectives into "them and us" categories oversimplify issues, marginalize people, and do not advance the creation of strategies and solutions. Most educators agree that systematic assessment and reflection has many benefits; determining the what, why, and how of effective assessment represents the real work of reflection and change.

Another area of dichotomizing related to "why" NCATE/CAEP accreditation is necessary or desirable is the monetary value of the credential for recruiting students or enticing donor contributions to programs. The value of the "seal of approval" may outweigh whatever pedagogical concerns exist. As the number of accredited institutions has grown, the luxury of challenging the system or voluntarily dropping accreditation has been limited to institutions that are financially secure and can afford to do so. Transparency about the multiple lenses, including pedagogical and financial, enables more transparency in conversations, and greater ability to explore perspectives in non-dichotomous ways.

Identify and calculate real accreditation costs within an institution to more accurately assess costs and benefits

Few faculty members are aware of the direct and indirect costs of accreditation. Estimates of travel and personnel expenses can be used to determine the direct costs. For, example, if a full-time NCATE coordinator position has a salary of $100,000/year (including benefits), the total salary is a million dollars in a 10-year cycle. Add support personnel, including administrative assistants, graduate assistants, and technical support, plus the direct costs of travel to state and national meetings for both the NCATE coordinator and faculty creating the reports, as well as the costs of site visits and visitors, and myriad categories that are obvious in an institution, and the direct costs alone will be surprising.

The privileging of some types of academic work over others, while at the same time requiring work that is not valued in the system, is difficult to challenge without knowledge of costs. The indirect costs of faculty time spent on accreditation are rarely considered, nor are the "opportunity costs" of what the faculty and staff could be doing instead with the time spent on accreditation. Faculty members typically have the burden of writing reports, creating and scoring of assessments, and entering data. In many cases, the workload is unevenly distributed across faculty members. Further, given the standard academic reward system for "teaching," "scholarship," and "service," accreditation compliance work, typically in "service," has little reward value.

Making costs of accreditation compliance transparent will likely yield sobering and staggering numbers at many institutions. Without a true assessment of the costs, it is impossible to identify the economic and human impact, or implement decision-making processes about productivity, cost effectiveness, workload distribution, and many other factors.

Identify and challenge "tail wagging the dog" mandates

When the previously asked questions, "What do *students* need?" and "What does *the accreditation organization* need?" conflict, a process should be in place at every institution to address and deal with issues. Statements such as "We can't do that because of NCATE/CAEP" or "We have to do that because of NCATE/CAEP" are, in most cases, inaccurate, and are often a means to silence voices or use the most expedient solutions. Such statements should never be allowed to stand unchallenged as justification for any decision that adversely affects curricula, pedagogy, or the best interests of students.

Identify and challenge fallacies of presumption

There are presumptions about accreditation of teacher education and the assessment of teacher candidates that are related to how such measures impact the quality of teaching. It is assumed that the cost of accreditation yields better teacher education programs and, thus, better teachers. Independent research to explore that assumption would benefit from more transparency from the accrediting organizations about exactly what it is intended to measure, and why, including transparency about the process used to determine what is and is not included in selecting and developing standards.

A related assumption is that accreditation standards and recommendations are firmly grounded in educational research. The research link on the NCATE site (NCATE, 2013) provides links to the following categories of "Research/Reports": NCATE initiatives, NCATE Data, Reports by Teaching Disciplines, Teacher Preparation Research, ETS Research, Articles, and Other Data. Links within most of the categories are reports, testimonials, and public relations materials that are *written by NCATE staff or commissioned by NCATE*. Independent research related to NCATE, such as scholarly, refereed journal articles or bibliographies of sources, are not included.

The ETS research link on the NCATE website includes a few ETS research studies and reports, but the relationship between NCATE and ETS is hardly independent. For example, one report in the link, an ETS study entitled "NCATE Makes a Difference," defines "the difference" as pass rates for ETS Praxis II content examinations (NCATE, 2013).

The use of ETS Praxis II pass rates as an indicator of NCATE effectiveness is flawed for at least two reasons. First, the Praxis II series measures "subject-specific content knowledge," as well as general and subject-specific teaching skills that K-12 educators need for beginning teaching (ETS, 2013), which is only part of the "content, skills, and dispositions" trilogy of NCATE.

Second, many institutions have learned to "play the game" to increase their reporting of Praxis II pass rates by requiring passage of Praxis II prior to student teaching. Therefore, students who do not pass do not student-teach and do not graduate. The pass rate of students *attempting* is not reported.

Take back appropriate levels of local level responsibility

Each of the previous strategies in this section respond to the big issue of what makes sense at the institutional level for program review and reflection. In higher education workplaces that are increasingly fragmented with additional responsibilities in teaching, scholarship, and service, time is filled (and overfilled) with immediate and concrete needs. Deciding how best to assess programs is a huge and abstract process, which is likely part of the reason it has been allowed to be "outsourced" to external control.

Swinging back the pendulum requires both leadership and investment of faculty and staff. The transition to CAEP may provide new opportunities for institutions to participate in redefining how accreditation is done; faculty and staff should be vigilant in guiding the development of those opportunities. Accreditation of teacher education programs is not going anywhere. Debates about its value and existence are related, but not central to, the more relevant questions about what local responsibility can and should be within the context of what is.

EXAMPLE 3: THE IMPACT OF PREVIOUS EDUCATIONAL EXPERIENCE, STATE STANDARDS, AND K-12 STANDARDIZED TESTING ON FUTURE TEACHERS

The Issue

Teachers are in the unique position of having 17 or more years of intensive experience as consumers of their profession before entering their profession. Given that the experience takes place throughout childhood and young adulthood, the impact of the experience on beliefs about what schools and teachers should be like is even greater. Since many of those aspiring to be teachers have had success in schools as they are structured, often the perceived "ideal" corresponds to what they experienced. As a result, many teacher candidates are predisposed to be unaware of systemic issues.

Two other factors related to the impact of one's own educational experiences on perceptions of the educational system are the narrowing of curricula and teaching practices to conform to standards developed by State Departments of Education (DOEs), and the pervasive use of standardized testing in schools. As more teacher candidates who are the products of standardized testing enter teacher education programs and the field of teaching, the more compliant they will likely be to such practices in their education and professions. Given that they were educated in, accustomed to, and, in most cases, successful in a standard testing culture, envisioning another way of operating may be difficult.

The familiarity of the structure from a student's K-12 experience will continue in college for those selecting teacher education programs, since the post-secondary programs are also in large part determined by DOEs. This often results in teacher education programs that are highly structured with few electives or choices that can be made by the student about their college education. The indirect message of a structured and inflexible curriculum full of "musts" is that the requirements are sufficient, and that nothing else is valuable. The "forced march" of many teacher education curricula is discouraging for potential students who envision college as having exploratory opportunities beyond their majors Those students are put into the unfair position of having to choose between their desire to be teachers and their desire to have a more diverse college experience.

Standards-driven curricula also emphasize subject area content and classroom skills, and are not generally influenced by political and economic forces. Teacher candidates want to be excellent teachers, and they depend on their education to give them what they need to be the best teachers possible. Increasingly, teacher candidates are aware of the loss of teacher autonomy, assaults on curriculum, teacher accountability, and anti-union sentiments. These problems, which are given increased attention in the media, are used to erroneously blame teachers as being the problem in schools. Recently, many of my teacher candidate students have been reporting that they are being discouraged by family members and former teachers from entering teacher education because of the public debates and, in some cases, the experiences of teachers who themselves are discouraged. It is a disservice to teacher candidates for teacher education programs to exclude systemic factors in education as part of teacher training; such exclusion makes teachers vulnerable to forces that adversely impact their ability to work with students and families in the most effective ways possible.

Strategies for Change

Include student voices to move from "self" to "other"

Allowing teacher candidates to articulate their own experiences as consumers of education is an important precursor for them to understand and analyze differences in educational experiences for their future students. If teacher candidates define their own, typically successful, childhood and young adult experiences as normative and ideal, they are likely to privilege elements of the educational system that were beneficial to them, and be unaware of the elements that perhaps disadvantage others. Assisting teacher candidates in moving from student to teacher in teacher education programs is a developmental process that is important in allowing teachers to be effective.

Include student voice to explore benefits and limitations of testing in teacher education curricula

Similarly, using the personal experiences of teacher candidates in their own education to guide discussions about testing can be a useful framework for examining standardized testing. In my conversations with my students, most of them were good "at taking the tests" that were required in their K-12 and teacher education admission processes, and, if they were in affluent schools, the standardized testing preparation and processes were not as intrusive on a daily basis as in lower-resource schools. Peer voices representing other more negative personal and school experiences are a powerful glimpse into the range of school cultures.

Analyze state and discipline-specific standards to examine what is or isn't valued and privileged in curricula

Looking at the meaning of what is and is not included in curricula is a skill that will enable teacher candidates to think critically about how curricula are developed, and, as importantly, enable them to recognize social, political, and economic influences. Specific examples of what is included in curriculum within content area (e.g., social studies, science) can illustrate links to controversial topics. Conversations about which content areas require standardized tests and which do not (e.g., reading and math versus social studies, science, arts) are connected to what is valued and what is emphasized. Analyzing state standards with a lens of what emphasizes facts and what emphasizes thinking (and how that thinking is constructed) is another useful activity in critical review. Infusing "thinking about thinking" can be included with minor adjustments to existing standards-based conversations, activities, and assignments, including simple prompts for teacher candidates such as "Why are there no standards on…?" "Why do you think this standard is included?" or "What are multiple ways you could teach this standard to enhance student thinking?"

Assist students in exploring the context of issues. Critique educational case studies of models of education reform

Understanding context can improve decision-making on classroom practices, and can buffer teacher candidates and teachers from political assaults. Context provides an alternative to dichotomous thinking, which was discussed earlier. Context can be included as an integrated part of teacher education curriculum. For example, when teaching strategies are being discussed, context is part of differentiating for individual students, as well as exploring benefits and limitations of options. Controversial content such as evolution, choice of books, and some topics in history, can be discussed more fully using context. At the broader levels of educational reform (e.g., standardized testing, for-profit schools, teacher accountability, alternative teacher education licensure programs), context can provide a benefit-limitations lens that emphasizes analysis.

K-12 STUDENTS: A LEGION FOR CHANGE

This chapter emphasizes the responsibility of teacher education to explore the impact of practices and policies of teacher education programs on the training and empowerment of future teachers, and the reductionist practices that hinder that responsibility. A fitting conclusion to the chapter is to encourage the extension of that empowerment to engage student voices in the conversation about the "content, skills, and dispositions" of teaching.

The lack of K-12 student voices is the ultimate example of reductionism, in that they are usually neither acknowledged nor tolerated. Students are on the front line, and are the consumers of education. They observe and experience the best of schools, as well as the injustices and inconsistencies in policies and behaviors by teachers, administrators, and external mandates. High school students frequently have considerable clarity in articulating those behaviors if asked about them in authentic ways, although they rarely are. Their perspectives can be unique, insightful, and sophisticated. They see a disconnect between stated policies and actual behaviors. They feel the sting of disrespectful actions. Like most of us, they know when they are being marginalized or discounted. They can provide a variety of perspectives based on personal and observed behaviors on everything ranging from a comparison of math teachers' requirements for student problem-solving to the meaning of failing graduation tests for individual students who do not pass. In my work with teacher candidates, they can easily describe injustices that they experienced or observed in their own schooling; those examples can then be used to help them understand injustices that may happen to their own future students.

Students know which teachers know their content *and* know how to effectively teach all students. They know how teachers make them feel about themselves and their ability to learn. They know who is fair and consistent in their treatment of all students. They know who cares.

When teacher candidates are given a voice as part of their learning, and are shown how their voice is important in analyzing, thinking, and learning, they are likely to use that model in their own teaching. This increases the academic achievement of their own students—academic achievement that includes content mastery and ability to think divergently in a complex world.

REFERENCES

CAEP Commission on Standards and Performance Reporting. (2013, February 1). Retrieved from http://caepnet.org/commission

Ede, A. (2006). Scripted curriculum: Is it a prescription for success? *Childhood Education, 83*(1), 29–32.

Educational Testing Service. (2013, February 10). About The Praxis Series tests. Retrieved from http://www.ets.org/praxis/states_agencies/about

Foundation for Individual Rights in Education. (2013, October 13). Retrieved from http://thefire.org

Haberman Foundation, The. (2013, February 2). Retrieved from http://www.habermanfoundation.org/

Hagopian, J. (2013, June 11). Seattle test boycott: Our destination is not on the MAP. *Rethinking Schools Online*. Retrieved from http://www.rethinkingschools.org/archive/27_03/27_03_hagopian.shtml

National Association of Scholars. (2012, October 13). Retrieved from www.nas.org

National Council for the Accreditation of Teacher Education. (2013, February 8). Retrieved from www.ncate.org

National Council for the Accreditation of Teacher Education. (2013, February 10). Unit standards in effect 2008. Retrieved from http://www.ncate.org/Standards/NCATEUnitStandards/UnitStandardsinEffect2008/tabid/476/Default.aspx

National Network for the Study of Educator Dispositions. (2013, February 2). Retrieved from http://coehs.nku.edu/content/coehs/centers/educatordispositions.html

Occupy Together. (2013, January 18). Retrieved from www.occupytogether.org

Quinn, S. (2012, November 10). 5 questions with Dr. Cornel West on Occupy Wall Street. *The Washington Post*. Retrieved from http://www.washingtonpost.com/blogs/on-faith/post/cornel-west-keeps-the-faith-for-occupy-wall-street/2011/11/10/glQAZxhk8M_glog.html

Seattle Education. (2012, December 21). The letter from the teachers at Garfield High School regarding the MAP test. Retrieved from http://seattleducation2010.wordpress.com/2013/01/11/the-letter-from-the-teachers-at-garfield-high-school-regarding-the-map-test/

Seattle's teacher uprising: High school faculty faces censure for boycotting standardized MAP tests. (2013, January 29). Retrieved from http://www.democracynow.org/2013/1/29/seattles_teacher_uprising_high_school_faculty

ThinkProgress. (2013). www.thinkprogress.org

Wasicsko, M. M. (2006). Determining dispositions to teach: A hiring strategy. *Principal*. Retrieved from https://www.naesp.org/resources/2/Principal/2006/S-Op51.pdf

We Are the 99 Percent. (2013). Retrieved from www.wearethe99percent.tumblr.com

CHAPTER EIGHT

Ways OF Being AS AN Alternative TO THE Limits OF Teacher Dispositions

MATTHEW J. KRUGER-ROSS

INTRODUCTION & OVERVIEW

In this chapter, the language given by teaching dispositions is contrasted with an alternative way of discussing teaching: ways of being a teacher. After a description of the context of inquiry, a brief overview of the methodology of the researcher-bricoleur follows. Next, disposition is tentatively defined before determining the limits of dispositional language. Two ways of being, teacher buy-in and fear towards technology, are developed and analyzed to identify the opportunities provided by using these ways of being to frame understanding the professional teacher. The chapter concludes with closing remarks and suggestions and implications for future inquiry.

BACKGROUND

To begin a journey you must know where you are coming from and where you are headed. My background fully informs my practice as an educator and researcher, and is the ground for the current examination of teacher dispositions and ways of being. Therefore, a brief description of my background is necessary before an overview of the methods that guide and frame the inquiry. I am trained as a middle school social studies and language arts teacher who taught math, social studies, and music for grades five to eight at an independent school for 4 years. I am an avid proponent of educational technologies, and I am often called on to provide training sessions for my fellow staff members on integrating technologies into their classrooms. In helping my colleagues explore emerging web-based technologies and their implications in teaching and learning, I uncovered a number of positive and negative assumptions that we possessed regarding the uses and nature of technology. These presuppositions included the transformative power of information and communication technologies, hesitations regarding issues of privacy and identity, and the relationship between the ideal and the real implications of teaching with technologies. Reformulating these unexamined assumptions as questions led me to the study of instructional technology. Are technologies transforming teaching and learning as we know it? How can we honor and respect the privacy of others and our own identities? With the integration of technology, what *truly* has changed? What makes some teachers embrace technology and what drives others to push it away? Not surprisingly, my research focused on teacher assumptions related to technology and, like most researchers and graduate students, my initial questions led to more complex and direct questions: (1) What assumptions do educators hold about technology and its use in teaching and learning? (2) How do educators' assumptions about technology influence their teaching practice? My current work includes utilizing qualitative and philosophical/conceptual methodologies to explore the being of education, teaching, and learning, with specific attention paid to educational technologies. I also have the privilege of simultaneously pursuing doctoral studies while serving as a virtual professional development coordinator for a group of online STEM-focused teachers. With a better grasp on the beginning of our journey, we move to the tools that will guide us along our path towards distinguishing dispositions and ways of being as they relate to the teaching profession.

THE BRICOLEUR'S TOOLKIT

The methodology that frames the current inquiry can be best defined as bricolage, thereby casting the researcher in the role of bricoleur. Joe Kincheloe (2001) traced the lineage of bricolage from Claude Levi-Strauss through its grounding in qualitative research (Denzin & Lincoln, 2000) and his own work (Kincheloe, 2005). "The French word, *bricoleur*, describes a handyman or handywoman who makes use of the tools available to complete a task" (Kincheloe, 2001, p. 680). These tools are selected by the researcher in order to explicate the phenomenon under study. As Kincheloe wrote:

> Ethnography, textual analysis, semiotics, hermeneutics, psychoanalysis, phenomenology, historiography, discourse analysis combined with philosophical analysis, literary analysis, aesthetic criticism, and theatrical and dramatic ways of observing and making meaning

constitute the methodological bricolage. In this way, bricoleurs move beyond the blinds of particular disciplines and peer through a conceptual window to a new world of research and knowledge production. (p. 323)

To describe and explore teacher dispositions and ways of being, the following tools will guide the current inquiry: phenomenology, ontological hermeneutics as informed by Heidegger, and Wittgenstein's later distinction of language games. Each tradition or research methodology gives a point of view from which to view the phenomena under study.

Phenomenology, as a philosophical tradition, champions the everyday, lived experience of human subjects embedded contextually. Human beings experience phenomena as they move through their lives and phenomenology takes this observation as primary. Bentz and Shapiro (1998) noted that "phenomenology attempts to take seriously the fact that we are conscious beings and that everything we know is something that we know only in and through consciousness" (pp. 40-41). Edmund Husserl, the founder of phenomenology, used the phrase "back to the things themselves" to focus on the objective of phenomenology. As a philosophical framework and methodology, phenomenology validates the first-person perspective and perceptions of researchers, acknowledging that all scientists' work begins with their own consciousness. "Things to human beings are experienced by and through consciousness. This fundamental reality had been ignored in the twentieth century in the rush to develop social sciences to parallel the natural sciences" (Bentz & Shapiro, 1998, p. 172). Phenomenologists utilize a method known as "bracketing" to approach phenomena in such a way that the taken-for-granted is uncovered (Husserl, 1962).

Bentz and Shapiro (1998) argued that phenomenological research is not based on subjective experience. Rather, "phenomenology aims to get beneath the ways in which people conventionally describe the experience to the structures that underlie them, which may be quite different from everyday consciousness" (p. 97). As phenomenology provides access to "the things themselves," the path it carves also reveals questions related to what is real and what exists outside of our minds or consciousness. For these questions we have to turn to ontological hermeneutics.

Ontology is a philosophical distinction that denotes the study of reality, of all that is. More specifically, and in the spirit of Martin Heidegger, it is often referred to as the study of being as such and in general. Hermeneutics, or the process of interpretation, is a term used to describe how human beings interpret and make meaning of their lived experiences. In a way unlike anyone prior, Heidegger brought together ontology and hermeneutics to provide a phenomenological explication of being.

Heidegger's deep ontology brought with it a major break in the hermeneutic tradition. To Heidegger, interpretation comes not by forceful analysis, an act of aggression, but by allowing an opening or clearing to occur. In this clearing, new "beings" may appear that were in hiding during the previous era of interpretation. (Bentz & Shapiro, 1998, p. 52)

In the text that follows, a clearing is created whereby teacher dispositions and ways of being will be allowed to "show up." As they are revealed, we will explore how each distinction gives a specific context, or *world*, where teaching and learning occur. *World* in this sense is not the physical world, but rather the day-to-day environment that frames our lives: *the world as experienced, as lived*. For example, teaching and researching within a university or college could be referred to as the *world* of academia. Ontological hermeneutics seeks to move beyond, or better yet, before, traditional concerns of the subjective-objective binary. "According to Heidegger, being is neither an object nor a concept, but rather something that we relate to through our existence in a way that makes being accessible or available to us" (Bentz & Shapiro, 1998, p. 172). It is language that will create an opening for the exploration of the ways of being a teacher.

Recent increased interest in language-based research can be traced, at least in part, to the work of Ludwig Wittgenstein, a philosopher of language. Wittgenstein created the distinction of "language game" to describe a phenomenon somewhat similar to Heidegger's *world*.[1] Every day humans speak, write, sing, and otherwise use language to communicate. Each time an utterance is made, it follows a particular set of rules that determine the understandability of the utterance. The sum of all the rules of a particular utterance is termed a "language game." In Wittgenstein's distinction, all language is always already part of, and subject to, the rules of a language game. Lyotard (1984) made three observations about language games:

> The first [observation] is that their rules do not carry within themselves their own legitimation, but are the object of a contract, explicit or not, between players (which is not to say that the players invent the rules). The second is that if there are no rules, there is no game, that even an infinitesimal modification of one rule alters the nature of the game, that a "move" or utterance that does not satisfy the rules does not belong to the game they define. The third remark is suggested by what has just been said: every utterance should be thought of as a "move" in a game. (p. 10)

Imagine a classroom setting and the dialogue in discussing a book. Within this classroom setting there are unwritten rules that give the teacher and students guidance to know what, when, and how to say whatever they want to say. Language games are everywhere, like the air we breathe or like water for a fish. If the text that the teacher and students are reading makes sense, then they are actively participating in a language game already! The distinction *language games* provides one pathway to access and communicates about teacher dispositions and ways of being in such a way that the following inquiry is rendered intelligible.

Bounded by phenomenology and ontological hermeneutics, and made accessible via language games, the next section begins the inquiry by situating dispositions before determining the rules of the language game that the language of dispositions provides.

SITUATING DISPOSITIONS

A clear definition or a list of key elements of a concept is necessary to adequately understand, communicate, and ultimately question the concept. Dispositions are notoriously difficult to define and this may have resulted in the multitudinous ways the term is used and employed in research literature. This section selects and reviews attempts to frame dispositions, followed by an analysis of the language game of dispositions, in order to better understand what is meant by the term "disposition."

Siegel (1999) framed disposition as "a tendency, propensity, or inclination to behave or act in certain ways under certain circumstances" (p. 208). Within educational research, dispositions grew from a call for greater teacher accreditation on behalf of the National Council for Accreditation of Teacher Education (NCATE) (2001). This call for accountability has also been strengthened by federal legislation, beginning with the Elementary and Secondary Education Act and continuing to the present-day No Child Left Behind Act. According to NCATE (2001), dispositions are the values, commitments, and professional ethics that influence behaviors toward students, families, colleagues, and communities, and that affect student learning, motivation, and development as well as the educator's own professional growth. A disposition is therefore founded on, and guided by, attitudes and beliefs possessed by the teacher. Taylor & Wasicsko (2000) described dispositions as the totality of an individual's attitudes, beliefs, interests, appreciations, and values. More specifically, Schulte, Edick, Edwards, and Mackiel (2004) framed disposition as patterns of behavior that are intentional, consciously controlled, and constituted in a habit of mind.

The recent calls for greater student accountability via standardized tests and other measurements (i.e., Adequate Yearly Progress) have resulted in shifting the focus of teacher preparation to the *professional* disposition(s) of teachers. In response to the call for accreditation made by the NCATE report (2001), teacher education programs have adjusted their coursework and program requirements to incorporate specific attention to the professional dispositions of pre- and in-service teachers. These adjustments include revisions of course syllabi and added or dropped required courses, as well as the changing of words in course goals or assignments.

While the intent of implementing and evaluating professional dispositions with teachers is honorable, in practice it gets trickier. Within the world of K-12 education, the phrase "teaching to the test" is often used as a warning against standardized assessment and accountability measures. What might teacher preparation look like were we to "teach to the disposition"?

Dispositions in this context are understood as things-in-themselves, qualities possessed and embodied by teachers that assist in determining their status as professionals (not to mention the assumption that professional dispositions are teachable and learnable). For example, Borda (2007) drew on the hermeneutical work of Hans Georg Gadamer to reflect on the dispositions necessary for the teaching and learning of scientific concepts. To be a "true man of science," a person must possess three dispositions: (1) absent-mindedness, (2) doubt, and (3) humility (Gadamer, 1947, cited in Borda, 2007). Espousing these dispositions "gives us an idea of specific dispositions the scientist must have in order to foster a consciousness between the familiar and the strange, and an openness to questioning her preconceptions" (Borda, 2007, p. 1032). Even a hermeneutical account of dispositions needed for the effective scientist leaves the practitioner (and teacher educator) wondering how on earth doubt or humility (much less absent-mindedness) could be taught and assessed as a professional disposition. While this may seem an extreme example, it is not too far off from the language being used to describe some of the dispositions needed to be a professional educator.

Stephen Smith (2004) shared a unique and alternative perspective on the process of integrating "dispositional inquiry" into the teacher education program at Simon Fraser University. In addition to a general disposition towards teaching, four teaching dispositions were identified that guide and permeate the teacher education program: pedagogical sensitivity, other directedness, reflective capacity, and critical mindedness. Rather than focusing on the more cognitive and intellectual understandings of dispositions, Smith detailed the ways that the teacher education program embraced dispositions "more physically as felt tendencies, body inclinations, postural leanings and alignments which, in turn, allow for the physical positions, motions and expressions of working with and living alongside children and youth" (p. 10). Building on the four teaching dispositions, the program is infused with variations of positionality in addition to dis-positions (i.e., pre-dispositions, bodily position-ing, presup-positions, etc.) and affects the hiring of staff, the acceptance of teacher candidates, and required coursework.

Not surprisingly, one result of the introduction of the dispositions of professional teachers by NCATE (2001) includes the development of surveys and scales to determine whether or not teachers have a particular disposition, or what their existing dispositions are exactly (Shiveley & Misco, 2010). In addition, the possibility of evaluating teacher dispositions emerged, and questions related to the ability to adopt new (or adapt existing) dispositions came into focus for researchers. The motivation for evaluating dispositions has depended mostly on the individuals responsible for implementing and revising teacher education programs. Some approach the evaluation strictly in terms of acquiring accreditation, while others (Smith, 2004) choose to use dispositions as a way into a deeper understanding of what it means to be a teacher. The lack of clarity in defining dispositions, identifying and fleshing out the *professional* dispositions of teachers, and the mixed intent and approaches toward implementing dispositions into teacher education programs, continues to trouble education professionals. Therefore, over a decade later, teacher education and educational researchers are still attempting to grasp and understand what dispositions are, and what that understanding means for preparing, nurturing, and developing teachers (Ruitenburg, 2011).

While these inquiries have been fruitful and interesting, the aim of this chapter is to reflect on the taken-for-granted assumptions that frame and constitute the *world* of dispositions. In employing the cognitive and intellectual phenomena of dispositions, assumptions are made and limitations are set that are helpful to consider. It is important to note that this inquiry is not aimed at determining the truth of the distinctions (dispositions, ways of being) nor does it claim to provide a *right* interpretation. The following offers one way to explore the way dispositions and ways of being are framed by assumptions that give ways of speaking, thinking, and writing that are necessary for understanding, but also limit access to alternatives or possibilities.

DISPOSITIONS AS GIVING A LANGUAGE

Professional teacher dispositions give teachers, teacher educators, administrators, and educational researchers a language that can be used to talk about and describe what teachers do and what makes them do what they do. Following Wittgenstein's idea of "language games," dispositions and the language that come with them can be reframed and viewed as a particular kind of game, the rules of which give dispositions their meaning. A simple example of a rule guiding and bounding the dispositions game is "Dispositions have something to do with the behavior and actions of people." When speaking from the context of dispositions, it makes sense (by playing the game correctly) to reference a person's attitude or behavior as a particular disposition. Rather than being constrained or restricted by the language game, the rules provide boundaries and limits to what can be talked about and, in turn, thought about and reflected on. Language, and, in this instance, a language game, creates a context that allows for communication about particular phenomena. The distinction "language game" provides the ability to see that the language of dispositions is one of many possible conversations that might be used to talk about what teachers do, how they think, how they act, and so on. Other conversations might include teacher attitudes, beliefs, goals, or, as we will consider later, ways of being a teacher.

Since teacher dispositions emerged from national accreditation standards, it is often administrators and upper-level educational staff that engage in conversations regarding dispositions specific to teaching. Above it was noted that there are researchers and practitioners who are working to identify and align an understanding of dispositions with a variety of concepts (values, beliefs, attitudes, or habit of mind, to name a few). While teachers are usually involved in the process of identifying and assessing dispositions, it is the researcher (or administrator) who ultimately collects and shares this information. In turn, it seems that teacher education programs and school administrators have been most intrigued by, and swept up in, the *how* of integrating dispositions into their schools and programs.

Given this experience, it is plausible that another rule of the disposition game is that dispositions are assigned externally, from outside-in. Some will argue that methods and specific framing strategies can help adjust for this bias in research. In the spirit of the physical and natural sciences, dispositions could be gleaned from observations of master teachers by multiple observers, therefore obtaining validity. The dispositions identified could then be shared and affirmed with the observed teachers for further confirmation. However, regardless of these efforts, it seems unlikely that teachers would be asked to identify their own dispositions towards teaching. If these efforts were made, even polling or surveying teachers to develop a list of effective dispositions for professional teaching would result in generalizing from a sample population of teachers to all teachers, everywhere, regardless of context. Do we want to standardize teaching to this extent? If we were to ask practicing teachers to identify their own dispositions, what would that reveal? How would validating the lived experience of teachers compare to the dispositions identified by a researcher? The outside-in rule of this language game limits the available answers to these questions and reflections.

From a global perspective, another interesting rule for the game is its focus on *teacher* dispositions. This is understandable given the mandate from teacher accrediting associations. However, one wonders what might become of the conversation surrounding dispositions if other essential educational groups explored their own dispositions. What about student dispositions related to learning? Key administrator dispositions for effective management and leadership? Dispositions of successful parents, in relationship to their child's school/education? To follow the same trajectory as professional teaching dispositions, viewing students, administrators, and parents via a dispositional lens would need to consider the implications of such a view. Dispositions would need to be identified for successful students, including specific positionalities related to content areas, academic skills, and social understandings. Administrators and parents would also need to be screened for their dispositions and measures would have to be developed to evaluate the fulfillment of the ascribed dispositions. Are administrators ready to have their disposition(s) assessed by their staff? Who would assess the parents? How would such an endeavor be implemented and administered?

Dispositions considered outside the realm of teaching reveals a slippery slope of unintended outcomes that must be critically analyzed. These trajectories are not good or bad, right or wrong, but are, rather, *real* possibilities given by, and constituted in, the language of dispositions. Again, the question is not whether these are good or bad, but rather, are we comfortable continuing down this path?

Dispositions language is useful and can be helpful in talking about the enigma that is good teaching. Within the context that this language provides, over a decade of dialogue has been initiated that has created new tools and structures for assisting pre- and in-service teachers aligned with appropriate behaviors, attitudes, and beliefs that support student learning. Dispositions also added dimension beyond knowledge and skills to evaluating and understanding the teaching profession. Teacher education programs have redeveloped curricula and assessment protocols have been rewritten to include a more holistic view of what it means to be a teacher.[2] When utilized mindfully, the language of dispositions can be used to empower teachers, to help them speak in ways that encapsulate their often difficult-to-describe sense of what they do moment by moment in the classroom.

But what does the language of dispositions not allow? Language games were described above as possessing a number of rules that limit what can be spoken of, and ultimately what can then be thought of. What lies beyond the bounds of dispositional language? What cannot be spoken of or remains inaccessible within the dispositional context? When we speak and act with the language of dispositions, we limit ourselves to the words that we have available to us that can be used to label visible features. Behaviors, actions, gestures, and voice have all been the focus of study as indicators of disposition. Invisible qualities such as attitudes, beliefs, and values have been rendered visible through surveys administered to teachers or identified in the observations made by administrators or supervisors in semi-yearly reviews. There is danger, however, in taking these (in)visible qualities and converting them to objective, quantifiable, and measurable phenomena. Even conducting observational research regarding teacher dispositions involves interpretation and meaning-making. While the researcher strives for objectivity, it is impossible to remove underlying assumptions that scholars bring to their research. As a profession, are educators and educational researchers truly comfortable with a teacher being "qualified to teach" if they score 80% or better on a disposition assessment? The objectifying of the qualities of beliefs, values, attitudes, behaviors, and actions is only a small step away from such a reality. While this may seem extreme, it is most troublesome that vital meaning is missed when we speak only in the language of dispositions.

A few questions may help further probe the limits of dispositional language: Are dispositions singular? Can an educator possess more than one? How so? Can dispositions be taught or are they innate? If they can be taught (and changed), in what ways, and to what extent? How do administrators and teacher educators navigate the moral ambiguity of changing or challenging teacher dispositions? Where does the responsibility lie with regard to a teacher's disposition? For example, is it the teacher educator's responsibility to evaluate and address, or is it the pre-service teacher's? Does a teacher have a disposition or does a disposition somehow belong to a teacher? What if administrators or teacher educators *force* a disposition upon teachers? If it is forced, then does a teacher really "own" it or is it something that is tolerated? If a disposition is not owned, not fully embodied, then how does it impact teaching?

What may seem like simple language games and word play are attempts to demarcate an area of study outside the language of dispositions. These important questions, and various others, need to be considered should dispositions continue to be a dominant thread within teacher education research. In the next section, we move outside dispositions to an alternative context; another way of speaking about teaching and learning: ways of being.

ANOTHER POSSIBILITY: WAYS OF BEING

If dispositions are difficult to define and agree on, ways of being, the topic of this section and of the remainder of this chapter, is even more so. The phrase "way of being" is harder to describe in the language that is normally used in academic writing, much less within the field of educational research, which is still dominated by the cognitive, intellectual, and epistemological. Other distinctions, such as *habit of mind*, have been integrated into adult education (Cranton, 2005) but remain focused on the mind and can be even more limiting than dispositional language. *Being*, while abstract, tends to honor the body-mind, lived experience, whereas the ethereal *habit of mind* maintains the mind-body dichotomy by focusing primarily on the psychological or cognitive. The following is an attempt to fully explain what is meant by ways of being. Further, *ways of being* is used to give access to an area of being a teacher that is not readily accessible via dispositional language.

Being, and the phrase "ways of being," is almost always transparent and assumed because it is at its core human existence. Ways of being are sometimes referenced as contexts or *worlds*, but this is misleading. Being cannot be collapsed into context or world because it negates the being of existence, of *human* being(s). Even more challenging, being is taken for granted because it is the basis of our language abilities. "To be" and its variations—is, are, am, was, and were—are clues to how pervasive and subtle being is to humans. In using the phrase *way of being,* "way of" is included purposefully to ease in the accessibility and understandability of the concept of being as used in this context.

Being evades description through language and resists attempts at codification. The moment a working definition of being is penned it conceals itself; being cannot be turned into an object or a thing. Being can defy explanation, it can be maddening, mostly (and simply!) because it *is*. The earlier distinction "language game" is useful here in metaphorically bounding being. To talk about and explore being, the rules listed above about description, resisting codification, and so on must be followed. When playing by the rules in the language game of being it will be possible to talk about what it means to *be* a teacher.

The German philosopher Martin Heidegger (1962) is the most well-known contributor to the conversation of being via his ontological hermeneutic phenomenology. His magnum opus *Being and Time* is one of the key texts of modern philosophy and the foundation for multiple traditions of scholarship. In *Being and Time*, Heidegger conducted a phenomenology of the being of Being (Dasein) and in so doing created the language game now being used to approach being a professional teacher. Three decades after the publication of *Being and Time*, the educational philosopher Donald Vandenberg (2008) developed an exploration of the relationship of being to education and educating in general. Through a lifetime of scholarship, Vandenberg traced the implications of Heidegger's *Being and Time* within the educational context. This thread of inquiry is known by many names but most often falls within existentialism or ontology.

Educational researchers have only recently brought Heidegger's philosophy and thought to bear on educational contexts and challenges. This is due to a number of factors, including the difficulty of grasping Heidegger's contributions to philosophy, increased availability of English translations of his later works (1945–1967), and a gradual lessening of the stigma associated with studying and analyzing Heidegger's work while acknowledging his association with the Nazi Party. Similarly, understanding of professional competence in a wider context is just now including a more existential ontological perspective and framework guided by Heidegger's work (Sandberg & Pinnington, 2009). Gloria Dall'Alba's research into ways of being in higher educational settings is also representative of this growing trend in applying Heidegger's phenomenology of being into teaching and learning (2005; 2007; 2009).

An example will help to better ground an understanding of being. At a superficial level it is easy to understand a way of being a teacher. Imagine walking into a classroom. You would quickly (1) understand that you were in a classroom, (2) identify common classroom elements or objects (board, desks, chairs), and (3) know who were the students and who was the teacher. Regardless of the obvious age difference between teacher and student (assuming an elementary classroom), describing "being a teacher" is readily accessible. Being a teacher means writing on the board, answering questions, leading discussions, guiding instruction, creating a safe and caring environment, and so on. If an alien landed next to an elementary teacher in the classroom and asked you who the tall person at the front of the room was, you would immediately reply, "She's the teacher." (Notice that in your response the "is" gets condensed and muddled with the pronoun and thus makes overlooking the "is" more likely.) Even without recognizing it, being is there in the speaking about teaching. Being and being a teacher, of course, involve much more than observable behaviors. This example is obviously focused on the external or outward, observable aspects of being a teacher to help distinguish being while not turning it into an object or a thing.

The phrase *way of being* is used rather than simply *being* because beyond the superficial and obvious level of being things get more complicated. Recent research into *ways of knowing* may provide additional understanding of the "way of" of way of being. *Ways of knowing* creates a context (or language game) whereby educators and researchers can talk about different kinds and types of knowing in such a way that each knowing or knowledge is respected and honored. Being, however, does not reduce to knowing and they are not synonyms. Another factor contributing to the difficulty surrounding conversations of being is the status of knowledge and knowing in the educational endeavor. Some would argue that teachers are primarily in the business of knowing and knowledge; most of the current climate of schooling would seem to validate this aim of schooling. Current pressure for standardized curriculum (e.g., Common Core), which prescribes learning objectives and "measurable" skills according to age and grade, demonstrates quite dramatically that schools should be in the business of cramming information into children's heads. But being is different from knowing; knowing at present has evolved into a technical understanding. Knowing something is considered an on/off positioning—once you know something, you know it, no need for further review or work. Even though teachers may speak as if this is not the case, a quick scan of public dialogue and educational research journals would override this speaking. The language used to describe and talk about dispositions exists in the same way that we speak of knowing, and the continued instrumentalization of teachers and the teaching profession is alarming.

A way of being is not on or off, it cannot be recorded and subsequently analyzed via a survey or questionnaire. Ways of being literally and figuratively are who we are. At any given moment we *are* a way of being. Returning to a surface-level example: I am a man. It is who I am. When I wake up in the morning, I do not have to think, "I'm a man," because it is just *who I am*. Making available ways of being that are usually taken for granted requires a radical and substantial shift in reflective capacities, and it is language that helps us to gain access. There is a language game, a question, which can assist in triggering this shift to accessing the being of teaching: "Who am I being such that …?" Consider the following example.

Mrs. Jackson calls on Shirley after demonstrating a math concept on the board. Shirley asks: "Where did the 5 come from? I don't get it." Mrs. Jackson responds: "What do you mean, 'I don't get it'? It's right there on the board and I've worked this problem out twice now," and moves to erase the math concept on the board.

Who is Mrs. Jackson *being* such that this is her reaction to Shirley's question? Since the topic at present concerns ways of being a teacher, the student's way of being will not be addressed. This may, at first, sound like a nonsensical question, but once it is truly grasped, its radical access to being becomes clearer. Who is Mrs. Jackson being? What was an esoteric, ethereal concept suddenly becomes a practical matter. Mrs. Jackson was being someone who assumes understanding comes from seeing numbers on a board, who considers working out a problem twice as sufficient for Shirley, and who does not take student questions and concerns seriously. Mrs. Jackson's way of being, now uncovered, also reveals the responsibility that Mrs. Jackson has taken for granted. Ways of being are anything but static; they transform moment by moment, but are based in patterns, in habits. Mrs. Jackson's way of being in this situation is not good or bad, right or wrong; it simply *is*. But in being distinguished, this way of being can be recognized as *one* way of being. Mrs. Jackson could now choose an alternative way of being that would give an entirely different context or world. Consider the situation repeated with Mrs. Jackson being someone who respects and honors student feedback, who understands that learning happens beyond the board.

How might this scenario play out with the language of professional teacher dispositions? Would teacher educators or administrators be able to determine Mrs. Jackson's disposition(s)? What would happen once the troubling disposition(s) were identified? First, Mrs. Jackson's disposition would most likely be identified as a negative (i.e., *not* a supportive environment for learning, *not* a caring relationship/disposition). If the disposition(s) in question were determined, a *treatment* plan (also known as a professional development plan) would be prescribed to change Mrs. Jackson's behavior, beliefs, attitudes, and, hopefully, her disposition. Would this process really change Mrs. Jackson's teaching practice? Considering *ways of being* and *dispositions* side-by-side, addressing Mrs. Jackson's way of being speaks directly to *who she is* as a teacher, while focusing on her disposition seems to only scratch the surface of her professional identity as a teacher.

To further explore the language that ways of being provides, the next two examples focus on the integration of technology into the classroom and two ways that teachers often *are* in relation to technology: being bought-into technological initiatives and being fearful toward technology.

Ways of Being a Teacher: Examples with Technology

It is now cliché to speak of teaching and technology. Statistics about the explosion of information and communication technologies available to teachers, students, and other educational stakeholders abound. The assumption that technology and education should go together is foundational to these studies; and this assumption is rarely questioned. Research into teachers' roles in integrating technology into their practice has been based on such an assumption. Explorations of teacher attitudes, beliefs, knowledge, and dispositions towards technology and its uses in education have become the main thrust in figuring out how to best integrate new technologies into the classroom. In this section, I draw on my own research into teachers and technology to see how ways of being might provide another angle from which to approach dialogue surrounding teachers and technology (Kruger-Ross, 2012). Specifically, we will look at "teacher buy-in" as a way of being and "fear" as a way of being toward technology in the classroom.

Teacher buy-in as a way of being

North American readers will most likely be familiar with the phrase "buy-in," but for our purposes here it is helpful to frame this phenomenon. One may have heard the phrase used in different contexts, such as: "For this initiative to be successful, we must have teacher buy-in" or "The program flopped because the most influential teacher never really bought-into the pedagogical strategies." Were we to examine a disposition of "buy-in," we would jump to creating bulleted lists and descriptions of behavior. We want to use our understanding of being to go beyond what might be understood within the language of dispositions.

This remains a difficult feat since ways of being are hard to articulate. However, using what we have already experienced as educators and teachers/leaders of educators, buy-in as a way of being should be readily accessible. If teachers "buy-into" a program, curriculum, or initiative, they believe in the goals and aspirations. While they possess knowledge of the program, their buy-in supersedes mastering knowledge about the program. They are, or they become, the program. Being "bought-in" comes with a way of being in the world that embodies the principles of the program in an almost unthinking or pre-reflective way. Teachers who are bought-in are easy to spot, and not just because of their observable behaviors or attitudinal dispositions. Teacher buy-in as a way of being gives a complex context that enables the teacher to show up as committed to the project not only through her behaviors and attitudes, but also through her bodily stance and the words she uses. Teacher buy-in as a way of being is neither right nor wrong and, in this instance, has little to do with the validity of the project or program. These are important considerations and quite worthy of critique, but they are of no concern to us now.

At the same time, locating and identifying a teacher who has not "bought-in" to a particular project is readily available. As a way of being "not-bought-into" a teacher is disinterested in the project and any engagement with the principles is superficial and inauthentic. While dispositionally a teacher may have fulfilled the criteria of being bought-into a project, looking at the same teacher for her way of being bought-in would quickly demonstrate the usefulness of the distinction.

What would this look like in the classroom? A common scenario might look like this: Researchers at a local university have received grant funding to explore the uses of mobile devices in a nearby middle school. The school administration partners with the university researcher to work out the particulars and announces at the next staff meeting that the entire seventh grade will be receiving mobile devices in 2 weeks, and that teachers should start planning to integrate these devices into their lessons. By watching the reactions to this news, one could almost instantaneously identify who in the room "bought-into" the project. (Interestingly, consider this scenario in your own situation. Could you already identify those teachers who would and would not buy-in?)

For teachers who are not "bought-in," there would be complaining and gossiping about the added work and the lack of support for professional development in technology. In the classroom, this would appear as poor pedagogical choices regarding the integration of the mobile devices. Even if professional development is offered in the 2-week interim before the devices arrive, those teachers who attend who are not bought-in are already at a disadvantage to truly gain what they can from the training. In this example, we are assuming a great deal—that mobile devices are wanted, are useful, will be supported through training for students and staff, and so on. However, approaching this experience as how teachers *are* in relation to the project (being-bought-into or being-not-bought-into) leaves a space for other teachers, administrators, and researchers to ask important questions: Why not buy-in to the initiative? What is keeping teachers from fully buying-into the mobile devices? Taking these questions to another level—Who are the administrators and university researchers "being" such that the seventh-grade teachers do not have buy-in to the project? These are difficult questions, and are new to the realm of educational research. They push for answers; not THE final answer, but an answer to the specific situation: context. Ways of being urge us to take account of who we are in a given situation. Beings are responsible to themselves and to others.

Being fearful towards technology

Another related phenomenon is that of fear. Fear is often the emotion expressed when there exists a misunderstanding towards the feared person, thing, or object. Separating the *reason* for being afraid from the *experience* of being afraid will help us gain access to these phenomena. There are many reasons why one might fear technology: Concerns for security of personal information; worry regarding the posting of videos and photos; invasion of privacy; fear of looking ignorant or uninformed, of breaking or misusing something, of causing irreparable damage, or of being overwhelmed. The reasoning for being fearful toward technology is not our concern here. We are focused on the experience of being fearful toward technology. This does not negate the reasons for possessing fear, but it does provide a way of talking about a way of being such that we can explore what to do with it.

As we saw with teacher buy-in as a way of being, fear can also be a way of being. However, a teacher who is being "in fear" creates a context where his reality, his experience, and his way of being are controlled by the relationship with fear. He experiences, behaves, possesses attitudes, and speaks in the language of fear: Computers and software are objects to be feared, that can cause physical or emotional harm, that are best stayed away from. To some extent, any intervention used to address the integration of technology into teaching and learning will not matter; if a teacher is "being someone who is afraid of technology," this will control the experience for him or her. Being fearful here might not actually manifest itself as running away; being afraid often involves a shutting down or politely disengaging when encountering the feared.

Utilizing our mobile devices initiative from teacher buy-in, a teacher may appear bought-into the initiative. But fear is a powerful way of being and could overcome buy-in. The mobile devices would sit unused in the back of the classroom, only to be pulled out when researchers and administrators arrive for observations. In professional training sessions, the fearful teacher will filter and understand most information as a threat. Teachers understand that when someone is afraid or does not feel safe, his or her ability to learn and understand new information plummets. Tips, tricks, and techniques are experienced as threats. Sometimes the being fearful might become transferred to administrators or even other teachers who had previously "bought-into" the initiative.

How do you move forward when a staff member's way of being is of fear toward technology? Obviously, the place to work this out is not in the classroom. Understanding and approaching fear towards technology as a way of being, however, helps give a language that can be used to communicate with the fearful teachers to understand how they experience their fear. Usually in this conversation space opens for teachers such that they are able to see their fear as just one way to be toward technology.

This section could be interpreted as operating on an implicit assumption that technology is good and resistance to technology is bad, but this is not necessarily so. Ways of being are not good or bad, right or wrong—they simply *are*. The expositions above on buy-in and fear toward technology are not about technology, its affordances or drawbacks. Rather, buy-in and fear are presented to sketch out how conversations about technology might be understood in a different context. Teachers (as well as students and administrators) have a myriad of other responsibilities both inside and outside the classroom. However, unquestioned fear of technology, much in the same way as unquestioned adoption of technology, cannot be a way of being/disposition for teachers. By acknowledging their being in relation to technology, teachers can take responsibility for, and take on, a new way of being regarding technology for themselves and their relationship to technology.

Doing so enables and empowers teachers to critically and radically evaluate the integration of technologies into their classrooms.

CONCLUDING THOUGHTS

"Most thought-provoking in our thought-provoking time is that we are still not thinking" (Heidegger, 1968, p. 6). Thinking about being is difficult and can be limiting if approached like any other object, subject, or phenomenon of study. The slipperiness of being becomes even more apparent as language is used to describe it. The best we can hope for when engaging in the language of ways of being is that we can see beyond existing language games to explore other possible ways of being educators. This final section provides some reflections on the limitation-strengths of ways of being as well as some concluding thoughts.

A common approach might include a concluding comparison between Dispositions and Ways of Being in a two-columned chart to list out the pros and cons of each. However, as soon as the lines are drawn, being evaporates and becomes an empty concept. It is best to trace the boundaries of being to experiment with what is possible when using the language of ways of being. Can ways of being be assessed? Yes, but it depends on what is meant by assess. Can another individual, through conversation and observation, identify another person's way of being? Absolutely. But if assess means the realm of quantification and measurability, then no, ways of being cannot be assessed. Can ways of being be identified and ranked? Identified? Yes. Ranked? Absolutely not. Rather than understanding these questions as determining the limitations of *ways of being*, consider that in bounding the *way of being* language game the strengths of *ways of being* have been identified.

As with philosophers and their philosophies, ways of being must be approached and understood on their own terms. Ways of being resist categorization and definition. Ways of being might be able to be prescribed or taught, but they are best understood when lived or experienced. The language we use to talk about teaching, learning, assessing, educating, and so on, is not as helpful in fully embracing what it means to *be* a teacher. In the future, it would be helpful to include the thoughts of one of Heidegger's students, Hans Georg Gadamer, whose work on truth, language, and method would provide insight to Wittgenstein's distinction of language games. Gadamer (1994), more than anyone else, built on his mentor's fundamental ontology and provided access to Heidegger's more abstract thought. This phenomena that is so close, yet so far away, is one of the reasons why education could use ways of being to help move the ongoing dialogue along. Teacher buy-in and fear toward technology, when approached as ways of being, can empower teachers to honor their profession by declaring that they cannot be objectified and decontexualized. Understanding the being of teaching can also ground the profession *as a profession* that is highly valued and deserving of respect. What *does* it mean to *be* a teacher? What ways of being ground good teaching? These are not questions to be answered but questions to be lived.

NOTES

1 This is not entirely true and scholars of Wittgenstein and Heidegger will strongly disagree with my attempt to render language games and world as synonyms. However, I believe that for our current purposes the drawing of a tentative connection between the two concepts may be helpful in grounding them both in the understanding of the reader. Regardless, one should realize that these terms are *not* synonyms and represent enormous differences in bodies of literature.
2 See, for example, Smith (2004).

REFERENCES

Bentz, V. M., & Shapiro, J. J. (1998). *Mindful inquiry in social research.* Thousand Oaks, CA: Sage.

Borda, E. J. (2007). Applying Gadamer's concept of disposition to science and science education. *Science & Education, 16*(9–10), 1027–1041. doi:10.1007/s11191-007-9079-5

Dall'Alba, G. (2005). Improving teaching: Enhancing ways of being university teachers. *Higher Education Research and Development, 24*(4), 361–372. doi:10.1080/07294360500284771

Dall'Alba, G. (2009). Learning professional ways of being: Ambiguities of becoming. *Educational Philosophy and Theory, 41*(1), 34–45. doi:10.1111/j.1469-5812.2008.00475.x

Dall'Alba, G., & Barnacle, R. (2007). An ontological turn for higher education. *Studies in Higher Education, 32*(6), 679–691. doi:10.1080/03075070701685130

Gadamer, H.-G. (1994). *Heidegger's way* (J. W. Stanley, Trans.). Albany, NY: SUNY.

Heidegger, M. (1962) *Being and time* (J. Macquarrie & E. Robinson, Trans.). New York, NY: Harper and Row. (Original work published 1927).

Heidegger, M. (1968). *What is called thinking?* (J. Glenn Gray, Trans.). New York, NY: Harper and Row.

Husserl, E. (1962). *Ideas: General introduction to pure phenomenology.* (W. R. Gibson Boyce, Trans.). New York, NY: Collier Books.

Kincheloe, J. L. (2001). Describing the bricolage: Conceptualizing a new rigor in qualitative research. *Qualitative Inquiry, 7*(6), 679–692. doi:10.1177/107780040100700601

Kincheloe, J. L. (2005). On to the next level: Continuing the conceptualization of the bricolage. *Qualitative Inquiry, 11*(3), 323–350. doi:10.1177/1077800405275056

Kruger-Ross, M. (2012). Toward a preliminary understanding of educators' assumptions about technology: a case study. Unpublished Masters thesis, NC State University, Raleigh, North Carolina. Available at http://catalog.lib.ncsu.edu/record/NCSU2671285.

Lyotard, J.-F. (1984). *The postmodern condition: A report on knowledge.* Minneapolis, MN: University of Minnesota Press.

National Council for Accreditation of Teacher Education (2001). *Professional standards for the accreditation of schools, colleges, and departments of education.* Washington, DC: Author.

Ruitenberg, C. W. (2011). The trouble with dispositions: A critical examination of personal beliefs, professional commitments and actual conduct in teacher education. *Ethics and Education*, *6*(1), 41–52. doi:10.1080/17449642.2011.587347

Sandberg, J., & Pinnington, A. H. (2009). Professional competence as ways of being: An existential ontological perspective. *Journal of Management Studies*, *46*(7), 1138–1170. doi:10.1111/j.1467-6486.2009.00845.x

Schulte, L., Edick, N., Edwards, S., & Mackiel, D. (2004). *The development and validation of the Teacher Dispositions Index*. Unpublished manuscript, Department of Education, University of Nebraska, Omaha, Nebraska.

Shiveley, J., & Misco, T. (2010). "But how do I know about their attitudes and beliefs ?": A four-step process for integrating and assessing dispositions in teacher education. *The Clearing House: A Journal of Educational Strategies, Issues and Ideas*, *83*(1), 9–14.

Siegel, H. (1999). What (good) are thinking dispositions? *Educational Theory*, *49*(2), 207–221.

Smith, S. J. (2004). *The bearing of inquiry in teacher education: The SFU experience*. Burnaby, BC: Simon Fraser University.

Taylor, R. L., & Wasicsko, M. M. (2000, November). *The dispositions to teach*. Paper presented at the meeting of SRATE, Kentucky.

Vandenberg, D. (2008). A guide to educational philosophizing after Heidegger. *Educational Philosophy and Theory*, *40*(2), 249–265. doi:10.1111/j.1469-5812.2007.00313.x

Wittgenstein, L. (1953/2001). *Philosophical investigations*. Oxford, England: Blackwell.

Practicing What We Teach

CHAPTER NINE

Seeking Balance

Rethinking Who Decides the Role of Dispositions in Teacher Evaluation

TIM MAHONEY AND JOHN WARD

INTRODUCTION

There has been much discussion of the definition of professional dispositions in education. Teacher educators, educational policy makers, practicing teachers, and school administrators have all identified the habits, beliefs, and values of teachers as part of what makes an effective professional educator. Despite this attention, there is also some confusion about how one defines dispositions, which dispositions are of value in teaching, whether dispositions are stable or can be developed, and whether dispositions can or should be evaluated (Diez, 2007). In this chapter, we will come at the topic from a different perspective: Who decides what dispositions matter for teaching? And if those dispositions are defined, then who should provide insight and, possibly, assessment of an individual teacher's dispositions? It is our thesis that the answer to the "who" question inevitably frames answers to the "what" or "which" questions.

We also believe that teacher education is at a critical juncture in regards to dispositions. Historically, educational theorists considered dispositions from the standpoint of standardization, centered on the work of experts searching for the right dispositions in teacher candidates that would lead to successful careers (Borko, Liston, & Whitcomb, 2007; Cochran-Smith & Fries, 2005; Bullough, Clark, & Patterson, 2003). As will be shown below, these efforts lead to a reductionist and instrumental view of dispositions. Other scholarship has recast the search to define dispositions into a more teacher-centered framework of reflection (Strong, Ward, & Grant, 2011; Loughran, 2002; Zeichner, 1987). This more individualistic approach involves teachers themselves thinking about their effectiveness with students. Until very recently, the standardization and reflection movements served as counter-balancing forces in the evaluation of certification students and beginning teachers. However, current trends toward high-stakes teacher accountability have given the standards new power and influence over how the work of teaching is defined. We believe unless serious attention is given to "who decides" what dispositions matter for teaching, there will be two possible outcomes for the current accountability movement regarding dispositions:

1. Dispositions are removed from the discourse on teacher evaluation, become unimportant to teachers, and marginalized in teacher education programs.
2. Dispositions are co-opted by teacher accountability, become standardized both in terms of description and measurement, with independent observers rating teacher dispositions.

It is our position that possible outcome #1 would be bad and possible outcome #2 would be worse. We will argue that a more desirable outcome is for teachers and teacher educators to value reflection on dispositions as a critical component of meaningful evaluation. The difference between this vision and possible outcome #2 is in "who decides and describes."

While our arguments and examples are limited to pre-service and beginning teachers, we believe all teachers are affected by the shift in the accountability systems, and removing teachers from deciding how their work is defined, supervised, and evaluated can lead to limitations on the success of all teachers in the new accountability systems.

While we are not attempting to develop an in-depth list of dispositions we think are most important (in fact we are arguing that such attempts can do more harm than good), much of the discussion that follows will make more sense if we are explicit about our perspective. Agreeing with Whitehead (1989), we consider dispositions to be internal values that are difficult to put in propositional form and that, instead, are embodied in practice over a long period of time. We think it is important to emphasize holistic and foundational dispositions rather than discrete dispositions that are aligned with knowledge and skills. Two examples that illustrate this fundamental and holistic perspective would be Dewey's (Rodgers, 2002) four dispositions of reflection—wholeheartedness, directness, open-mindedness, and responsibility, and Van Manen's (1994) description of the quality of the pedagogue— "caring for a child as he or she is, and by caring for a child for what he or she may become" (pp. 135–136).

We believe such frameworks provide grounding while enabling individual teachers to understand and assert their own selfhood. We agree with LaBoskey (1993) that critical reflection should coincide with instrumental reflection on pedagogy and content because both are consequential, and likewise believe that teacher accountability is important and should include multiple facets. Our view that dispositions are deeply held values, however, means that we see them as belonging to interpretative and transformational realms of teacher reflection and should not be treated as part of technical reflection for instrumental purposes.

POTENTIAL OUTCOME #1: TEACHER ACCOUNTABILITY MARGINALIZES DISCOURSE ON DISPOSITIONS

For a glimpse of what the teacher accountability movement could mean in the near future, we would suggest looking at the 2013 Measures of Effective Teaching (Bill and Melinda Gates Foundation MET Project, 2013a) brief suggesting how the findings of their research reports might be used. This brief provides a colorful example of a teacher report-card charting value-added scores, student surveys, and observation data using not-so-subtle red-yellow-green colors to portray percentile rankings comparing individual teachers to other teachers in the same school and district. The MET study is bolstered in spirit by the 2013 Our Responsibility, Our Promise report of the Council of Chief State School Officers (CCSSO) (2011), which proposed that states develop licensure standards that "include multiple measures of educators' ability to perform, including the potential to impact student achievement and growth."

Holistic dispositions embodied in practice over time do not lend themselves so easily to quantification. In the face of accountability programs that have high-stakes implications for teachers, many educators will naturally have the tendency to try and figure out the most expedient ways to meet those standards. As teacher certification programs, supervisors, and evaluators are put under increasing pressure, it is easy to imagine dispositional qualities of teachers receiving less attention in favor of competencies that are more easily measured.

Why dispositions matter and why eliminating them from teacher evaluation would be a bad idea begins with the concept of "teacher selfhood" (Palmer, 1998). Palmer's (1998) central argument is that "good teaching cannot be reduced to technique; good teaching comes from the identity and integrity of the teacher" (p. 10). In Palmer's (1998) view, when teachers develop this identity and integrity, they become whole, real, and present to their students. When the identity and integrity are violated, teachers become fragmented, uncertain, and ineffective, primarily because they do not believe in what they are doing.

By allowing certification students and beginning teachers to develop and act on their identity and integrity, we believe it is possible to create a deeper commitment in teachers to deconstruct and reconstruct initial images of how teachers work in classrooms. As Palmer wrote, "as we learn more about who we are, we can learn techniques that reveal rather than conceal the personhood from which good teaching comes" (p. 24). As teachers become aware of these techniques, as they practice methods and develop curricula consistent with their identity and integrity, teacher selfhood can develop and flourish. This is not to say that questioning methods of instruction, content knowledge, or generalized truths about teaching and learning leads to a subjective evaluation of teaching. In our supervision, we do not excuse poor technique, sloppy assessment, or incomplete content while urging teachers to "just be themselves" and find their own selfhood. Nothing could be further from the truth, in both our efforts in teacher education and Palmer's conception of teacher selfhood (p. 62). However, without the understanding of how teachers develop their identity and integrity, evaluation and supervision can be rendered ineffective, unhelpful, and counter-productive.

Stories of Selfhood in Action

To evaluate the role teacher selfhood plays in how teachers from certification programs actually teach after they graduate, we conducted a longitudinal study that tracked beginning teachers from their last year of certification coursework into their first 2 years of teaching. Although this study began as an investigation of the durability of the content of the certification coursework in the first years of teaching, the data also provided compelling stories about the "who decides" question: how beginning teachers are evaluated, what they are being evaluated on, and how they could be evaluated in ways that would maximize their potential for growth and improvement. These stories represent an interpretive search for who decides what dispositions matter.

Sixteen beginning teachers were the subject of the investigation, all of whom had experienced coursework that emphasized the development of teacher selfhood. Each of these beginning teachers also self-selected to continue thinking about their selfhood through study groups and informal conversations with the certification faculty. These teachers worked in a wide variety of content areas in diverse middle and high schools. They were also diverse themselves; five men and 11 women made up the subjects; one teacher identified herself as Hmong, one male as African American, two women and two men as Mexican American and one male and one female as Portuguese American. The remainder identified themselves as White. All teachers were between 24 and 28 years old at the time the study began.

Data for the study involved recording and transcribing study group discussions centered on student work, observations in their classrooms, recorded and transcribed interviews after observations, and field notes from both informal conversations and study group meetings. Data were analyzed using the constant comparative method (Glaser & Strauss, 1967), where categories centered on the holistic description of individual teachers, their reactions and responses to the certification program, and their ongoing development and growth as teachers.

Antonio

Antonio taught Spanish in a high school with a high percentage of English language learners and a prevailing school climate of academic disinterest. In contrast, his classroom was a place of hope and activity, and it was consistently filled with students working on projects, doing homework, or just spending time with him. In his second year teaching, Antonio said this in an interview:

> I need to be the kind of unconditional teacher we talked about. I need to fill my room with passion and energy. I can't think of myself another way. I know most of the people here don't understand, but you know what? I don't care. I have results. My students feel safe in here, feel welcome. That's the way I always imagined it. They know I am serious, that I expect a lot from them. I push a lot of them pretty hard, much harder than anyone around here thinks is possible. They think I am crazy, but they come in here and see what is happening, and that shuts them up real quick. (Personal communication, February 24, 2011)

Although, in many ways, Antonio was a very traditional teacher from a methodological standpoint (desks in rows, teacher-centered instruction, strict classroom management policies and expectations), his identity as an ELL student himself and his integrity to question and reject the perception that his students could not achieve academically were readily apparent in his teaching. While his colleagues and administrators warned him not to expect much from his students, he staged and directed Spanish plays for the community, partnered with the Art teacher (also part of this research) to decorate the school hallways with cultural murals, and, as he said, created a safe space for his students to show what they could do. So, while a detached observer might evaluate Antonio as using defensible methods, demonstrating content knowledge as a fluent Spanish speaker, and employing appropriate and effective classroom management skills, by neglecting the dispositions behind his practice, that evaluation could miss most of what defines and animates Antonio's classroom, rendering the evaluation incomplete and, in many ways, ineffective for Antonio's continued growth as a teacher.

Peter

The study showed that many of the beginning teachers developed articulate ways to describe their practice. As Antonio expressed, many of these articulations were generally contrary to the stated expectations for their teaching, particularly from their new teacher induction evaluators.

In one interview, after a long description of his vision of himself as a teacher who prides himself on defying convention and using creative materials and technology in his teaching, Peter described this perspective in this way:

> You know, just last week, I just was evaluated by [his new teacher induction mentor], I was, and well, I did the note thing, I had them taking notes, but that was supplemented by video slides, I had some video slides, and some music from the time period, images… so it was a lecture, a standards-based lecture, but it wasn't a stand at the podium in front of the room and talk while everyone else is silent. No. It was still pretty interactive. (Personal communication, January 17, 2011)

> When asked what the reaction to his lesson was from his induction mentor, Peter said, It wasn't clear to me she was awake during the class. I had music and slides and I talked about how baseball and nationalism created this idea that America was invincible, and all she asked me about was the standards that were met in the lesson. It was like she wasn't even there. (Personal communication, January 17, 2011)

Again, the perspective of the detached and expert observer might evaluate Peter's practice as competent, even exceptional. He consistently demonstrated a comprehensive content knowledge, was very engaging and interactive in class, and students responded to his teaching through eager participation in class and in projects and extra work outside of class (such as State History Day and service projects in the local community). However, as he noted, this detached evaluation missed the heart of Peter's practice, and he didn't consider the evaluation helpful for his development or growth.

David

Further evidence of evaluation that misses the mark comes from a conversation with David, a biology teacher in a high-performing suburban/rural high school. David also demonstrated an expansive content knowledge and was very interactive and engaging when teaching. In his first year of teaching, he was put on an "improvement plan" by his supervisor, in his case a vice principal, because his classroom observations consistently did not match the lesson plans David submitted at the beginning of the week. He attended to the mandatory meetings required in his improvement plan, mostly centered on the organization of curriculum and classroom management, but did not change his practice in any observable way. By the end of his second year, he said this about his evaluations:

> Well, I am kind of a laid back person, so being stern and strict just doesn't work for me. But I am changing somewhat, as students who are used to all the detentions and referrals can tend to take advantage of me, and because they are so used to the model where the teacher talks and they listen, that when we are talking as a class, when subjects get brought up, and they ask questions, and it's not as formal, they don't know what to do with that right away.

Some don't speak, like they are asking themselves, "Should I speak? Is it my turn?" And others just go bonkers and can't be quiet. So, I am starting to think about using more structure in discussions. But, if I become totally standards-driven, silent-room, crack-the-whip, then that would be the end of me. I wouldn't enjoy my job. I would *not* enjoy it. I would go home every day thinking "Why am I doing this? I have no connection to the kids. I don't even know them." That is not how I want to be. And there are teachers like that here—that have no interaction with the students. When (his evaluator) tries to tell me what to do, or tries and help with how to keep the class quiet, it's hard not to laugh at him. I mean, that is my strength, interaction and conversation. Does he think he can make me another way? Change who I am? (Personal communication, April 21, 2011)

While David recognized that he might need more structure in his teaching, he also realized, as Palmer noted, that teaching practices work best when they reveal, rather than conceal, the identity and integrity of the teacher. If his evaluator took his teacher selfhood—in essence his dispositions—into account, it may have been possible to help David structure class discussions so that he could retain what made his teaching real while enabling students to understand the expectations and conventions of classroom interaction. It isn't hard to imagine that if that had happened, David might have found their meetings more productive and would have had a more positive view of his supervisor. As the evaluator did not ask David about his deeply held values, he continued to provide structured guidelines, mostly from classroom management textbooks, on how to manage classroom discussions and David continued to struggle with facilitating discussions and communicating his expectations while gradually and independently figuring out ways to prevent his classroom from becoming chaotic.

Elizabeth

Elizabeth taught English at a suburban high school. A significant part of her induction program was to observe more experienced teachers (although the teachers were chosen by the induction mentors without asking Elizabeth what kind of teacher she might want to watch). One of the teachers selected was the English Department Head at another high school in the district, a seasoned teacher who had a reputation for running an extremely efficient classroom, where time was never wasted and students were constantly working. Having observed in this classroom ourselves, we knew it contained very little conversation and was almost entirely centered on the teacher lecturing, assigning work, and correcting errors. Although the curriculum was not scripted, there was very little deviation from the standard-based, content-driven lesson plan and almost no room for student input during the day. Reflecting on this observation, Elizabeth said:

I need to talk to kids about different things than just English. About society and culture and power, and not just be a teacher of English and that's it. Plus I get protective of my students, and I want to help them in here, but also outside as well. Most of that time it is a lot about listening and giving them some advice. If I say, "You know what, I don't want to talk to you about that," then the class won't be as opened as I feel is necessary, the atmosphere that fosters the best kind of education. What I'm doing isn't just about English; it's about being with each other. They need to be able get their ideas out there, and that is more important than knowing what a predicate nominative is or identifying prepositional phrases. I know I can do a quiet classroom, but I also know that the kids learn more by being active, and I have some evidence to prove it. (Personal communication, January 9, 2011).

The evidence Elizabeth produced was as varied as student awards for creative writing and increases in standardized test scores. In her first year of teaching, Elizabeth was assigned a remediation class for students who had failed the English portion of the state-mandated high school exit exam. Many of her students passed the test after her course, although Elizabeth rarely used the district's study guide. Elizabeth was also the teacher parents frequently requested for her Advance Placement English courses (in which a large percentage of students passed the AP test).

As with many of the students in this research project, Elizabeth's classroom was decorated with student work. Although her methods are somewhere in between Antonio's structure and David's lack of it, her evaluators urged her to adopt some of the methods of the department head she observed. As suggested in her comments, she felt her mentors and evaluators profoundly misunderstood the beliefs and values at the core of her teaching.

Susan

Susan, also an English teacher in the same district as Elizabeth, offered this insight into her identity and integrity as she taught:

Honestly, I care very little if my students leave the classroom remembering the plot, characters, and activity arc of the books and poems and stories we read. I know that I have no idea about most of this stuff, and I was someone who loved English. But I do know that reading taught me to ask questions like "What does the author want me to think?"; "Who has the power to believe this statement is true?"; "Does this match up with other evidence?"; "Is this ethically acceptable or not?" That is what I want the kids to do. So, they make me ask the silly questions in the [district-adopted literature series] books, but I just pass through them, and get on with the more important discussions. When students can question things they hadn't thought of before, and examine people, philosophies, and ideas in a more critical way, I know that I have taught them something far more valuable than the content of any text. (Personal communication, January 10, 2011).

What is remarkable about Susan's classroom practice is that she maintained these beliefs despite the constant pressure from her department head who, as noted above, felt that content and organization were the highest priorities in any classroom. In every observation, Susan was living these dispositions by asking questions, encouraging thinking, and modeling the kind of behavior she thought was important for her students. She was aware that she was taking risks, both professional and personal, in conducting herself in a way that encouraged thinking, but she felt the benefit was worth the risk. As she explained:

> I agree that all this questioning is a little dangerous. First, because it put me and all my own values up to scrutiny—not only in how I answer questions, but that I chose to answer questions at all—because they know how it is in other sections. But, I am sure my students are growing stronger, more confident. If they can examine the world around them critically, using some of the tools we use in class, then they have the chance to navigate the world as discerning young adults rather than passengers. (Personal communication, January 13, 2011).

We share these stories to illustrate the case that teacher selfhood is a critical component of how teachers construct their classroom. It is clear that the teachers we have studied view their personal identity—defined by their most important values—as the central quality of the instruction they deliver, and the quality most often overlooked in how they are evaluated.

Because of these stories, and many others like them, we believe ignoring dispositions and eliminating them from teacher evaluation will have a subtractive effect on the main purpose of teacher evaluation: the improvement of practice. If these teachers were forced to adopt practices that were contrary to their identity and integrity, they would lose the power that motivates their practices.

Further, it is hard to imagine how the teachers in the study would have entered their first classroom if they did not have the chance to develop their selfhood in the certification program. We would encourage pre-service teachers to develop and articulate what Fried (1995) called a "stance"—"a philosophy, an attitude, a bearing, a way of encountering students based on a set of core values about kids and their learning potential" (p. 139). As students develop their stance, we try to convey that this can be the focal point of their instruction. What is important to note here is that as the pre-service teachers developed their stance, their dispositions emerged in practice. As these dispositions emerged, they had the freedom to try them out, modify them, and arrive at decisions about what they would do and how they would be in their classrooms. This, we believe, is a compelling reason to emphasize teachers in the "who decides" question of dispositions.

FROM SELFHOOD TO SOLIDARITY

We want to avoid the pitfall of ignoring teacher voice in the rush to develop high-stakes accountability measures for teachers. Although we want to help teachers articulate their values, we do not believe that teachers are free to invent themselves in ways that supersede the need to care for students. And this grounding is made meaningful in practice through critical reflection on student perspectives and fulfilled by establishing solidarity with students.

Like many parents, we often hear students talk about teachers with statements such as "I like her because she is fun"; "I like him because he cares"; and "He never listens to me, so I don't like his class." We also hear fellow parents talk about teachers by saying "She was really hard on my daughter, but in a good way"; "My son loved her class"; and "That teacher seems so boring." These comments indicate that parents and students see the internal qualities of teachers, those values that are embodied over a long period of time, more than their external characteristics such as their daily methods, their academic preparation, or the classroom curriculum. We think they are on to something important.

Unlike school leaders and university supervisors, students see their teachers every day, and in many ways know their teachers better than an observer who comes into the classroom only occasionally. Perhaps the teacher is "putting on a show" for the observer, or the observer, by chance, sees examples that don't capture the essence of the teacher's nature. This explanation is consistent with the idea that dispositions are strongly held values and attitudes of teachers that are expressed in many unscripted ways (Whitehead, 1989). Students are likely to see their teachers differently than an independent observer because of their strong knowledge of the context of their classroom. So, while an expert might see a teacher partially losing her temper with a student and consider it a poor example of practice, students may see the same incident through the light of the extreme patience they have seen their teacher display in other situations with the same student. It may be the incident that helps the students see the prior caring attitude of the teacher for what it was, understanding that the loss of patience today is an expression of the frustration of a teacher who cares about a peer who is not living up to his potential.

Student voice is important for a more fundamental reason: students do not always interpret teacher actions the way their teachers intend them. Students may see the genuine efforts at caring as inauthentic or contrived. It is also possible (but less likely) that a teacher could effectively feign caring. Brookfield (1995) gave several examples where teacher intentions may be seen differently by students and educators. Whereas an adult observer might see the use of learning contracts with students as a wonderful approach to developing a positive classroom environment, students may see it as teacher laziness if the groundwork was not properly developed in advance. An observer will want to see a teacher moving from group to group when students are collaborative or in cooperative learning activities; students may see this as overly intrusive.

In a sense, this seems unfair to teachers. We would have great sympathy (having been there from time-to-time) for a misunderstood teacher working diligently for her students. The responsibility of the teacher, though, is to understand the perspective of students. Brookfield (1995) argued that it is vital for teachers to engage in reflection with an understanding that their intentions are not always understood and to engage in a constant emotional audit of how instruction is experienced by students.

The propensity to take on the perspective of others, and particularly those of students, can be seen as a fundamental disposition in its own right or as a quality that gives fullness to other dispositions. So, for example, the disposition of responsibility is tempered by an understanding of how actions are interpreted by others. This quality of insight into the perception of others is sometimes described as tact (Van Manen, 1991), or could be described using other dispositional qualities such as discretion, or judgment (Sockett, 2009).

Palmer (1998) argued that to make the shift toward understanding teaching from the standpoint of the expert to understanding from the perspective of the students involved a two-step process: first, teachers must confront their assumptions about themselves, and secondly, they must move beyond those assumptions and consider the experiences of their students. Palmer began his description of Teacher Selfhood by explaining what he considered self-knowledge:

> When I do not know myself, I cannot know who my students are. I will see them through a glass darkly, in the shadows of my unexamined life—and when I cannot see them clearly, I cannot teach them well. When I do not know myself, I cannot know my subject—not at the deepest levels of embodied, personal meaning. I will know it only abstractly, a congeries of concepts as far removed from the world as I am from personal truth. (p. 2)

Rorty (1989) developed a conception of solidarity that helps join the selfhood of the teacher with the effect on students. Solidarity is a powerful framework to understand how dispositions such as selfhood, or caring for students in the present and in the future, are practical and observable dimensions of teaching. In describing what solidarity is, Rorty wrote:

> Human solidarity is not about clearing away prejudice or burrowing into repressed anger or fear, but rather as a goal to be achieved through imagination—the ability to see unfamiliar people as fellow travelers—it is not only discovered through reflection, but is created by increasing our sensitivity to their circumstances—this renders it difficult to marginalize people as "other"—as we have created bonds that make them—us. (p. xvi)

One key component to a strong sense of teacher selfhood is this expansive sense of self that reaches out to include different kind of students in classrooms. This is a stronger movement than empathy or sensitivity, as there is still a demarcation between "self" and "other" in those dispositions. Solidarity is a stronger sense of common ground. Rorty (1989) also wrote that our sense of solidarity is strongest when we think of those with whom solidarity is expressed *as one of us*, where us is defined as something smaller and more local than the human race. In this way, solidarity enables teachers to go beyond some vague obligation to become an effective teacher for all their students, or past altruistic notions of helping kids or serving as a positive role model.

Those ideas persist in placing the teacher at the center and the students at the margin. Rorty (1989) wrote that we can transcend such vague and fleeting obligations with something far more durable when we consider solidarity not as a recognition of ambiguous commonalities with all human beings, but "as the ability to see more and more traditional differences (of tribe, religion, race, customs, and the like) as unimportant when compared with…the ability to think of people wildly different from ourselves as included in the range of 'us'" (p. 192). This translates into classroom practices when teachers, over extended periods of time, become resiliently and robustly inclusive in their efforts to teach all their students. What we reject is the propensity to take ideas such as solidarity and fold them into a standards-based accountability system where the individual efforts at solidarity become less important than the observable and quantifiable practices endorsed by frameworks such as Danielson's (2007), which include rubrics for components such as "setting instructional outcomes," "designing coherent instruction," and "using assessments in instruction." To her credit, Danielson kept the rubrics general, but we consider it an incomplete answer and misleading to believe that effective classrooms can be reduced to a few general qualities that should be applied to all teachers in the same way. This frames teacher accountability as something that can be standardized across all classrooms. Van Manen (1977) saw this danger clearly. In critiquing the influence of science and quantification on the evaluation of teaching, he wrote:

> In education, the scientific consciousness is visible in the obsession of bringing the primary domains of the thoughts, values and feelings of the student under the effective control of the school curriculum. This obsession is, no doubt, a function of the fact that accountability is most readily translated into the obligation to be "countable." (p. 223)

While we are compelled by the ideas of solidarity, we realize there is much to be wary of when teachers assume they can fully understand the perspective of their students. Margolis (2007) expressed this caution by rejecting the idealism that teachers can somehow dismiss existing relations of power and privilege, particularly in classrooms, and somehow merge positions with their students. Similarly, we do not believe it is possible to see and understand events beyond our own experience. What is possible, however, is to imagine and create classroom practices that enable every student to learn. These practices will only be recognized and appreciated by supervisors and evaluators if the dispositions supporting those practices, selected by the teachers, themselves play a role in the conception of effective teaching.

POTENTIAL OUTCOME #2: STANDARDIZING MEASUREMENT OF DISPOSITIONS

So far we have argued that marginalizing the role of dispositions in teacher evaluation leads to a dry and incomplete understanding of teachers. Next we will argue that going the opposite route, attempting to standardize, quantify, and reliably measure dispositions so as to heighten their importance, would be even worse. It is one thing for teachers to feel their most central values are not part of the conversation; it is worse to feel that those values are part of the conversation and must be changed to fit what has been defined in advance as the ideal.

There is a long history of theoreticians and other educational experts attempting to describe teacher dispositions. The 1929 Commonwealth Teacher-Training study provides an early example of this effort (Charters & Waples). The study, with its list of over 1000 skills for teaching, has been used as an example of the ultimate in reductionist approaches to teacher development. A less-well-known aspect of the study, however, is the development of a list of the 26 most important traits a teacher should possess. Without asserting that the list is precisely what we would today call "dispositions," it certainly contains many qualities that are frequently cited as dispositions, such as open-mindedness, courage, and good judgment. It is interesting to read the study to see how valued qualities have changed or remained the same over time, but we raise it here not for what it said were preferred qualities, but as an example of the idea that dispositions are defined from the perspective of the expert. In fact, this is an explicit point made in the study:

> It is obvious enough that any determination of personal traits is at present dependent upon judgment. There is no other available means of identifying the personal qualities that make for success or failure in teaching. Such judgments are secured by two methods: first, by analysis of the literature wherein the writer's judgments are expressed; and second, by oral interviews with expert judges. (p. 52)

The assumption implied by the methodology of the Commonwealth study is that positive dispositions are not specific to individual teachers, but can be defined in a way that is standardized across teachers. In the introduction to the Commonwealth study, Capen (1929) wrote that the standardization movement in teacher education had started about 25 years earlier, and with great foresight wrote that "Indeed, it promises to last for some years to come" (p. xiv). After more than a century of effort and attention, we remain subject to Capen's prediction. The current interest in dispositions has been linked to the inclusion of dispositions along with knowledge and skills in the Interstate New Teacher Assessment and Support Consortium (InTASC) in 1992. The inclusion of dispositions by InTASC later led to the adoption of dispositions as an element of teacher evaluation in at least 30 states, and was recognized in the National

Council for the Accreditation of Teacher Education's (NCATE) 2002 standards, which called for teacher education institutions to assess the dispositions of their candidates (Diez, 2007; Sockett, 2009).

The current InTASC approach defines 43 specific dispositions across 10 standards (CCSSO, 2011). The dispositions parallel knowledge and skill standards, but are analytically separated. None of the dispositions are objectionable, but the highly specific nature of the dispositions leaves little room for individual teacher identity. The National Board for Professional Teaching Standards (NBPTS), in contrast, integrates dispositions in a more holistic fashion; more importantly, evaluation depends in large measure on teacher reflection (Lustick, 2011). The delineated nature of the InTASC approach can be traced directly to the fact that the standards were defined by a group that wanted to influence teacher evaluation by independent observers. Diez (2007), who was part of the original InTASC group, wrote that she personally believed that knowledge, skills, and dispositions work together in a holistic way that shouldn't be analytically separated. Nevertheless, she reported that she argued for analytic separation in the InTASC standards "to assure that teacher educators and policy makers would attend to assessing more than knowledge" (p. 392). The "who decides" in this case clearly influenced the "what and which" questions.

The act of defining dispositions for the purpose of evaluation creates problems even for well-intentioned efforts. Sockett (2012; 2009), for example, proposed an elegant framework for dispositions of character, intellect, and care and recognized and articulated the need for flexibility of definitions and strong teacher self-awareness. Such a framework is consistent with the case we are making. However, Sockett went a step further in citing the need for transparency and a clearer articulation of the specific qualities that define character, intellect, and care so as to achieve transparency under the premise that there will be instruments devised for "diagnosis and assessment." The language of "diagnosis and assessment" opens the door to standardized approaches that work against teacher selfhood.

The teacher standardization movement, now more than 100 years old, should be seen alongside the counter-balancing influence of the teacher reflection movement. Teacher reflection is frequently associated with Dewey (Rodgers, 2002) who, ironically, was the thesis advisor for W.W. Charters, lead author of the Commonwealth study. In modern times, the groundwork for acceptance of teacher reflection came during the 1970s and the recognition that qualitative methods, particularly those borrowed from anthropology, allowed for legitimate investigation of teacher beliefs, providing an alternative to behaviorally defined competency-based teacher education (Richardson, 1990). Of course, the movement took off in the 1980s with Schön's work (Schön, 1987; 1983) and teacher reflection became a near-ubiquitous banner for teacher education by the 1990s (Lyons, 2010). On a very broad scale then, the "who decides" teacher dispositions question has been pushed in different directions by the teacher standardization and teacher reflection movements for a very long time.

One could argue that the prominence of both trends has led us to a place where today's standards provide useful guidance while still maintaining appropriate flexibility for teachers (Zeichner, 2012). In addition, it seems essential to seek evaluation standards that are influenced by teacher reflections on deeply held beliefs. The National Board for Professional Teaching Standards approaches this balance, but in our view the InTASC standards go too far in defining in detail what dispositions matter. Despite Zeichner's optimism, we remain very concerned that the growing sophistication and influence of the teacher accountability movement tip the "who decides" question further away from teachers when it is combined with the assumption that accountability depends on highly reliable quantitative measures.

We are not sure if there is a way to balance accountability with meaningful teacher reflection, but the emphasis on quantitative measures is powerful and challenges the heart of teacher reflection. Only a clear vision by the profession will prevent teacher evaluation and teacher reflection from becoming a purely technical endeavor. While the co-opting of teacher reflection by instrumental approaches has long been an issue (Smyth, 1992), it is all the more poignant when reflection and teacher evaluation explicitly involve deeply held commitments and values.

A Caveat

We have cited the MET studies several times and return to them now because they represent probably the most extensive effort at teacher evaluation to date. The conclusion of the MET studies that good teaching can be identified and that value-added assessment scores are the most reliable predictor of effective teaching, has been challenged (Darling-Hammond, Amrein-Beardsley, Haertel, & Rothstein, 2012), but if true, would seem to undermine our thesis. The MET study makes value-added assessment scores sine qua non of teacher evaluation. Other measures are considered useful only if they are demonstrably related to student achievement scores.

Another more straightforward interpretation of the findings, however, is completely consistent with our ideas. The clearest conclusion from the MET studies is that the greatest part of the explanation of why some teachers are more effective than others is still not known (even when defining effective teaching using the limited criteria of value-added scores). The finding that past value-added scores predict future value-added scores much better than either student surveys or experienced observers only begs the question: What is the X factor that would explain how strong value-added scores were achieved in the first place? Since expert evaluations do not correlate well with value-added scores, we know that the answer is not to be found in very well-developed instruments such as *A Framework for Teaching* (Danielson, 2007; Danielson & McGreal, 2000). We would argue it is the artistry of the teacher and the human power of teacher character coming through to students in profound ways. And if that *is* true, then it would be backwards to adopt analytic frameworks for dispositions that mirror standards for knowledge and skills. This would take away a potentially powerful explanation and double-down on the incomplete explanation that we already have. And so, by rejecting such approaches, we also reject the attempt to develop reliable forms of assessment of dispositions that could be carried out by independent observers. Any attempt to do so will inevitably lead to a dehumanization of the profession, and even worse, to a poor understanding of what makes for good teaching. The true work of reflection and disposition development must be in the hands of teachers, their students, and non-evaluating peers and coaches.

Digging deeper into the MET studies, there is a fascinating finding that supports the importance of student insight. The studies found a modest relationship between the Tripod survey of student engagement and value-added test scores, and what is surprising is that surveys of students predict value-added scores slightly better than scores from expert observers (Bill & Melinda Gates Foundation MET Study, 2013b). As experienced student teacher supervisors who believe in our insights about good teaching, this is somewhat disconcerting. How can the results of a short survey given to children predict standardized scores better than an expert using an instrument that, at least in some sense, represents the accumulated wisdom and research of hundreds of researchers and practitioners?

The finding is consistent with our ideas of teacher selfhood and solidarity with students. It makes sense that students are responding to something more fundamental than the discrete behaviors that observers are able to document using observation rubrics. It is also possible that students have a deeper understanding of teacher character because they see them in many different situations over a long period of time. Finally, expert observers understand teacher behavior from an adult perspective. Students see through their own perspective and, regardless of the intention or skill of the teacher, the interpretation of the student is what makes a difference in how they respond. Unfortunately, the finding that standardized observations correlate poorly with value-added scores has been obscured by the debate over the use of value-added scores in the first place. If this fact were to be well understood, it could help professionals see the limitations of standardized approaches to evaluation and open the door to more well-rounded approaches that include teacher voice.

There are several possible explanations for why this has not yet happened. First, it could be that there actually is a closer alignment between the Tripod survey and the kind of teaching that leads to results on narrow tests of learning—perhaps experienced observers are looking for more fundamental qualities that transcend results on standardized tests. Common sense would say that students do not value teachers who have a narrow focus, and the seven key questions of the survey would also make this explanation implausible. While the survey includes the key question, "My classmates behave the way the teacher wants them to," most of the questions focus on broader qualities, for example, "My teacher seems to know if something is bothering me," "My teacher knows when the class understands," and "My teacher wants us to share our thoughts."

Other possible explanations are consistent with our view that students have important insights. It is possible that students are responding to something more fundamental than the discrete behaviors that observers are able to document on standardized forms. It is also possible, as suggested in our initial conception of dispositions, that students have a deeper understanding of teacher character because they see them in many different situations over longer periods of time. A fourth possible explanation is that expert observers understand teacher behavior from an adult perspective. Students see through their own perspective, and regardless of the intention or skill of the teacher, the interpretation of the student is what makes a difference in how they respond. Perhaps student voice is just as important as teacher voice in the answer to who decides what matters.

The METs study is widely understood as proposing that good teaching can be identified and that value-added assessment scores are the most reliable predictor of effective teaching. Another interpretation of the findings, however, is that the greatest part of the explanation of why some teachers are more effective than others is still not known (even when defining effective teaching using the limited criteria of value-added scores). The fact that prior-year value-added scores do predict next-year value-added scores better than either student surveys or experienced observers only begs the question: What is the X factor that would explain the predictive power of prior-year value-added scores if not the extensive set of qualities documented on instruments such as the Framework for Effective Teaching (Danielson, 2007)?

Until there is a sufficient answer to this question, we reject attempts to develop reliable forms of assessment of dispositions that could be carried out by independent observers. The true work of reflection and disposition development must be in the hands of teachers, their students, and non-evaluating peers and coaches.

A More Preferred Outcome: Balance

Over the history of teacher education, much has been written about the knowledge, skills, and dispositions of effective teachers (see Darling-Hammond & Bransford, 2005; Cochran-Smith & Zeichner, 2005). The years of research, much of it fitting into the quantitative and "scientifically based" models prominent within federal policy, have generated many frameworks and lists of the qualities of effective teachers and the practices effective teachers employ. However, while these lists of qualities and practices may describe *effective teaching*, they do not explain why teachers in possession of them do not necessarily become *effective teachers*. Perhaps the most striking conclusion that should be drawn from the MET study is that we know that we do not know why some teachers are more predictably effective than others.

While we do not want to make an argument critiquing existing research on effective teaching, we have tried to argue that asking this question in a different way can yield productive results. In thinking about who should define and evaluate effective teaching, we have concluded that the teachers themselves must play an important role in explaining who they are and what they value. Using conceptions like a stance, and teacher selfhood and solidarity, we have illustrated how, when the teachers themselves have a voice in their evaluation, much can be revealed about how to help them grow into more effective educators.

We have also shown how students should have a voice in how effective teaching is defined and evaluated. Based on evidence ranging from anecdotes from our own experiences to the far more systematic MET study, neglecting student voice in the evaluation process misses important dimensions of the effectiveness of classroom practices.

So where does this leave us? Given that a standards-based evaluation of teacher effectiveness is inevitable, and that value-added assessment is likely to become more widely used, what can be done to advocate for both the necessity of including dispositions in evaluations while not subjecting these dispositions to the standardization that would render evaluations both dangerous and unhelpful? The teachers we have described provide evidence that balancing individual dispositions with standardized expectations would be the most beneficial to the ultimate outcome of improved practice, but we remain skeptical that such a balance can exist within a framework of quantitative evaluation.

Within a discussion about how her middle school was moving toward a more standardized evaluation program that included checklists of expected practices (lesson objectives visible in the front of the room and mandated five-step lesson plans, among other structures), Julia said this:

> I think the way I contest those standards is in how I plan. I really learned not to rely on someone else's opinion about what I should be doing, and I guess learned to be confident, sort of confident, in my own plans. There are a couple other teachers who are really sticking to the book and buying the whole ball of wax in there about what to study. That isn't history, and that isn't teaching. It's not like I feel I am better than them, maybe those teachers wants kids to learn too, I don't know, but I do know that if you asked me why I taught this lesson today, I can usually tell you. I can talk about where it fits into the larger thing I am working on. I know you want to hear that but it is true. I know, and I am not sure they do. So, when [her department head] calls me in and makes me feel like a 10 year old, I can talk

about my big picture and where I want to go, and when he really starts blowing smoke, I'll pull out the standards and show him. And I won't cry, not even later. (Personal communication, January 13, 2011).

Ultimately, what Julia's story illustrates is that when conversations that appreciate her motives and values are considered along with other forms of evaluations, her practice becomes effective in a more meaningful way.

REFERENCES

Bill & Melinda Gates Foundation MET Project. (2013a). *Feedback for Effective Teaching: Nine Principles for Using Measures of Effective Teaching*. Retrieved from http://www.metproject.org/downloads/MET_Feedback%20for%20Better%20Teaching_Principles%20Paper.pdf

Bill & Melinda Gates Foundation MET Project. (2013b). *Ensuring Fair and Reliable Measures of Effective Teaching: Culminating Findings from the MET Project's Three-Year Study: Brief.* Retrieved from http://www.metproject.org/downloads/MET_Ensuring_Fair_and_Reliable_Measures_Practitioner_Brief.pdf

Borko, H., Liston, D., & Whitcomb, J. A. (2007). Apples and fishes: The debate over dispositions in teacher education. *Journal of Teacher Education, 58*(5), 359–364.

Brookfield, S. D. (1995). *Becoming a critically reflective teacher*. San Francisco, CA: Jossey-Bass.

Bullough, R.V., Clark, D. C., & Patterson, R. S. (2003). Getting in step: Accountability, accreditation and the standardization of teacher education in the United States. *Journal of Education for Teaching: International Research and Pedagogy, 29*(1), 35–51.

Capan, S. (1929). *Introduction*. In W. W. Charters & D. Waples (Eds.), *The Commonwealth teacher training study* (pp. i–xxxi). Chicago, IL: University of Chicago Press.

Charters, W. W., & Waples, D. (1929). *The Commonwealth teacher training study*. Chicago, IL: University of Chicago Press.

Cochran-Smith, M., & Fries, K. (2005). *Researching teacher education in changing times: Politics and paradigms*. In M. Cochrane-Smith & K. M. Zeichner (Eds.), *Studying teacher education: The report of the AERA panel on research and teacher education*. Mahwah, NJ: Lawrence Erlbaum.

Cochran-Smith, M., & Zeichner, K. M. (Eds.) (2005). *Studying teacher education: The report of the AERA panel on research and teacher education*. Mahwah, NJ: Lawrence Erlbaum.

Council of Chief State School Officers. (2011). *InTASC Model Core Teaching Standards: A Resource for State Dialogue*. Retrieved from *http://www.ccsso.org/Documents/2011/InTASC_Model_Core_Teaching_Standards_2011.pdf*

Council of Chief State School Officers. (2013). *Our Responsibility, Our Promise*. Retrieved from http://ccsso.org/Documents/2012/Our%20Responsibility%20Our%20Promise_2012.pdf

Danielson, C. (2007). *Enhancing professional practice: A framework for teaching*. Alexandria, VA: ASCD.

Danielson, C., & McGreal, T. L. (2000). *Teacher evaluation to enhance professional practice*. Princeton, NJ: ETS.

Darling-Hammond, L., Amrein-Beardsley, A., Haertel, E., & Rothstein, J. (2012). Evaluating teacher evaluation. *Phi Delta Kappan, 93*(6), 8–15.

Darling-Hammond, L., & Bransford, J. (Eds.). (2005). *Preparing teachers for a changing world: What teachers should learn and be able to do*. New York, NY: Jossey-Bass.

Dewey, J. (1933). *How we think*. Buffalo, NY: Promethus.

Diez, M. E. (2007). Looking back and moving forward three tensions in the teacher dispositions discourse. *Journal of Teacher Education, 58*(5), 388–396.

Fried, R. L. (1995). *The passionate teacher: A practical guide.* Boston, MA: Beacon.

Glaser, B. G., & Strauss, A. L. (1967). *The discovery of grounded theory: Strategies for qualitative research.* Chicago, IL: Aldine.

LaBoskey, V. K. (1993). A conceptual framework for reflection in preservice teacher education. In J. Calderhead & P. Gates (Eds.), *Conceptualizing reflection in teacher development* (pp. 23–38). Bristol, PA: Falmer Press.

Loughran, J. J. (2002). Effective reflective practice. In search of meaning in learning about teaching, *Journal of Teacher Education, 53*(1), 33–43.

Lustick, D. (2011). *Certifiable: Teaching, learning and National Board certification.* Lanham, MD: Rowman & Littlefield.

Lyons, N. (2010). *Reflection and reflective inquiry: Critical issues, evolving conceptualizations, contemporary claims and future possibilities.* In N. Lyons (Ed.), *Handbook of reflection and reflective inquiry: Mapping a way of knowing for professional reflective inquiry.* New York, NY: Springer.

Margolis, F. (2007). A relational ethic of solidarity? *Philosophy of Education Archive,* 62–72.

Palmer, P. J. (1998). *The courage to teach: Exploring the inner landscape of a teacher's life.* San Francisco, CA: Jossey-Bass.

Richardson, V. (1990). The evolution of reflective teaching and teacher education. In R. T. Clift, R. W. Houston, & M. C. Pugach (Eds.), *Encouraging reflective practice in education: An analysis of issues and programs.* New York, NY: Teachers College Press.

Rodgers, C. (2002). Defining reflection: Another look at John Dewey and reflective thinking. *The Teachers College Record, 104*(4), 842–866.

Rorty, R. (1989). *Contingency, irony and solidarity.* Cambridge, England: Cambridge University Press.

Schön, D. A. (1983). *The reflective practitioner* (Vol. 1). New York, NY: Basic Books.

Schön, D. A. (1987). *Educating the reflective practitioner.* San Francisco, CA: Jossey-Bass .

Smyth, J. (1992). Teachers' work and the politics of reflection. *American Educational Research Journal, 29*(2), 267–300.

Sockett, H. (2009). Dispositions as virtues: The complexity of the construct. *Journal of Teacher Education, 60*(3), 291–303.

Sockett, H. (2012). *Knowledge and virtue in teaching and learning: The primacy of dispositions.* New York, NY: Routledge.

Strong, J. H., Ward, T. J., & Grant, L. W. (2011). What makes good teachers good: A cross-case analysis of the connection between teacher effectiveness and student achievement. *Journal of Teacher Education 62*(4), 339–355.

Van Manen, M. (1977). Linking ways of knowing with ways of being practical. *Curriculum Inquiry, 6*(3), 205–228.

Van Manen, M. (1991). *The tact of teaching: The meaning of pedagogical thoughtfulness.* Albany, NY: State University of New York Press.

Whitehead, J. (1989). Creating a living educational theory from questions of the kind, "How do I improve my practice?" *Cambridge Journal of Education, 19*(1), 41–52.

Zeichner, K. (1987). Preparing reflective teachers. *International Journal of Educational Research, 11*(5), 29–44.

Zeichner, K. (2012). The turn once again toward practice-based teacher education. *Journal of Teacher Education, 63*(5), 376–382.

CHAPTER TEN

Professional Dispositions FOR Teacher Candidates

From Standardization to Wisely Effective Classrooms

SUSAN M. DUNKLE AND KELLY H. AHUNA

INTRODUCTION—TEACHING AS A PROFESSION

As a profession, teaching is undervalued in our society. This undervaluing is evidenced in teacher salaries, public opinion polls about teachers, and the general societal blame placed on teachers for the decline in U.S. competitiveness with other countries (Ornstein, Levine, & Gutek, 2011). Additionally, unlike other professions, many people think that they can teach—because they were students once and feel they have some intimacy with the practice (Ornstein et al., 2011).

This outlook is given credence every time a parent encounters a teacher behaving unprofessionally or an article about unethical teacher behavior appears in a newspaper. But if we are to improve our schools, we need to improve the societal value of those who work in them. This process must include raising the status of the teaching profession. Just as most people would not presume to know more about their health than their doctors (even though they inhabit their own bodies), so too should most people not presume to know more about how we should educate students than the teachers in schools (Ornstein, Levine, & Gutek, 2011). A striking difference between the way we think of teachers and doctors, however, is the weight we place on the value of medical school for doctors compared to Schools of Education for teachers. There is a general acceptance that medical school is selective and rigorous: not just anyone can be a doctor. But is there a comparable situation for our Schools of Education? We would like to argue that not just anyone can be a teacher. While teaching may appear to require less technical knowledge than medicine, it certainly requires more pedagogical and interpersonal knowledge. Pedagogy is the art and science of teaching, not just the science alone. While the science piece is the technical (or "effective"), the art (or "wise") aspect requires the additional non-technical proficiencies of interacting with students in a respectful manner and holding high expectations for all students. Only in this way can teachers achieve wisely effective classrooms and meet the needs of the whole student. Teachers interact with children, colleagues, parents, and supervisors every day. Each interaction requires application of various sets of skills (or dispositions) that we cannot take for granted because of their imperative nature. The question, of course, is: what are those dispositions and how do we teach them?

It is not too much to say that the ways in which a teacher interacts with a student can change that student's future. This results from more than the transference of content knowledge; it results from the messages the student receives from teachers about his or her self-worth and potential. Hence, Thornton (2006) argued that any discussion of teacher quality must move beyond instrumental skills and knowledge to include a "third element"—that of teacher dispositions (p. 53) since dispositions are the intangible piece that leads to the aforementioned change. There has been evidence for decades that student learning and development are influenced by teacher dispositions (Brewer, Lindquist, & Altemueller, 2011; Eberly, Rand, & O'Connor, 2007), but there has been no universal consensus about what constitutes the fundamental dispositions (Thornton, 2006). Kegan (as cited in Eberly et al.) recognized that the goal of teacher training is not just to ensure that teacher candidates outwardly behave toward students in certain ways but also to ensure that teacher candidates are motivated by an "inner feeling" of "responsibility towards others" (p. 31). It is this kind of abstract expectation, difficult both to label and to teach to others, that often falls under the heading of "dispositions." As a result, many Schools of Education attempt to make these expectations more concrete by generating lists of professional dispositions and demanding adherence to them. It has been our experience that this kind of compliance is valued over critical thinking.

Thornton (2006) synthesized the many approaches to assessing professional dispositions into five overall models. The first two models deal primarily with checklist-style expectations for behavior. The "standards language" and "professional behaviors" models are both concerned with teacher candidates behaving appropriately in the educational environment. These expectations can often include a list of minimal behavioral standards (e.g., dress, attendance, timeliness) and thus do not encompass the full spectrum of dispositions required for success. The third, a "self-reflection" model, asks teacher candidates to write journal-type responses to what they observe in the field, with the goal of increasing their self-awareness and metacognition toward dispositional issues. The self-reported nature of this model, however, makes its true effect questionable. In their attempt to make professional dispositions measurable, these initial three models suffer from distorting and over-simplifying what is really at stake.

The next two models take the issue of professional dispositions to a more complex level. With added attention to less concrete matters, what Thornton (2006) called the "ethics and equity" model focuses on teacher candidates' appreciation for diversity in the classroom and a true openness to different cultures and passion for educating all students: the prerequisites for authentic culturally responsive teaching. Finally, the "dispositions in action" model investigates the link between teacher candidates' dispositions (looked at here as moral inclinations and attitudes toward others) and actual actions in the classroom. What sets these last two models apart from the first two is a clear distinction between their demand for considering changes in attitude as well as observable behavior. This makes them more difficult to assess, but we would argue that without this attitudinal change, the goal of wisely effective classrooms will not be met.

In order to authentically embrace these attitudes, Thornton (2006) called for "dispositional intelligence" as a "requisite of quality teaching performance" (p. 56), and we would like to suggest that Schools of Education need to determine what constitutes such "dispositional intelligence." If we expect education to be the great equalizer that allows access to equal opportunities in the United States, we cannot take for granted that our teacher candidates ascribe to notions of social justice and culturally responsive teaching. Instead, we must find ways for our teacher preparation programs to promote a nurturing culture where authentic caring will become valued. This is not impossible, as there is evidence that, although difficult, dispositions can be changed through the use of case study exercises and other real-life scenarios (Brewer et al., 2011; Eberly et al., 2007).

ONE SCHOOL'S PATH TO PROFESSIONAL DISPOSITIONS

As educators of pre-service teachers, faculty in Schools of Education are charged by accreditation agencies, governmental mandate, and common sense to provide wide-ranging knowledge and skills to prepare teacher candidates for the class-room. Not to be taken for granted, professional dispositions are an integral factor in a teacher's success and subsequent outcomes for students. Because it cannot be assumed that teacher candidates come to their teacher training with professional dispositions in place, we agree with the charge from the government and accreditation agencies to include dispositions in teacher preparation.

According to the National Council for the Accreditation of Teacher Education (NCATE), dispositions are defined as the values, commitments, and professional ethics that influence behaviors towards students, families, colleagues, and communities and thus affect student learning, motivation, and development as well as educational growth. Dispositions are the beliefs and attitudes related to values such as caring, fairness, and the conviction that all students can learn. Educators should be committed to high and challenging standards as well as a safe and supportive learning environment (http://www.ncate.org). In our opinion, this cannot be overstated. Given the extensive research discrediting self-fulfilling prophecies (i.e., that students from the worst environments at home can still be highly successful at school and that students with every advantage can still fail), it is imperative that teacher candidates are coming out of school with the belief in the potential of all students (Jussim, 1989; Jussim, Eccles, & Madon, 1996; Weinstein, 1985).

At a small private college serving teacher candidates from the United States and Canada, School of Education faculty and administrators recently discussed the adoption of expectations for professional dispositions. This particular School of Education has a complementary mix of long-time practitioners in K-12 education and doctoral-level professors, each with valuable insights about what constitutes professionalism in the field of education. While the school has always held students to high standards, there were occasional student actions that did not seem to represent professional values, ethics, or behaviors. Although many infractions were not particularly dramatic (e.g., inappropriate attire, an informality in professional interactions with cooperating teachers and the staff at schools, or an inappropriate tone in professional electronic correspondence), each diminished the teaching profession in some way.

After committee meetings, drafts, discussions, redrafts, and a final meeting of the entire School of Education, consensus was reached to establish a list of professional dispositions. This document was provided for faculty to share with incoming and existing students. The adopted professional dispositions included, but were not limited to, five basic areas: attendance, conduct, expectations, accountability, and legal and ethical responsibilities. They consisted of what were considered basic elements of professionalism and common sense, such as arriving to class on time, not using cell phones during class, and not committing plagiarism. The faculty expected the list to be a potentially valuable tool to open a discussion about professionalism.

On the first day of any class, instructors are expected to discuss their syllabi, course assignments, and the professional dispositions expected of teacher candidates. The instructors are also tasked with distributing written "statements of understanding." These statements are signed by the students to indicate that they have read and understood the syllabus and requirements for the course. With this system in place, any violation of professional dispositions is also a violation of the agreement the student signed, enabling opportunities for discussion and disciplinary action if needed.

These School of Education expectations are intended to carry over into the Student Teaching practicum. Associate Teachers and College Supervisors evaluate teacher candidates on issues such as being able to demonstrate rapport with students and colleagues, using language appropriately for the workplace, working collaboratively with other professionals, taking responsibility for one's own actions, responding appropriately to feedback, and incorporating feedback into practice. The ultimate goal for teacher candidates is to engage in wisely effective teaching within their classrooms, balancing high academic expectations with a sincere investment in their students' lives. This is the culmination of a process that faculty begin at the initial class meetings when the professional dispositions are described to new teacher candidates.

Making Professional Dispositions Meaningful

As a program, this particular School of Education anchors its curriculum on Vygotsky's (1978) theory of constructivism. This constructivist perspective recognizes that students process information in relation to their existing life experience in order to make sense of it. Obviously, every student has a different life experience so each person's learning is an individual journey. These insights should not be neglected in the teaching of professional dispositions. But, this is very possible if professional dispositions are presented in a didactic manner—as a list to be read (and perhaps memorized). Hence, we believe that Schools of Education need to think through the manner in which they provide this instruction. If we want teacher candidates to understand and embrace the need for professional dispositions in the teaching field, we need to approach the task of presenting them in a consistently authentic manner.

Authentic learning may be described as "a pedagogical approach that allows students to explore, discuss, and meaningfully construct concepts and relationships in contexts that involve real-world problems and projects that are relevant to the learner" (Mims, 2003, p. 1). Authentic learning enables students to make connections between rote knowledge and how it can be applied in the real world. By making knowledge more meaningful, authentic learning increases student motivation (Newmann, Secada, & Wehlage, 1995). As well, it enables teachers to access students' prior knowledge on a topic and help students make direct connections between the new material and that prior knowledge. Authentic instruction differs from traditional teaching methods in that it expects students to be engaged in exploring, to use higher order thinking skills, and to experience social learning through discussion with fellow students and teachers (Donovan et al., 1999; Mims, 2003; Newman & Associates, 1996; Newmann et al., 1995; Nolan & Francis, 1992).

In this light, it makes sense for education faculty to provide teacher candidates with critical thinking and case study opportunities around professional disposition issues. By examining real life scenarios and commonly encountered concerns, pre-service teachers have the opportunity to learn about the dynamics and culture of classrooms before they even enter one. Through these more authentic experiences, future teachers can come to their own constructivist understanding of professionalism in the field of education. By providing our students with scenarios that problematize what it means to be more professional in their practice, we can make room for dispositions to be internalized rather than memorized. It is important for our students to understand the theoretical and philosophical underpinnings of our practice, but when they get to the classroom it is even more important for them to have a personal commitment to managing their classrooms and solving problems in a truly ethical way.

Part of critical thinking is to resist the natural human tendency toward egocentrism (Ahuna & Tinnesz, 2006). Teacher candidates are no exception to this tendency; like most people, they think their approaches and opinions are the "right" ones. Scenarios in which professional dispositions are disputed are typically scenarios for which there are many possible actions as opposed to only one correct response. As a result, many teacher candidates believe all responses to be equally valid. This is, of course, not true. Some responses will be "better" than others in that they more greatly respect the student, the social context of the situation, and the classroom learning community. By involving students in critical thinking scenarios and allowing them to hear divergent opinions and work through their own responses, we can hope to increase the teacher candidates' acceptance of the importance of professionalism. When education instructors attempt to indoctrinate students with certain professional dispositions, there is an understandable resistance. By introducing teacher candidates to the limits of their point of view, an analysis of their assumptions, and an exploration of consequences stemming from certain actions (Ahuna & Tinnesz, 2006), we can begin to reach some consensus on acceptable behaviors for the profession. This would require time dedicated to exploring who students are, what their life stories have been, why they believe what they believe, and what assumptions they make. Then students can delve into case studies and compare their various responses and why they vary.

At our School of Education, additional program requirements consisting of 100 hours of classroom observation and of writing a personal philosophy of education are further steps towards self-reflection before the student teaching experience. Through these incremental experiences pre-service teachers can begin to recognize the value and benefits for internalizing these professional dispositions.

A real-life scenario: Introducing professional dispositions

The following scenario was undertaken with the goal of addressing professional dispositions in an authentic manner. "If learning is authentic, then students should be engaged in genuine learning problems that foster the opportunity for them to make direct connections between the new material that is being learned and their prior knowledge" (Mehlinger, 1995, cited in Mims, 2003, p. 1). In a recent course with master's level students in elementary education, an open conversation highlighted how the content of professional dispositions can be approached in an authentic manner. The professor of the course began the discussion with the following questions for her 18 teacher candidates:

1. What are professional dispositions?
2. What professional dispositions are important for teachers to possess or practice in their classrooms?
3. Are professional dispositions important, and if so why?

The answer to the first question was rather direct: professional dispositions are the ways in which we ought to interact with our students, their families, and work colleagues. This led to a response to the second question that culminated in the construction of a list of criteria:

- No segregation of students either physically or conversationally
- Patience with self and students
- Ability to work with all students
- No profanity
- Separation of teacher's home and work life
- Appropriate level of response to situations
- Classroom management
- Professional development
- High expectations of all students
- Reflective practice
- Mutual respect of students, teachers, classmates, and colleagues
- Compassion for students; understanding of different backgrounds
- Respect of family and caregivers
- Knowledge of family situations and commitment to partnering with families.

The answer to the third question about the importance of professional dispositions was embedded within the rich discussion that surrounded the construction of such lists. Addressing each entry, students were also challenged to express why a particular criterion was integral to a successful classroom as they understood it.

At the end of the discussion on professional dispositions, one student remarked that she felt that "this activity and discussion helped her verbalize and reinforce her understanding of the concepts." Students also stated that in other courses they had been given the list of the college's professional dispositional expectations to read, but that it did not enter into their consciousness when planning lessons and units. Many students generally stated that this authentic learning activity helped them focus on articulating the meaning of dispositions and the way pedagogical theories actually have concrete social relevance that can be appreciated by the act of reflective and collaborative application. The larger implication of this activity is that these novice teachers will enter the field with a greater sensitivity for the need to reflect authentically on the meaning of professional dispositions. This will put them on track for leading wisely effective classrooms in which they are prepared to meet the needs of all of their students.

CULTURALLY RESPONSIVE TEACHING AS A PROFESSIONAL DISPOSITION

One component of meeting student needs is being culturally responsive. A strong argument can be made that professional dispositions are incomplete without consideration of our students' backgrounds (i.e., race, ethnicity, gender, social class, ability, etc.). If teachers are not responsive to the backgrounds of their students, both the learning environment and learning outcomes may be negatively affected. The National Council for the Accreditation of Teacher Education (NCATE) recognized this in its fourth standard dedicated to diversity. NCATE requires that teacher candidates exhibit proficiency in both understanding and dealing with diversity. As such, it becomes imperative that teacher preparation programs include issues of culturally responsive teaching in their dispositional expectations (Kerr & Dils, 2011). Culturally responsive teaching is a pedagogy that recognizes the importance of including students' cultural references in all aspects of learning (Ladson-Billings, 1994). Students' cultural references come from a variety of sources: parents and families, culture, language, and community. Each of these sources is considered when shaping instruction and determining what pedagogical methods to use. While examining and respecting each of these sources, teachers must relay positive feelings about each and set high expectations for students (Teaching Diverse Learners, 2006).

According to Nieto (1996, as cited on the Education Alliance at Brown University website, 2006):

> Culture is central to learning. It plays a role not only in communicating and receiving information, but also in shaping the thinking process of groups and individuals. A pedagogy that acknowledges, responds to, and celebrates fundamental cultures offers full, equitable access to education for students from all cultures. (para. 1)

Because there continues to exist a mismatch between the cultural make-up of teachers (predominantly white women) and an increasingly diverse student body

(Garmon, 2005; Vescio, Bondy, & Poekert, 2009; Eberly, Joshi, Konzal, & Galen, 2010), there is an understandable gap between the culture of the school and the culture of the home. Eberly et al. (2010) focused on how to prepare teacher candidates to establish more positive teacher-parent relationships. These researchers surveyed and held focus group discussions with current teachers, and then planned a series of three professional development sessions. The first session focused on teachers' self-awareness, the second introduced a panel of parents to discuss their families' cultures and educational experiences, and the third worked on the development of concrete skills teachers could use in working with diverse families. Although they experienced some moderate success, one finding of their study was that "transition from knowledge into practice is difficult and requires time" (p. 29). As individuals are introduced to "disequilibrium," they need time and opportunity to "build new schemas" (p. 29). Given that this study focused on professional teachers, it is reasonable to predict that this process may be even more complicated for teacher candidates.

At the same time, a true openness to diversity cannot be forced upon teacher candidates. Because they exhibit "individual agency" (Vescio et al., 2009, p. 5), teacher candidates are unlikely to adopt a culturally responsive attitude toward teaching simply because their instructors demand it. Rather, authentic learning experiences that are "learner-centered, participatory, interactive, and presented within the context of the students' lives" (Vescio et al., p. 6) are required to help teacher candidates move beyond the lens through which they have always viewed the world. Thompson (2009) discussed the need for instruction that "must simultaneously be aimed at the head (academic), gut (feeling), and heart (social change) levels" (p. 38). Clearly, this is a novel way of thinking about teaching teachers. It is not enough to present content, model pedagogical techniques, and demand adherence to a list of dispositions. While educating the head, gut, and heart is arguably the longer path, the outcomes might be well worth it. A move toward culturally responsive teaching might improve the educational experience for all students.

However, this will be difficult. Garmon (2005) addressed the need to consider the life experiences of teacher candidates. He discussed the relationship between pre-service teachers' "predispositions and prior experiences" (p. 282) and the likelihood that they will accept new information that may conflict with those predispositions and experiences. No matter how much information is presented and no matter how well it is taught, individuals are less likely to internalize it if it stands in contention with prior life experience. In the same vein, Thompson (2009) also reminds us that dispositions should never be "used as a hammer for program-related punishments" (p. 46), since such an approach could easily lead to the further entrenchment of predisposed attitudes and an enhanced reluctance to change.

THE ROLE OF CULTURAL CAPITAL IN ACHIEVING JUST CLASSROOMS

Another authentic entry point for a conversation about professional dispositions can be an exploration of "cultural capital" (Freire, 2000; McLaren, 2009) and the varying prestige value placed on behaviors. Because inequality is built into the societal structure, there is a hierarchy to the value of varying social norms and behaviors. When teacher candidates realize how behaviors are interpreted differently across contexts, there can be two positive results. First, teacher candidates can rethink the assumptions they may make about students based on differences in culture and social norms. Second, teacher candidates can begin to understand how their own conduct as teachers will be interpreted in the communities in which they teach. Both of these insights around the idea of cultural capital can enhance the work teachers do with their students.

In Gay's (2010) updated text, *Culturally Responsive Teaching: Theory, Research, and Practice*, the author highlights the work of Wang and Gordon (1999), which "provides a significant antidote to the cultural deficit paradigm and reveals the strength and resilience of the families, communities and cultures of students from diverse racial, ethnic, and linguistic groups" (p. x). This research reinforces the understanding that marginalized students do not have deficits, and instead focuses on the disparities in academic achievement between mainstream and marginalized students. As such, this theory guides teachers away from blaming students and their families for those academic disparities and encourages the promotion of high expectations for all students regardless of their economic, racial, ethnic, or other differences. While educators can have high expectations, there is still a possibility that students will fail. The important point is that teachers recognize that the failures stem from a complex combination of socioeconomic factors as opposed to individual deficits.

McLaren (2009) expanded on the academic gap between majority and minority students by suggesting that knowledge is organic and subjective; that is, he claimed that knowledge is the product of an ongoing conversation between members of a given society at a given time. McLaren further asserted that "[c]ritical pedagogy asks how and why knowledge gets constructed the way it does, and how and why some constructions of reality are legitimated and celebrated by the dominant culture while others clearly are not" (p. 63). Many students endure an education that seems to have little validation of their history or their lived experience. As a result, McLaren noted that "academic performance represents, therefore, not individual competence or the lack of ability on the part of disadvantaged students but the school's *depreciation of their cultural capital*" (p. 81).

Phuntsog (1999), in discussing culturally responsive teaching, extrapolated that "those students who do not feel valued in school settings are likely to develop lower self-esteem, alienating them further from school learning" (para. 22).

Culturally responsive theory, on the other hand, states that "the discontinuities" that children feel may be alleviated "through prescriptive pedagogy" (Allen & Boykin, 1992, p. 586). Because the contextual factors of children's cultural experiences can influence and harm their performance in school, it becomes the responsibility of culturally responsive teachers to bridge the gaps between home and school and make pedagogical choices that resonate with the student (e.g., reading books with characters that represent students' lived experience, providing mathematical word problems that are authentic to students' daily lives). In short, teachers must value the cultural capital students bring into the classroom with them.

This discussion highlights some complications in preparing teacher candidates for the education profession. Kaur (2012) pointed out that one of the most important questions in increasing the success of education is how to make schools more equitable for all learners in increasingly diverse classrooms. Unlike many occupations, performing well does not just require mastery of content. Teaching well requires educators to recognize their own preconceptions and biases, and importantly, work to overcome them. Part of this demands a reexamination of cultural capital and the divide between school and home cultures. Only then can teachers equally and effectively educate all of their students. Only then can the education profession claim to be working at its best, the end result of which would be the realization of social justice.

SOCIAL JUSTICE AND WISELY EFFECTIVE CLASSROOMS— THE END GOAL

Social justice is defined as "the fair and proper administration of laws conforming to the natural law that all persons, irrespective of ethnic origin, gender, possessions, race, religion, etc., are to be treated equally and without prejudice" (http://www.businessdictionary.com). Social justice in the classroom, then, calls for educators to equally and equitably teach all students without prejudice. While most teachers would say they are committed to this, actions do not always match words. It is arguable that the most basic professional disposition in education has to be a commitment to social justice, for without that, teachers may only best serve a certain population of students and not all of them—the antithesis of the foundational goal of what it is to be an educator.

Additionally, teacher candidates must be challenged to think critically about how their interactions with their students affect outcomes. Prospective teachers need to be taught intentionality in their practice, which simply means that they have to be thoughtful about their practice, determine ahead of time what they are hoping to accomplish with the students, and put all of their efforts into that pursuit. Teachers need to be ongoing reflective practitioners of the methods that they are using within their classrooms to be able to remediate, enrich, and provide instruction that meets the various learning styles of their students. Reflective thinking allows teachers and teacher candidates to evaluate what was successful, or not, in their practice and to be able to adjust their methods to meet their students' learning needs and to successfully teach new concepts. In doing so, teachers are using their developed skills to create wisely effective classrooms.

CONCLUSION—IMPROVING THE STATUS OF THE TEACHING PROFESSION

Over the past several decades, control of the educational process has increasingly moved from local districts to state agencies and then to federal oversight. With an increased focus on standards since the advent of No Child Left Behind (NCLB) in 2002 and now the Common Core Standards for Students and the expectations of the Annual Professional Performance Review (APPR) for classroom teachers, educators are under greater stress. They need to acquire knowledge of these expectations and assure they are taught and mastered to meet the assessment criteria for themselves and their students. More than ever, the teaching cadre demands professional individuals who are able to meet the ever-evolving challenges before them. Research shows that beginning teachers leave the profession due to unrealistic expectations of the classroom and the constraints that they face. The attrition rate within the first 3 years of teaching is 14%, and it rises to almost 50% after five years (Alliance for Excellent Education, 2004). Clearly, Schools of Education and the instructors within them are called to prepare our teacher candidates for the challenges that face them in this demanding career.

Ornstein et al. (2011) remind us that until the twentieth century, teachers were relatively untrained. In fact, formal training consisted of 1 to 2 years at a teacher's college, at most. Today, the profession of teaching and the requisite training has evolved dramatically. And although most teachers strive for professionalism in their work, education is often criticized in the media, by politicians, and by the general public. One such criticism questions whether teaching is truly a profession. As a response to this criticism, Orenstein et al. (2011) offered the following characteristics of a "profession."

First, a sense of "public service" is required (Ornstein et al., 2011). Because education is a service mandated by law to every child, this requirement is salient in teaching. It is imperative, however, that teachers practice culturally responsive teaching and social justice in the classroom. For without those components in the "public service" of education, existing institutional biases that disadvantage some groups of students will never dissipate and many students will continue to suffer a disservice.

Second, Orenstein et al. (2011) called for a "defined body of knowledge and skills" in a profession. Clearly, there is subject content to be mastered and pedagogical techniques to learn in education, but the set of "skills" required is more difficult to define. As argued in this chapter, educators must embody certain professional dispositions in order to be most effective. If internalized, professional dispositions can lead to true culturally responsive teaching and the realization of just classrooms. With this kind of conviction, teachers can move education towards being viewed more professionally and valued more highly.

Ornstein et al. (2011) also called for "an acceptance of responsibility for judgments made and acts performed related to services rendered" (p. 28). Because there is an inherent power differential in education when adults are working with minors, the need to take responsibility for judgment is all the more imperative. Judgments that teachers make about students can have self-confidence implications on students' self-image leading to long-term effects on aspirations and personal worth. As a result, the preceding discussion on cultural capital and the need for teacher candidates to evaluate their own assumptions and biases in an effort to best serve their students cannot be underscored strongly enough. Any one interaction with a student can have long-lasting effects that a teacher may never know.

Finally, Ornstein et al. (2011) called for "a code of ethics to help clarify ambiguous matters or doubtful points related to services rendered" (p. 28). This is an overt opening for professional dispositions to come into play. Of course, no profession can ensure that all of its practitioners subscribe to any set of ethics, but professional standards can hold individuals accountable to the highest ideals. In the case of education, where outcomes directly impact the quality of our society, it is imperative that those ideals are explicit and upheld. It is essential for teachers to maintain a code of ethics that ensures a safe, culturally responsive, and just environment for all students. These ethics cannot be negotiable.

REFERENCES

Ahuna, K. H., & Tinnesz, C. G. (2006). *Methods of inquiry: Applied critical thinking (2nd ed.)*. Dubuque, IA: Kendall Hunt.

Allen, B. A., & Boykin, A. W. (1992). African-American children and the educational process: Alleviating cultural discontinuity through prescriptive pedagogy. *School Psychology Review, 21*(4), 586–596.

Alliance for Excellent Education. (2004). *Tapping the potential: Retaining and developing high-quality new teachers*. Washington, DC: Author.

American Association of Law Libraries. (2012). *ARCHIVED: Writing Learning Outcomes*. Retrieved on January 1, 2013, from http://www.aallnet.org/Archived/Education-and-Events/cpe/outcomes.html

Banks, J., Cochran-Smith, M., Moll, L., Richert, A., Zeichner, K., LePage, P.,...McDonald, M. (2005). Teaching diverse learners. In L. Darling-Hammond & J. Bransford (Eds.), *Preparing teachers for a changing world* (pp. 232– 274). San Francisco, CA: Jossey-Bass.

Brewer, R. D., Lindquist, C., & Altemueller, L. (2011). The dispositions improvement process. *International Journal of Instruction, 4*(2), 51– 68. Retrieved from http://files.eric.ed.gov/fulltext/ED522684.pdf

Brown, D. (2002). *Becoming a successful urban teacher.* Portsmouth, NH: Heinemann.

Cochran-Smith, M. (1999). Learning to teach for social justice. In G. A. Griffin (Ed.), *The education of teachers: Ninety-eighth yearbook of the National Society for the Study of Education* (Vol. 1, pp. 114– 144). Chicago, IL: The National Society for the Study of Education.

Cochran-Smith, M. (2004). *Walking the road: Race, diversity, and social justice in teacher education.* New York, NY: Teachers College Press.

Danielson, C. (2009). A framework for learning to teach. *E-journal of Association for Supervision and Curriculum Development, 66.* Retrieved on September 29, 2012, from http://www.ascd.org/publications/educational-leadership/summer09/vol66/num09/A-Framework-for-Learning-to-Teach.aspx

Davis, B. M. (2006). *How to teach students who don't look like you: Culturally relevant teaching strategies.* Thousand Oaks, CA: Corwin Press.

Donovan, M. S., Bransford, J. D., & Pellegrino, J. W. (Eds.). (1999). *How people learn: Bridging research and practice.* Washington, DC: National Academy Press.

Eberly, J. L., Joshi, A., Konzal, J., & Galen, H. (2010). Crossing cultures: Considering ethnotheory in teacher thinking and practices. *Multicultural Education, 18*(1), 25– 32.

Eberly, J. L., Rand, M. K., & O'Connor, T. (2007). Analyzing teachers' dispositions toward diversity: Using adult development theory, *Multicultural Education, 14*(4), 31–36.

Florian, L. (2009). Preparing teachers to work in "schools for all." *Teaching and Teacher Education: An International Journal of Research and Studies, 25*(4), 533–534.

Freire, P. (2000) *Pedagogy of the oppressed: 30ᵗʰ anniversary edition.* New York, NY: Continuum.

Garmon, M. A. (2005). Six key factors for changing preservice teachers' attitudes/beliefs about diversity. *Educational Studies, 38*(3), 275–286.

Gay, G. (2000). *Culturally responsive teaching: Theory, research, & practice.* New York, NY: Teachers College Press.

Gay, G. (2010). *Culturally responsive teaching: Theory, research, & practice.* New York, NY: Teachers College Press.

Hollins, E. R., & Guzman, M. T. (2005). Research on preparing teachers for diverse populations. In M. Cochran-Smith & K. M. Zeichner (Eds.), *Studying teacher education: The report of the AERA panel on research and teacher education* (pp. 477–548). Mahwah, NJ: Lawrence Erlbaum.

Introduction: Creating classrooms for equity and social justice. (2013). In *Rethinking our classrooms, volume 1, new edition.* Retrieved on January 15, 2013, from http://www.rethinkingschools.org/publication/roc1/roc1_intro.shtml

Jussim, L. (1989). Teacher expectations: Self-fulfilling prophecies, perceptual biases, and accuracy. *Journal of Personality and social Psychology, 57*(3), 469–480.

Jussim, L., Eccles, J., & Madon, S. (1996). Social perception, social stereotypes, and teacher expectations: Accuracy and the quest for the powerful self-fulfilling prophecy. *Advances in Experimental Social Psychology, 28,* 281–388.

Kaur, B. (2012). Equity and social justice in teaching and teacher education. *Teaching and Teacher Education: An International Journal of Research and Studies, 28*(4), 485–492.

Kerr, J., & Dils, K. (2011). Meeting NCATE standard 4: One university's plan to help preservice teachers develop the knowledge, skills, and professional dispositions necessary to ensure that all students learn. *Educational Conversations, 38*(2), 13–19.

Ladson-Billings, G. (1994). *The dreamkeepers: Successful teachers for African-American children.* San Francisco, CA: Jossey-Bass.

Lynch, J., DeRose, J., & Kleindienst. G. (2006). Mentoring new teachers. *Techniques: Connecting Education and Career, 81*(6), 24–28.

McLaren, P. (2009). Critical pedagogy: A look at the major concepts. In A. Darder, M. P. Baltodano, & R. D. Torres (Eds.), *The critical pedagogy reader* (pp. 61–83) New York, NY: Routledge.

Mims, C. (2003). Authentic learning: A practical introduction & guide for implementation. *Meridian: A Middle School Computer Technologies Journal, 6*(1). Retrieved from http://www.ncsu.edu/meridian/win2003/authentic_learning/index.html

Newmann, F., & Associates (Eds.). (1996). *Authentic achievement: Restructuring schools for intellectual quality.* San Francisco, CA: Jossey-Bass.

Newmann, F., Secada, W., & Wehlage, G. (1995). *A guide to authentic instruction and assessment: Vision, standards and scoring.* Alexandria, VA: ASCD.

Nieto, S. (1996). A gesture towards justice: Small schools and the promise of equal education. In W. Ayers, M. Klonsky, & G. Lyon (Eds.), *A simple justice: The challenge of small schools* (pp. 13–18). New York, NY: Teachers College Press.

Nolan, J., & Francis, P. (1992). Changing perspectives in curriculum and instruction. In C. Glickman (Ed.), *Supervision in Transition* (pp. 44–60). Alexandria, VA: Association for Supervision and Curriculum Development.

Ornstein, A. C., Levine, D. U., & Gutek, G. (2011). *Foundations of education (11ᵗʰ ed.).* Boston, MA: Houghton Mifflin.

Phuntsog, N. (1999). The magic of culturally responsive pedagogy: In search of the genie's lamp in multicultural education. *Teacher Education Quarterly, 26*(3). Retrieved February 4, 2013, from http://www.teqjournal.org/sample_issue/article_6.htm

Richardson, V. (2003). Constructivist pedagogy. *Teachers College Record, 105*(9), 1623–1640.

Social Justice website (2011). Retrieved on February 1, 2013 from http://socialjusticeparadigm.wordpress.com/tag/cultural-capital/

Thompson, F. (2009). The instruction and assessment of multicultural dispositions in teacher and counselor education. *Journal of Invitational Theory Practice, 15*, 32–54.

Thornton, H. (2006) Dispositions in action: Do dispositions make a difference in practice? *Teacher Education Quarterly, 33*(2), 53–68. Retrieved from http://www.teqjournal.org/backvols/2006/33_2/volume_33_number_2.htm

Vescio, V., Bondy, E., & Poekert, P. E. (2009). Preparing multicultural teacher educators: Toward a pedagogy of transformation. *Teacher Education Quarterly, 36*(2), 5–24.

Vygotsky, L. S. (1978). M. Cole, V. John-Steiner, S. Scribner, & E. Souberman (Eds.), *Mind in society: Development of higher psychological practices.* Cambridge, MA: Harvard University Press.

Walsh, K. (2006). Teacher education: Coming up empty. In *Fwd: Arresting Insights in Education.* Washington, DC: Thomas Fordham Foundation.

Webster's Revised Unabridged Dictionary. (1998). Retrieved from http://machaut.uchicago.edu/websters

Weinstein, R. S. (1985). Student mediation of classroom expectancy effects. *Teacher Expectancies,* 329–350.

CHAPTER ELEVEN

Teachers AS Advocates FOR Democracy

Standardization of Public Education and Voter Participation

SHELLEY J. PINEO-JENSEN

Assessment of teacher dispositions in teacher education programs has been under attack as a mechanism by which progressive values are forced into the instructional practices of new teachers (Villegas, 2007). Misco and Shively (2007) argued that an appropriate goal of public education, "societal transformation" (para. 6) can be achieved with the preparation of teachers who promote equitable outcomes for students without any a priori goal in mind. They advocated for discussion as the means by which teachers can foster social justice; "deliberation is predicated on pre-service teachers formulating ideas, finding solutions, and bringing to light the non-recurring nuances of a particular circumstance ... [to refine] pre-service teachers' sense of justice, equity, and awareness of inequality" (paras. 16, 27).

This chapter is predicated on a different proposition. I argue that teachers armed with research that interrogates the role of K-12 public education in preparing students to vote, or more to the point, *not* to vote, will inform the dispositions of teachers such that they engage their students with the content and skills of active civic knowledge that will empower students to later participate in democracy at the most fundamental and most powerful level—by voting. In order for marginalized groups to achieve social justice they must obtain political power. Change in the distribution of power in the U.S. inevitably depends on the force of law; elected representatives play the key role in ensuring that the laws reflect the will of all the people and not just that small portion of the population who have greater economic, social, and political power.

This chapter presents a serious problem with U.S. voter turnout, describes the moderating effect of education on groups facing obstacles to voting, recounts the historical rise of educational standardization, and articulates the difference between standardization and differentiation in K-12 public education. It then reports the author's research finding of a weak but significant correlation between educational standardization and voter turnout for some recent years.

For social justice advocates, a key rationale for public financing of K-12 education is that public schools are a crucial site for the formation of citizen empowerment. The current standardization movement abdicates that responsibility in lieu of the education of citizens as workers in the global economy. One example is a 2013 Arkansas Department of Education administrative rule: "academic content standards are rigorous and equip students to compete in the global workforce" (para 4).

The study demonstrated that increased standardization of public education did not correlate with increased voter turnout. Given the varying levels of voter suppression in the U.S., K-12 teachers can play a critical role in empowering an informed electorate. In advocating for public education, Thomas Jefferson (1820) wrote:

> I know of no safe depository of the ultimate powers of the society but the people themselves; and if we think them not enlightened enough to exercise their control with a wholesome discretion, the remedy is not to take it from them, but to inform their discretion by education. (p. 278)

VOTER TURNOUT IN THE U.S.

Voting is a fundamental indicator of participation in a democracy. The literal definition of democracy is "rule by the people" (Dahl, 2012, para. 1). Voting is the "machinery of democracy" (Bird, Campbell, & Briggs, 2012, para. 1). In order for a democratic process to be viewed as legitimate, citizens must have the opportunity to determine their preferences, to communicate these preferences effectively, and to express these preferences without discrimination (Dahl, 1971). These opportunities depend on several institutional guarantees, including: the "right to vote ... alternative sources of information ... [and] free and fair elections" (p. 3). In other words, voter participation is the hallmark of a democracy.

Evidence of the reduction of access to counter-narratives can be found in the consolidation of media sources in the U.S. Since the Telecommunications Act of 1996 (Federal Communications Commission, 2013), the number of sources of reliable information has been shrinking (Common Cause, 2013b). Control of the television and cable media has been reduced to six major companies; radio has been similarly consolidated. This has increased the influence of large media conglomerates (Common Cause, 2013a) and decreased access to alternative information about public affairs, particularly elections. One obvious remedy to a decline in wide-ranging news and commentary is an educated populace capable of critical examination of corporatized media. Unfortunately, as Giroux commented, under standardized educational reform "the logic of routine, conformity, and standardization eliminates the need for critical thinking, historical analyses, and critical memory work" (Tristan, 2013, para. 10). The next section provides a discussion of voter turnout.

Voter turnout in other countries is higher than in the U.S. (International IDEA, 2012). Figure 1 provides a representation of voter turnout for selected countries from 1991 to 2000. Additionally, there is great variation of voter turnout among the states (U.S. Census Bureau, 2012). The electoral process in the U.S. is distorted by variety in voter registration laws and obstacles to voting. After improved voter participation by people of color in the 2008 presidential election, an "assault on voting rights that is historic both in terms of its scope and intensity… [of] restrictive voting measures … threaten[ed] to … suppress … the political participation of people of color, the poor, the elderly, and the young" (Haygood, 2012, p. 1019). The distribution of these voter suppression laws was concentrated in "the very same states that experienced high rates of minority population growth and political participation over the last decade" (p. 1030).

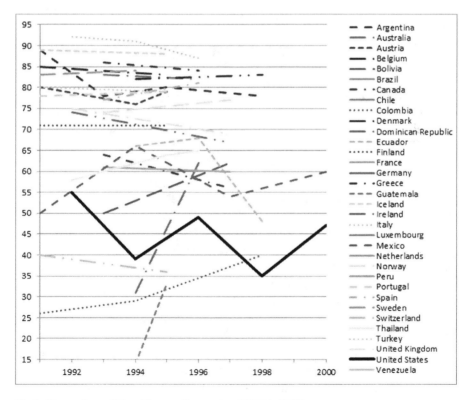

Fig 1. Comparison of Voter Turnout (International IDEA, 2012).

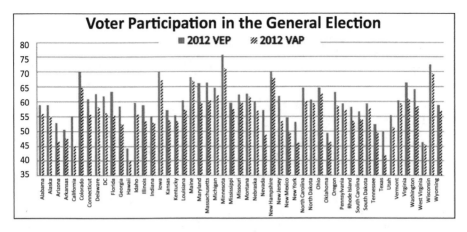

Fig 2. Voter Participation by State for the 2012 General Election (McDonald, 2012a).

As noted earlier, there is great variability of voter turnout among states. State voter participation is reported either as Voting Age Population (VAP) or Voting Eligible Population (VEP). VAP is calculated by dividing the number of votes cast by the number of state residents older than 18 as reported in the U.S. Census. VEP uses the same operation, except that the divisor is adjusted by the deduction of non-eligible voters such as felons and non-citizens, and the addition of those residents who are overseas (McDonald, 2012b). Figure 2 presents voter turnout in the 2012 general election for VEP and VAP, which ranges from approximately 40% to 75%.

An additional problem with voter turnout in the U.S. involves differences in voter turnout for particular demographic groups—including age and educational level (Baum, Ma, & Payea, 2010).

EDUCATION AND VOTER PARTICIPATION

Level of formal education, as a demographic variable that counts the number of years of education a person has achieved, is probably the single most important correlate to voting; "education is everywhere the universal solvent, and the relationship is always in the same direction" (Converse & Campbell, 1972, p. 324). The more education a person has the more likely that person is to vote (Burden, 2009; Dee, 2004; Freedman, Franz, & Goldstein, 2004; Lassen, 2005; Sondheimer & Green, 2010).

Tenn (2005) described a paradox, sometimes called "Brody's Puzzle" (Brody, 1978), in which an increase in the level of educational attainment for an individual increased the likelihood that the person would vote, but national increases in level of education did *not* increase the likelihood of an increase in national voter turn-out. He suggested that the relationship is relative; in other words, within a studied group (i.e., those who have recently moved), those who have more years of education relative to others within the group have been more likely to vote than those who have fewer years of education.

The importance of relative levels of education manifests itself in the role education plays in offsetting obstacles to voting. In the U.S., registration requirements, lack of access to polling places, and lack of mobility are all impediments to voting.

Mobility is an obstacle to voter registration. This occurs primarily when individuals move to a new precinct. This type of voter suppression is visited less on those with more education; "college graduates are decidedly less hindered by moving than people with less education" (Squire, Wolfinger, & Glass, 1987, p. 53). Consequently, the impediment of mobility to voter participation is overcome more easily by individuals who have more education than their peers.

Institutional impediments are another obstacle. A study of the relationship between education and voter participation between the U.S. and the United Kingdom found that there was "a strong and robust relationship between education and voting for the United States ... [where] registration rules present a barrier to participation" (Milligan, Moretti, & Oreopoulos, 2004, p. 1667). This effect was not found in the United Kingdom because similar registration impediments did not exist. In other words, in the U.S., those who are better educated have more resources to overcome obstacles of institutionalized voter suppression.

EDUCATIONAL STANDARDIZATION IN THE U.S.

The basic rationale for an education system that is financed by taxes is that it benefits society. How this public good is framed influences education policies and accountability systems. An examination of the roots of public education in the United States will help to understand how the goals of public education have drifted from the original intentions of the founders, and how the current emphasis on large-scale, high-stakes testing has been driven by an emphasis on efficiency, accountability, and the desire for standardization. The next section will describe the original rationale for public education, the influence of the Progressive Movement and subsequent rise of meritocracy, and the effects of the Cold War on the perception that public education is failing.

The influence of the Enlightenment fostered the earliest commitment to public education, which was seen as a basic requirement in the welfare of the state and the responsibility of the government, in order to guarantee citizen participation in a democracy, which required an educated populace (Heck, 2004). Thomas Jefferson articulated a rationale for a free public school system, arguing that "peace and stability in the new nation were best preserved by giving people access to education" (p. 46). Horace Mann promoted free public education in the early 1800s; "public schools became a means for ensuring the transfer of knowledge between generations" (p. 47). Up to this point, then, public education provided for the transmission of culture and the development of literacy as a prerequisite for voting.

During the late 1800s, the Progressive Movement was a response to industrialization, migration from rural to urban areas, and immigration. Public education acquired another domain of public utility beyond literacy for citizenship and communication of culture—health education. Education was conceptualized as a proactive tool for creating desirable social changes (Mintz & McNeil, 2012). Among other health initiatives in public schools in the early part of the twentieth century were massive programs of immunization of students (Rosen, 1958). In the early 1900s, John Dewey, an advocate for progressive education, sought to move educational practice away from rote learning to active learning, emphasizing the needs of the whole child.

With the rise of the Progressive Movement was a concurrent rise of the power of corporations. The election of William McKinley was supported by "commercial and manufacturing interests ... [using] the new political methods of mass advertising" (Heck, 2004, p. 86). "The cultural values of the corporate state were politically unassailable in twentieth century America" (Goodwyn, 1978, p. 278). As the twentieth century unfolded, Dewey's theories gave way to bureaucratic and meritocratic ideals that matched the business values of efficiency and accountability.

As school districts and states implemented free and compulsory education, public financing underscored the need for accountability and efficiency. Meritocracy became a popular concept, combining businesslike reforms in education with the belief that advancement based on merit would guarantee equity. "Municipal reform ... put the power in the hands of business elites ... with superintendents overseeing school operations as scientific educational managers" (Heck, 2007, p. 93). Efficiency became a dominant theme and corporate-ethic models were applied to educational systems. Testing became a critical component of meritocracy.

The predecessor to standardized tests in public education was the Stanford-Binet IQ test that had been used as a sorting tool by the U.S. Army during World War I. Following the war, the perceived success of this instrument led to the development of standardized achievement tests for public education; this was

> among the most important developments. [The tests] caught on quickly because of the relative ease of administration and scoring and the [perception of a] lack of subjectivity or favoritism.... [They were] less expensive and more efficient than essay tests. Their use proliferated widely. (Kaplan & Saccuzzo, 1989, pp. 15–16)

The goals of education had not changed, but differentiated high schools tracked students toward college and others toward blue collar jobs as determined by their scores on standardized tests. Testing students enabled educational systems to sort students efficiently but not equitably. This system did not benefit members of what we currently refer to as subgroups—who did not score as well on tests contextualized in the culture and norms of the dominant group (Shea, 1977). The stage was set for the standards-based movement.

Critiques of Public Education

The publication of *Why Johnny Can't Read* (Flesch, 1955) challenged the notion that our schools were effective. The launch of Sputnik in 1957 (Garber, 2007) built on Cold War anxieties to support the claim that U.S. education was inferior to that of the Soviet Union.

In a move that enlarged the federal government's role in education far beyond anything that had been done before, Congress passed the Elementary and Secondary Education Act of 1965 (ESEA) as part of President Lyndon B. Johnson's War on Poverty. Building on the goals of the civil rights movement and designed to improve educational equity, ESEA was "the first major social legislation to mandate project reporting" (McLaughlin, 2011, p. v). The evaluation requirement of ESEA was intended to provide political accountability so that local constituents would be able to see if the money from the federal government was being spent appropriately to improve the education of disadvantaged students. Among the goals was that federal management of education programs would be modeled on business accounting methods. Data would be presented in "cost-benefit terms … leading to more effective local practices and more efficient federal decision making" (p. v). There was opposition to ESEA policies by those who "contended that evaluation was inconsistent with best practice in that it consumed already limited program resources and employed invidious and inappropriate measures of 'success'—achievement scores" (p. v).

Concerns about the quality of public education in the U.S. crystalized with the publication of *A Nation at Risk* (Gardner, 1983), a product of the National Commission on Excellence in Education. The report was not described as a representation of scientific research; rather, it was framed as the opinions of the Commission. The Commission examined existing reports commissioned from experts, but it also depended on public hearings, symposiums, meetings, and letters. The report also relied on conjecture founded on "descriptions of notable programs and promising approaches" (pp. 2–3). The author commended the "public-minded citizens who took the trouble to share their concerns … [and noted the] diversity of opinion it received regarding the condition of American education, [commenting that] … how we have treated their suggestions is, of course, our responsibility alone" (p. 3).

When *A Nation at Risk* was published, it was considered reliable evidence of the failure of American education, and this perception remains, for the most part, widely accepted today. As recently as 2009, Educational Testing Service, a powerful advocate for the standards-based movement, claimed the report sounded the "call" for educational reform (Barton, p. 3). While *A Nation at Risk* was highly influential in stoking concerns about the quality of public education, a closer examination of the report reveals the flaws in its findings.

A Nation at Risk presented a series of claims that the United States was "being overtaken by competitors throughout the world" (p. 5), that American education was "mediocre" (p. 5), and that the country had "lost sight of the basic purposes of schooling" (p. 5). The document supplied a list of risk indicators: poor U.S. performance compared to international competitors on academic tests; high illiteracy; poor achievement on standardized tests; poor performance of gifted students; decline in the scores on the Scholastic Assessment Test (SAT), and low levels of higher order intellectual skills; a preponderance of remedial courses required for those entering college; lower college exit scores; and complaints from business and the military that entry level students lacked basic math and reading skills. Here, the report sounded a dire warning: "We are raising a new generation of Americans that is scientifically and technologically illiterate" (p. 10).

Researchers at Sandia Laboratories investigated the claims of the National Commission on Excellence in Education. Overall, their evidence contradicted *A Nation at Risk*, finding that "the present system [of education] has shown a steady or improving trend" (Huelskamp, 1993, p. 718). Their analysis of high school graduation rates found that when including students who took longer than four years to complete high school, or who later obtained a GED, graduation rates had remained stable, and were "among the best in the world" (p. 719). They evaluated SAT and National Assessment of Educational Progress (NAEP) and found gradual improvement in the NAEP scores, and misrepresentation of the *meaning* of the decline in SAT scores; that is, that the decline in scores was a natural consequence of a (desirable) *increase* in the participation of low-achieving students and those from formerly underrepresented groups. They dismissed the international comparisons as not meeting their expectations for the appropriateness of the comparisons. They concluded that U.S. students were performing well compared to their international counterparts.

Because of the lack of rigor associated with the data collection, analysis, and conclusions of *A Nation at Risk*, it is appropriate to discount it as political posturing. Nonetheless, *A Nation at Risk* was highly influential in driving the standards-based movement. Public education was now expected to be competitive. This new emphasis pitted the U.S. against international rivals in a contest to produce the largest gross national product and be the greatest influence on the world. This change in the *goals* of education came with the clamor for a dramatic reform of public education. Higher standards and testing would be key components of this movement. The next section will cover the rise of the privatization of testing, the increase in large-scale, high-stakes standards-based tests, and it will examine the most recent federal reform initiatives.

Current Standardization

Formerly relying on off-the-shelf standardized products from the testing industry, states now sought to match testing materials with their specific curriculum and standards. By the mid-1990s, test publishing companies were contracted by states to help design these assessment materials (Jorgensen & Hoffman, 2003). This rise of a profit-driven testing materials industry was a consequence of the refocusing of national and state education policies on standards and accountability.

With the 2002 reauthorization of ESEA as *No Child Left Behind* (NCLB) (No Child Left Behind Act of 2001, 2002), a new "accountability regime" (McGuinn, 2006, p. 194) completed the move from the War on Poverty's focus on equity to improved education for "all students … with increased accountability for school performance" (p. 194). While NCLB intended to reduce federal influence over education, it is widely accepted that it enlarged the federal role (Education Week, 2004). In order to continue to receive federal funding, states, districts, and schools were mandated to test virtually all students annually and to meet targets for achievement on the tests. NCLB mandated that all public school children be "proficient" (i.e., at grade level) in reading and math by the end of the 2013–2014 school year, as measured by standardized tests (ALSDE, 2011).

Criticism of the standardization movement persisted but, as of 2010, not much had changed since the publication of *A Nation at Risk* in the political framing of education in America as failing. In *A Blue Print for Reform* (U.S. DOE), national goals for education were articulated in terms of competition. President Barack Obama noted that "the countries that out-educate us today will out-compete us tomorrow" (p. 1), echoing the competitive/alarmist language of *A Nation at Risk*.

Comparing the educational system of the United States to that of other countries is an "apples and oranges" endeavor. A critical concept presented by Darling-Hammond (2007) is that "most high-achieving countries not only provide high-quality universal preschool and healthcare for children, they also fund their schools centrally and equally, with additional funds going to the neediest schools" (p. 3). Darling-Hammond reported that successful school systems in other countries had high-quality teacher preparation and professional development programs, while NCLB (ironically) called for "alternative routes that often reduce training for the teachers of the poor" (p. 3).

Furthermore, Herman (2008) suggested that "there is only so much that public schools can do to close an achievement gap that grows out of greater social and historical inequities" (p. 227). He recommended health care clinics at schools; comprehensive early childhood education, and intensive after-school/summer school programs; higher teacher salaries; and smaller class sizes.

The demands of the standards-based movement increased with the mandates of NCLB: states, districts, schools, administrators, teachers, and students were now to be evaluated on the basis of students' scores on annual high-stakes tests. A business model was applied to educational policies and practice. In a capitalistic culture, companies that cannot compete go out of business. In applying these principles to education, schools were labeled as "failing." Calls for parental choice and vouchers permeated the rhetoric of reform. Some schools were taken over by the state; others were closed (Wallis, 2008).

President Obama's *American Recovery and Reinvestment Act of 2009* (H. R. 1—111th Congress, 2012) provided funding for education in the form of the *Race to the Top* funding, which offered competitive grants for innovations that were expected to improve student outcomes as evidenced by "increased productivity and effectiveness" (U.S. DOE, 2009, p. 2). In recent years, attention has been focused on standards for high school graduates. Adoption of high school exit examinations attempts to certify what students have learned; the newest goal for high school students is that they graduate "college and career ready" (U.S. DOE, 2010a).

The goals of American education have slowly, incrementally, and inexorably been transformed from a system that produced an informed electorate to a system that efficiently prepared skilled workers.

STANDARDIZATION VERSUS DIFFERENTIATION

Educational pedagogy can be divided into two contrasting practices, standardization and differentiation (Noddings, 2010). Proponents of standardization have successfully advocated for state adoption of common core standards, benchmark assessments, and rigorous tests as prerequisites to earning a high school diploma (Achieve, 2012). The theory that underlies standardization is instructionism (Papert, 1993). Instructionism is a vision of knowledge as a collection of facts and procedures that teachers transmit to students. One assumption of instructionism is that "the way to determine the success of schooling is to test students to see how many of these facts and procedures they have acquired" (Sawyer, 2006, p. 1). The U.S. Department of Education (US DOE) advocated for standardization (U.S. DOE, 2010a, 2010b; U.S. DOE Office of Vocational and Adult Education, 2012) in the latest round of education reform. Other powerful advocates for standardization, American corporations and business leaders, have:

> articulated a powerful and steady vision for the standards-based reform movement to policymakers, educators, parents, students and the public about the urgency of school reform. This school reform movement rests on high academic standards, rigorous assessments that measure achievement and real accountability for results at all levels of the education system. (Business Tools for Better Schools, 2012, para. 2)

While some promote standardization, others argue for differentiation (Noddings, 2010). Teachers rarely teach in homogenous classrooms; usually their students have "significant differences in learning styles, skill and ability, and linguistic and cultural background. These differences make the 'one size fits all' principle inoperative" (Smutny, 2003, p. 7). General education teachers face the additional challenges of inclusion of children with disabilities and greater numbers of students for whom English is a second language. "Without question, one of the primary concerns of classroom teachers throughout the nation is how to meet the ever increasing diverse learning needs of students in our classrooms today" (Wood, 2002, p. 155).

The theory that underlies differentiation is constructivism (Piaget & Gabain, 1932; Vygotsky & Cole, 1978). Constructivism is antithetical to instructionism. Rather than seeing a student as a recipient of knowledge, in a constructivist classroom, a student *constructs* knowledge by interacting with the environment in developmental stages such as concrete and abstract operations (Piaget & Gabain, 1932).

A student constructs meaning as a result of interacting with content that is within that individual's zone of proximal development (Vygotsky & Cole, 1978). Cognitive or learning science elaborates on these theories. The learning sciences incorporate "the importance of deeper understanding ... focusing on student learning in addition to teaching ... creating learning environments ... the importance of building on a learner's prior knowledge, [and] ... the importance of reflection" (Sawyer, 2006, p. 2). Sawyer contrasted instructionism with "learning knowledge deeply [based on] findings from cognitive science" (p. 4).

The binary (Derrida, 1976; Saussure, Bally, Sechehaye, & Riedlinger, 1949) is an analytic tool that reveals the power assigned and denied to the two sides of a dichotomous sort. It has been used to explain the power of racial assumptions (Said, 1978) and the rationalization of gender as a natural phenomenon, as contrasted to the constructed assignment of personality traits (West & Fenstermaker, 1995; West & Zimmerman, 1987). Table 1 presents a binary that sorts into two categories standardized and differentiated educational practices and the policies that support these visions. The half of the binary that assumes a more prestigious and powerful position in this binary sort is standardized education, which comes at the expense of the attributes of differentiated education.

Narrowing the Curriculum

As a result of the standards-based movement—and in service of producing higher scores on standardized tests—the curriculum has been narrowed (Gunzenhauser, 2003; King & Zucker, 2005; Mathis, 2003; Pedulla et al., 2003; Vogler, 2003). The greatest effect has been in the schools with the highest proportion of minority populations (Von Zastrow & Janc, 2004). Content that does not relate directly to tested objectives is reduced or eliminated, and social studies is among the casualties (Duncan, 2011, p. 124). Social studies curriculum, as defined by the National Council for the Social Studies guidelines, is the location of instructional

Table 1 Dichotomous Sort of Accountability Concepts

Standardized	Differentiated
Commerce; business; industry; technological innovation; blueprint	Educated populace; enlightened participation; respect for the individual; personal agency
Cost-benefit; inputs/outputs; efficiency	Optimal outcomes for individuals
Produces workers; world markets	Individual responsibility, freedom, and benefits
Competition to succeed; winners and losers	Collaboration among peers
Accountability; blame, failure	Support; professional development
Sanctions, punishment; choice, privatization	Funding; opportunity to learn; equitable facilities
High standards; setting the bar high	Zone of proximal development (ZPD); Response to Intervention (RTI)
High expectations for all students	Optimal outcomes for each student
High school diploma based on passing proficiency exams (Algebra II, etc.)	Various levels of diplomas with certifications for Algebra II and other gateway courses
Meritocracy/sorting of students by "ability" to prepare them for jobs in business and industry	Respect for the individual; play is the work of children; constructivism; active learning; higher-order thinking skills, creativity, entrepreneurship
Quantitative research	Qualitative research
Large-scale testing; accountability	Needs of the whole child; school climate
Summative assessments drive performance	Formative assessments inform instruction
Measuring for effective teachers (VAM)	Teacher-learning communities
Testing; measurement	Active learning; SEL, developing human consciousness, social responsibility, life skills
Teacher-dominated classroom	Student-centered classroom
Science, Technology, Engineering, and Mathematics (STEM)	Foreign languages, vocational shops, history, political science, art, music, theater, sports, citizenship, philosophy, physical education, health education, family and consumer studies
B.F. Skinner, Adam Smith, *A Nation at Risk*	Vygotsky, Piaget, Dewey, Jefferson, Du Bois

themes including "power, authority, governance" (2013, para. 32). Narrowing the curriculum to exclude social studies is not likely to have a positive effect on voter participation. The next section will describe a study that analyzed the relationship of variables that represented standardized education and voter turnout.

THE STUDY

The study was an exploratory investigation that examined the relationship between states' educational standardization and voter turnout using cultural and critical theory lenses and quantitative methods. The study developed a tool for measuring states' levels of educational standardization, the *Standardized Education Index* (SEI), drawing on the *Creativity Index* developed by Richard Florida (2002). While Florida's creativity index identified four contextual or environmental indicators that correlated with the presence of what he termed the *creative class*, the SEI identified nine indicators of standardized education to measure states' level of educational standardization (see Table 2 below). Florida described a set of places that he termed "creative centers" (p. 218). His research showed that the geographic

Table 2 SEI Indicator Descriptions

Indicator	Title	Description
1	Standards	Align high school standards with the expectations of college and careers
2	High school diploma	Align high school graduation requirements with college- and career-ready expectations
3	Assessment	Develop college- and career-ready assessment systems
4	P-20	Develop P-20 longitudinal data systems
5	Accountability	Develop accountability and reporting systems that promote college and career readiness
6	College- and career-ready goals	Member of Achieve's American Diploma Project Network
7	Standardized growth model across states	Member of Partnership for Assessment of Readiness for College and Career
8	Leader in standardizing science	Next Generation Science Standards Lead Partner
9	Common core standards	Adopted Common Core Standards for math and English language arts

areas that qualified as creative centers were magnets for the creative class and primed these regions for economic growth. The SEI was used to investigate relationships between states' SEI scores and their levels of voter turnout. A state's SEI score was calculated using a counting system ranging from 0 to 9, with zero assigned to a state with no indicators of a standardized educational context, and 9 being the strongest indicator of a standardized educational context.

The other variable in the study was state voter turnout. The United States Election Project (USEP) (McDonald, 2013) reported voter turnout by state for national elections. USEP data from the four presidential general elections from 2000 to 2012 for both VAP and VEP participation levels were used.

The study asked the question: is there a relationship between a state's level of educational standardization (as measured by the SEI) and its voter turnout in national general elections? Correlation analysis was run for all U.S. states to discover any relationships between state SEI scores and McDonald's report of state VEP and VAP turnout for 2000, 2004, 2008, and 2012.

A weak correlation was found between the SEI and voter turnout in all eight analyses; when the SEI score decreased, voter turnout *increased* with between 6% and 14% of variability explained. While some of these results may have been due to random sampling variability, four of the correlations were significant ($p < .05$): VEP and VAP for 2000 and VAP for 2004 and 2008. While this evidence did not provide compelling support for a significant correlation between low SEI and higher voter turnout in general, no evidence of a positive relationship between higher levels of SEI and higher voter turnout was found. With currently articulated goals of global economic competiveness, it is not surprising that the standards-based movement was not correlated with voter participation.

Figure 3 displays regression lines that trend from the upper left to the lower right; the higher the voter turnout, the lower the SEI score. The problem of low, varying, and fluctuating voter turnout remains a problem that can and should be addressed by K-12 public education.

DISCUSSION

The literature and research reported in this chapter made the case that there is a problem with voting in the U.S. evidenced by low voter turnout compared with other nations, variability of voter turnout among states, fluctuation in turnout from year to year, and variation in participation between groups.

That higher levels of education result in increased participation in elections has been a common assumption based on unidirectional nature of a proven relationship, but relative education explains more variation than absolute education. Being better educated than peers predicts more successful outcomes as compared

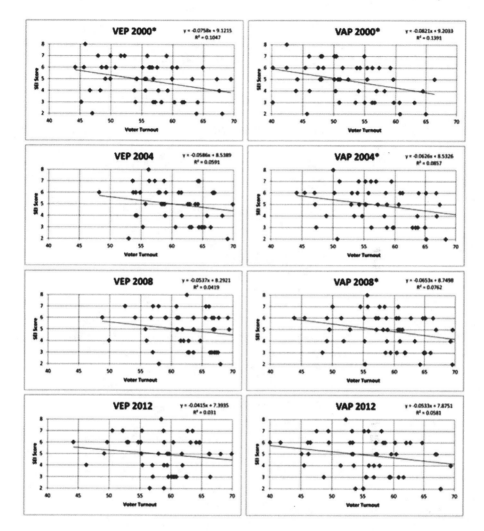

Fig 3. Correlations for VEP and VAP 2000–2012 with SEI score.
* Correlation is significant, p< .05.

to those peers for a variety of measures, including voter participation. The importance of relative education was highlighted as a proven moderator to obstacles to voting including mobility and institutional impediments.

Evidence was presented that traced the transformation of the goals for public education from producing an informed electorate to producing skilled workers efficiently in service of global economic competitiveness. What is lost in the emphasis on standardization of public education is differentiation of instruction to meet the unique needs of learners. Narrowing of the curriculum was described as a natural consequence of standards-based reform that has led to a reduction in social studies instruction. For social justice advocates, the marginalizing of social studies instruction is problematic because civic knowledge is part of the expected content of that discipline.

The study found a relationship between a state's level of standardization of education, as measured by the SEI, and its level of voter participation. While no causal relationship was claimed, it can be said that there is some evidence that the more *standardized* a state's educational system is, the more likely it is that the state has a *lower voter turnout*. The exploratory nature of the study enables it to serve as a baseline for further investigation of the relationship of educational standardization to voter participation. However, teachers with a disposition to promote social justice can work to gain a higher level of equity for marginalized groups through participation in democracy (i.e., voting).

CONCLUSION

This chapter can contribute to the discussion of educator dispositions in several ways. It enables current teachers, future teachers, and those who direct teacher education programs to recognize the need for a greater commitment to instruction in the skills and attitudes associated with active participation in a democracy. The K-12 public education system, rather than continuing to serve a tool of corporate dominance (as is arguably the effect of the standards-based movement), can be a source of renewed urgency to foster democracy.

When Dr. Martin Luther King (1947) advocated for the educational goal of "intelligence plus character" (para. 5), he warned that "education which stops with efficiency may prove the greatest menace to society" (para. 3). Standardization of education is premised on faith in efficiency as the ultimate arbitrator of what works in K-12 public education. What is lost in the reframing of educational goals is the opportunity to empower our students. Empowerment in a democracy ultimately depends on voting, and voter participation in the U.S. is subject to great variability in part due to unequal access to the process of voting. Education has a powerful moderating effect that can increase the probability that an individual will vote. The standardization movement is designed to prepare workers for the global economy, and evidence shows that it does not improve the chances that citizens will vote.

In 1906, W. E. B. Du Bois (1970) delivered the *Niagara Address*. Du Bois called for real education for Blacks, by which he meant "the development of power and ideal ... a right to know, to think, to aspire" (p. 172), which he contrasted with schools whose purpose is "to educate black boys and girls simply as servants and underlings, or simply for the use of other people" (p. 172). We should take heed of Du Bois' challenge to provide education that leads individuals out of servitude. With the engagement of dispositions that embrace democratic ideals of personal empowerment, teachers have the power to teach the thought processes and behaviors that lead to active civic participation.

REFERENCES

Achieve. (2012). Achieving the common core. Retrieved May 20, 2012, from http://www.achieve.org/achieving-common-core

ALSDE. (2011, July 2009). Accountability: Frequently asked questions. Retrieved June 21, 2011, from https://docs.alsde.edu/documents/91/Accountability%20FAQs%202009.pdf

American Recovery and Reinvestment Act of 2009 (2012). Retrieved March 26, 2012, from http://www.gpo.gov/fdsys/pkg/BILLS-111hr1enr/pdf/BILLS-111hr1enr.pdf

Arkansas DOE. (2013). Comprehensive Testing, Assessment and Accountability Program and the Academic Distress Program. Arkansas, AR: Arkansas Department of Education.

Barton, P. E. (2009). National education standards: Getting beneath the surface. Retrieved from the Education Testing Service website: http://www.ets.org/research/policy_research_reports/publications/report/2009/hhor

Baum, S., Ma, J., & Payea, K. (2010). Education pays 2010: The benefits of higher education for individuals and society. Retrieved July 18, 2012, from Trends in Higher Education website: http://trends.collegeboard.org/sites/default/files/education-pays-2010-full-report.pdf

Bird, W. L., Campbell, K., & Briggs, N. (2012). Vote: The machinery of democracy. Retrieved August 24, 2012, from http://americanhistory.si.edu/vote/intro.html

Brody, R. A. (1978). The puzzle of political participation in America. In S. H. Beer & A. King (Eds.), The new American political system. Washington, DC: American Enterprise Institute for Public Policy Research.

Burden, B. C. (2009). The dynamic effects of education on voter turnout. Electoral Studies, 28(4), 540–549.

Business Tools for Better Schools. (2012). Business leadership of education reform. Retrieved May 23, 2012, from http://www.biztools4schools.org/what_business_has_already_done

Common Cause. (2013a). Facts on media in America: Did you know? Retrieved July 21, 2013, from http://www.presidency.ucsb.edu/ws/?pid=15545

Common Cause. (2013b). Media and democracy reform initiative. Retrieved July 21, 2013, from http://www.commoncause.org/atf/cf/%7Bfb3c17e2-cdd1-4df6-92be-bd4429893665%7D/M&DOVERVIEW.PDF

Converse, P. E., & Campbell, A. (1972). The human meaning of social change. New York, NY: Russell Sage Foundation.

Dahl, R. A. (1971). Polyarchy: Participation and opposition. New Haven, CT: Yale University Press.

Dahl, R. A. (2012). Democracy. Retrieved August 24, 2012, from http://www.britannica.com/EBchecked/topic/157129/democracy

Darling-Hammond, L. (2007). Evaluating "No Child Left Behind." The Nation. Retrieved from http://www.thenation.com/article/evaluating-no-child-left-behind#

Dee, T. S. (2004). Are there civic returns to education? Journal of Public Economics, 88(9–10), 1697–1720. doi: 10.1016/j.jpubeco.2003.11.002

Derrida, J. (1976). *Of grammatology*. Baltimore, MD: Johns Hopkins University Press.

Du Bois, W. E. B. (1970). *W. E. B. Du Bois speaks: Speeches and addresses*. New York, NY: Pathfinder Press.

Duncan, A. (2011). The social studies are essential to a well-rounded education. *Social Education*, *75*(3), 124–125.

Education Week. (2004). No Child Left Behind. Retrieved June 21, 2011, from http://www.edweek.org/ew/issues/no-child-left-behind/

Federal Communications Commission. (2013). Telecommunications Act of 1996. Retrieved July 21, 2013, from http://transition.fcc.gov/telecom.html

Flesch, R. (1955). *Why Johnny can't read*. New York, NY: Harper & Row.

Florida, R. L. (2002). *The rise of the creative class: And how it's transforming work, leisure, community and everyday life*. New York, NY: Basic Books.

Freedman, P., Franz, M., & Goldstein, K. (2004). Campaign advertising and democratic citizenship. *American Journal of Political Science*, *48*(4), 723–741.

Garber, S. (2007). Sputnik and the dawn of the space age. Retrieved August 5, 2012, from http://history.nasa.gov/sputnik/

Gardner, D. P., & Associates (1983). *A nation at risk: The imperative for educational reform. An open letter to the American people. A report to the nation and the secretary of education*. Retrieved from the United States Department of Education website: https://www2.ed.gov/pubs/NatAtRisk/risk.html

Goodwyn, L. (1978). *The Populist moment: A short history of the agrarian revolt in America*. New York, NY: Oxford University Press.

Gunzenhauser, M. G. (2003). High-stakes testing and the default philosophy of education. *Theory into Practice*, *42*(1), 51–58.

Haygood, R. P. (2012). The past as prologue: Defending democracy against voter suppression tactics on the eve of the 2012 elections. *Journal of Law & Education*, *64*(4), 1019–1064.

Heck, R. H. (2004). *Studying educational and social policy: Theoretical concepts and research methods*. Mahwah, NJ: Lawrence Erlbaum Associates.

Heck, R. H. (2007). Examining the relationship between teacher quality as an organizational property of schools and students' achievement and growth rates. *Educational Administration Quarterly*, *43*(4), 399–432.

Herman, J. L. (2008). Accountability and assessment: Is public interest in K-12 education being served? In K. E. Ryan & L. A. Shepard (Eds.), *The future of test-based educational accountability* (pp. 211–231). New York, NY: Routledge.

Huelskamp, R. M. (1993). Perspectives on education in America. *Phi Delta Kappan*, *74*(9), 718(714).

International IDEA. (2012). International voter turnout, 1991–2000. Retrieved May 3, 2012, from http://archive.fairvote.org/turnout/intturnout.htm

Jefferson, T. (1820). Educating the people. Retrieved May 12, 2012, from http://www.famguardian.org/Subjects/Politics/ThomasJefferson/jeff1350.htm

Jorgensen, M. A., & Hoffman, J. (2003). History of the No Child Left Behind Act of 2001 (NCLB). Retrieved June 21, 2011, from http://images.pearsonassessments.com/images/tmrs/tmrs_rg/HistoryofNCLB.pdf?WT.mc_id=TMRS_History_of_the_No_Child_Left_Behind

Kaplan, R. M., & Saccuzzo, D. P. (1989). *Psychological testing: Principles, applications, and issues*. Pacific Grove, CA: Brooks/Cole.

King, M. L. (1947). The purpose of education. Retrieved from http://www.drmartinlutherkingjr.com/thepurposeofeducation.htm

King, K. V., & Zucker, S. (2005). Curriculum narrowing. Retrieved January 15, 2013, from http://images.pearsonassessments.com/images/tmrs/tmrs_rg/CurriculumNarrowing.pdf?WT.mc_id=T-MRS_Curriculum_Narrowing

Lassen, D. D. (2005). The effect of information on voter turnout: Evidence from a natural experiment. *American Journal of Political Science, 49*(1), 103–118.

Mathis, W. J. (2003). No Child Left Behind: Costs and benefits. *Phi Delta Kappan, 84*(9), 679–686.

McDonald, M. (2012a, December 31). 2012 General Election turnout rates. Retrieved January 16, 2013, from http://elections.gmu.edu/Turnout_2012G.html

McDonald, M. (2012b). Voter turnout. Retrieved December 18, 2012, from http://elections.gmu.edu/voter_turnout.htm

McDonald, M. (2013). United States elections project. Retrieved January 9, 2013, from http://elections.gmu.edu/index.html

McGuinn, P. J. (2006). *No Child Left Behind and the transformation of federal education policy, 1965–2005.* Lawrence, KS: University Press of Kansas.

McLaughlin, M. W. (2011). Evaluation and reform: The Elementary and Secondary Education Act of 1965, Title I. Retrieved June 20, 2011, from http://www.rand.org/content/dam/rand/pubs/reports/2009/R1292.pdf

Mintz, S., & McNeil, S. (2012). Progressivism. Retrieved February 13, 2013, from http://www.digitalhistory.uh.edu/disp_textbook.cfm?smtID=2&psid=3132

Misco, T., & Shiveley, J. (2007). Making sense of dispositions in teacher education: Arriving at democratic aims and experiences. *Journal of Educational Controversy, 2*(2). Retrieved from http://www.wce.wwu.edu/Resources/CEP/ejournal/v002n002/a012.shtml

NCSS. (2013). *National Curriculum Standards for Social Studies: Chapter 2—The Themes of Social Studies.* Retrieved March 16, 2012, from http://www.socialstudies.org/standards/strands

No Child Left Behind Act of 2001, 1425, Pub. L. No. 107–110 U.S.C. § 115, Stat. 1425 (2002).

Noddings, N. (2010). Differentiate, don't standardize. Retrieved May 20, 2012, from http://www.edweek.org/ew/articles/2010/01/14/17noddings-comm.h29.html

Papert, S. (1993). *The children's machine: Rethinking school in the age of the computer.* New York, NY: Basic Books.

Pedulla, J. J., Abrams, L. M., Madaus, G. F., Russell, M. K., Ramos, M. A., & Miao, J. (2003). Perceived effects of state-mandated testing programs on teaching and learning: Findings from a national survey of teachers. *National Board on Educational Testing and Public Policy.* Chestnut Hill, MA: Boston College.

Piaget, J., & Gabain, M. (1932). *The moral judgment of the child.* London, England: K. Paul, Trench, Trubner & Co.

Rosen, G. (1958). *A history of public health.* New York, NY: MD Publications.

Said, E. W. (1978). *Orientalism.* New York, NY: Pantheon Books.

Saussure, F. D., Bally, C., Sechehaye, A., & Riedlinger, A. (1949). *Cours de linguistique générale.* Paris, France: Payot.

Sawyer, R. K. (2006). *The Cambridge handbook of the learning sciences.* Cambridge, England; New York, NY: Cambridge University Press.

Shea, T. E. (1977). An educational perspective of the legality of intelligence testing and ability grouping. *Journal of Law & Education, 6*(2), 137–158.

Smutny, J. F. (2003). *Differentiated instruction.* Bloomington, IN: Phi Delta Kappa Educational Foundation.

Sondheimer, R. M., & Green, D. P. (2010). Using experiments to estimate the effects of education on voter turnout. *American Journal of Political Science, 54*(1), 174–189.

Squire, P., Wolfinger, R. E., & Glass, D. P. (1987). Residential mobility and voter turnout. *The American Political Science Review, 81*(1), 45–66.

Tenn, S. (2005). An alternative measure of relative education to explain voter turnout. *The Journal of Politics, 67*(1), 271–282. doi: 10.1111/j.1468-2508.2005.00317.x

Tristan, J. M. B. (2013). Henry Giroux: The necessity of critical pedagogy in dark times Retrieved July 21, 2013, from http://truth-out.org/news/item/14331-a-critical-interview-with-henry-giroux

U.S. Census Bureau. (2012). Elections: Voting-age population and voter participation. Retrieved May 23, 2012, from http://www.census.gov/compendia/statab/cats/elections/voting-age_population_and_voter_participation.html

U.S. DOE. (2010a). *A Blueprint for Reform: The Reauthorization of the Elementary and Secondary Education Act.* Washington, DC: U.S. Department of Education. Retrieved from http://www2.ed.gov/policy/elsec/leg/blueprint/blueprint.pdf

U.S. DOE. (2010b). *College- and Career-Ready Standards and Assessments.* Retrieved May 18, 2012, from http://www2.ed.gov/policy/elsec/leg/blueprint/faq/college-career.pdf

U.S. DOE Office of Vocational and Adult Education. (2012). Investing in America's Future: A Blueprint for Transforming Career and Technical Education. Retrieved May 17, 2012, from http://www2.ed.gov/about/offices/list/ovae/pi/cte/transforming-career-technical-education.pdf

Villegas, A. M. (2007). Dispositions in teacher education: A look at social justice. *Journal of Teacher Education, 58*(370), 370–380.

Vogler, K. (2003). Where does social studies fit in a high-stakes testing environment? *The Social Studies, 94*(5), 207–211.

Von Zastrow, C., & Janc, H. (2004). *Academic atrophy: The condition of the Liberal Arts in America's public schools.* Washington, DC: Council for Basic Education.

Vygotsky, L. S., & Cole, M. (1978). *Mind in society: The development of higher psychological processes.* Cambridge, MA: Harvard University Press.

Wallis, C. (2008). No Child Left Behind: Doomed to fail? Retrieved February 29, 2012, from http://www.time.com/time/printout/0,8816,1812758,00.html#

West, C., & Fenstermaker, S. (1995). Doing difference. *Gender and Society, 9*(1), 8–37.

West, C., & Zimmerman, D. H. (1987). Doing gender. *Gender and Society, 1*(2), 125–151.

Wood, K. D. (2002). Differentiating reading and writing lessons to promote content learning. In C. C. Block, L. B. Gambrell, & M. Pressley (Eds.), *Improving comprehension instruction: Rethinking research, theory, and classroom practice.* San Francisco, CA: Jossey-Bass.

CHAPTER TWELVE

CSFE Principles

Wise and Effective Mechanisms to Translate Social Foundations Content to K-12 Classroom Practice

JACQUELYN BENCHIK-OSBORNE

DIFFERENT CONCEPTS—DIFFERENT PERSPECTIVES

As a scholar of social foundations of education (SFE), I struggled with the connection of dispositions, standards, and SFE as a way to serve teachers. The three concepts share a common thread: They focus on strengths and qualities of good teaching. But what constitutes good teaching?

SFE grounds itself within a field committed to students and teachers in community. SFE studies

> schools and explore[s] why we do the things we do, where current practices come from, what values they reflect, and what alternative options exist. That is, as we often say, we help people to think interpretively, critically, and normatively about education. As part of doing this work, we offer narratives of hope and possibility within education. We also share overlapping commitments: to democracy, diversity, equity, inclusion, empowerment, reflexivity, and equality of opportunity. We foreground the political nature of all educational choices and seek out the most ethically defensible pedagogical practices. (Hytten, 2010, p. 156)

SFE looks "to examine fundamental and urgent social problems and issues" (Warren, 1998, p. 120). The problems and the people involved in solving the issues are embedded within community. Issues arise and achieve resolution within the social context of learning (Murrell, 2002).

Dispositions study the person, but the emphasis shifts. Where SFE focuses its efforts on the teacher within the social fabric of the classroom, dispositions examine the person as an individual. Villegas (2007) defined dispositions as "tendencies for individuals to act in a particular manner under particular circumstances, based on their beliefs" (p. 373). The study of beliefs opens the door to look at how and in what ways the individual thinks and acts. The tasks of the person influence the group but the priority is committed to the type of individual the teacher is.

To understand these tendencies of belief, Shiveley and Misco (2009) operationalized and assessed dispositions. They mapped teacher success as exhibited within the vocabulary of dispositions. They coordinated a teacher education program to specific courses, providing students opportunity to rehearse skills committed to individual qualities such as reflection, leadership, and critical analysis, based on frameworks devised by governing bodies, such as the National Council of Accreditation of Teacher Education (NCATE).

SFE, focused on community learning and problem solving, differs from dispositions, concentrated on the beliefs of the individual teacher. Standards take on another distinct angle, varying in perspective from both dispositions and SFE. Lubinski and Otto (2004) explained that use of standards provides a richer grasp to processing content.

For example, instead of memorizing math formulas to plug in correct answers, pre-service teachers saw an increase in the level of analytical depth when multiple problem-solving strategies, matched to explicit math standards, were incorporated within math instruction (Lubinski & Otto, 2004). Malina, Plunk, and Lindell (2006) identified a similar outcome when instructing pre-service teachers with the use of a standards-based science curriculum:

> Student perceptions of the course indicated that activities helped them learn the science content, science techniques and methods, and how to use technology. Students indicated that the activities helped them think for themselves about a level and amount of content that was appropriate for their background. (p. 22)

Standards-based instruction explicitly applies content, and encourages the development of thinking independently. Teachers analyze subject matter, plan instruction, and design assessment with greater insight and intensity.

But, the specific tasks outlined within standards challenge both SFE and the study of dispositions. Standards imply a set path to task completion with clear understanding of content and instructional delivery (Mulcahy, 2011). Dispositions seek further, deeper meaning for what it means to be teacher (Splitter, 2010). And, SFE is focused on the classroom context in which teacher and students take an active social role to support and enhance the classroom learning context through question and analysis (Laird, 1998; Giroux, 1985). These many-layered distinctions are what make SFE, dispositions, and standards hard to navigate in an integrated fashion. These three specific concentrations contain distinct and separate content, points-of-view, and perspectives.

Will the use of standards inform the depth of dispositions as well as respect the variation and difference valued within the community context of SFE? How could this triad of concepts work in concert with one another?

DO STANDARDS HELP SUPPORT TEACHERS?—BALANCING THE PRAGMATIC AND THE CIVIC FOCUS

The integration of standards, dispositions, and SFE requires teacher educators to map different vocabularies and concepts to support classroom teachers. How do instructors apply the language of SFE to their instructional practice? Is that bridge between theory of SFE and dispositions operationalized to explicitly assist teacher candidates and experienced instructors alike? Dottin, Simpson, & Watras (2005) spoke to this challenge: The avenue to attain such a goal may be the application of standards.

The precise use of standards helps teachers identify what is important to say and do when instructing (Baker & Digiovanni, 2005; Andrzejewski, Baltodano, & Symcox, 2009). For example, Bailey (2010) identified that when teachers engaged in well-organized professional development to plan math lessons matched to standards-based instruction at the second-and third-grade level, the following data were noted:

> Only 31% of teachers indicated that their ability to prepare interactive homework assignments, design assessments and engage students in instruction was effective on the pretest, while 78% deemed their ability to complete these same tasks "highly effective" on the posttest. (p.130)

After the intervention of clearly matching instructional planning to standards, the almost 50% increase in ability to provide instructional delivery and assessment design was striking. Helping teachers to become conscious of standards remarkably enhanced instructional delivery.

The explicit use of standards to SFE content is much needed (Dottin, 2011). But, not all SFE scholars want to see a match between the field and standards-based instruction. As Dottin et al. (2005) explained:

> To many advocates of social foundations, the idea of standards and the processes of accreditation contradict the aims of deep thought and careful analysis that foundations scholars pursue…. Other critics argue…teaching appear(s) to be a list of skills and information prospective candidates must master. These are exactly the kinds of questions that foundations scholars should raise. (p. 253)

However, Tozer and Miretzky (2000) argued that a relationship between standards and SFE serves one another extremely well. Standards help inform instruction (Tozer & Miretzky, 2005). Inclusion of SFE standards provides an opportunity for teachers to explicitly identify and apply content rooted in the social lives of the children served. Dottin (2011) indicated that SFE standards situate the teacher as scholar to judge such measures as a tool, while also employing the instrument to her practice. As an example, Murrell (2001) and Ladson-Billings (1994) illustrated how teachers connect books and historical events based on the needs of their group. Food, music, clothing, and reading materials familiar to the neighborhood community help to contextualize the grounding of the curriculum for the students. The content is learned but then also analyzed to the social fabric of the everyday experiences the children encounter.

In tying standards to SFE within a practical and applicable frame, the Principles from the Council of Social Foundations of Education (CSFE, 2000) may be that needed anchor for experienced instructors, future student teacher candidates, and teacher educators. The intent of the CSFE Principles, from its inception, connects theory of SFE to the practice of classroom teaching. Its commitment to integrate the social world to content results in rich analysis, critique, and substance.

For teacher educators, especially, the CSFE could be the vehicle to demonstrate to student teachers how to combine the social world within teaching practice. The Principles offer a way to identify the extent to which teacher candidates connect the social world to classroom content.

CSFE PRINCIPLES INFORM SFE STANDARDS

The CSFE Principles, listed below, function as a service to support both student teachers and classroom instructors as they incorporate SFE content overall and democratic practice in particular:

- *Principle #1:* The educator understands and can apply disciplinary knowledge from the humanities and social sciences to interpreting the meanings of education and schooling in diverse cultural contexts.
- *Principle #2:* The educator understands and can apply normative perspectives on education and schooling.
- *Principle #3:* The educator understands and can apply critical perspectives on education and schooling. The educator uses critical judgment to question educational assumptions and arrangements and to identify contradictions and inconsistencies among social and educational values, policies, and practices.
- *Principle #4:* The educator understands how moral principles related to democratic institutions can inform and direct schooling practice, leadership, and governance.

- *Principle #5:* The educator understands the full significance of diversity in a democratic society and how that bears on instruction, school leadership, and governance.
- *Principle #6:* The educator understands how philosophical and moral commitments affect the process of evaluation at all levels of schooling practice, leadership, and governance.

These Principles operate as a collection of dispositions. They require educators to analyze their instructional delivery and, at the same time, reflect upon their role in the classroom as leaders within wise and effective frameworks. Content is presented, and concurrently questioned and analyzed, between both the teacher and the students.

Each Principle works as a mechanism to think deeply about practices sought in the classroom within democratic structures. As an example, to look at Principle #3, teachers need to make explicit the assumptions as to why students complete individualized paper-and-pencil tasks. If preparation in an engaged and involved society were significant, then, would straight rows in classrooms with isolated, individual tasks be the most beneficial use of time? On the other hand, the teacher needs to ask herself the question: If students engage in constructive dialogue to solve a problem, what skill sets do they need to best succeed at completing such a task among the community of learners? Is the straight-row model appropriate to achieve that end? If not, what other content and skills need to be made explicit within the frame of classroom practices and instructional delivery? These questions, predicted on the language of the Principles, direct the instruction offered in the classroom and the content studied. The hope is that the work in classrooms will operate in a richer and fuller way, as a result.

The CSFE Principles serve three purposes. First, the Principles, anchored within the SFE tradition, identify the connection between schooling and society. Second, the CSFE concepts embody the meaning of dispositions. The work acknowledges qualities needed within teachers to educate and prepare children for life in a democracy. Third, the explicit and transparent language helps to clarify how and in what ways instruction specifically connects skills and content alongside the social aspects of students' lives.

DEMOCRACY: THE ROOT OF SFE

When analyzing dispositions, standards, and SFE, one significant point emerges: Teachers need to be aware of the community in which they teach. The learning context is not an isolated endeavor but matched to the beliefs and values of the teacher, as well as embedded in the social world of the school within community

(Tozer, Senese, & Violas, 2012). That teachers, in the U.S., live and work in a democracy needs to be analyzed, studied, applied, and explicitly practiced.

Commitment to democratic instruction is not simply an array of abstract concepts memorized for course study in a history of education class. SFE specifically focuses on preparation for life in a democratic society (Butts, 1993). For example, at a minimum, regardless of socio-economic or cultural context, all children identify, at some level, the social understanding that citizenry of democratic practice in the United States, upon completion of schooling, is required (Butts, 1995).

Embedded throughout the CSFE Principles, contextualized within the SFE tradition, is a rich understanding of the meaning of democracy. However, SFE does not perceive democracy solely as a government structure. It sees, instead, a broader construct that develops the talents of all to the fullest. Through the lens of Dewey (1920):

> Democracy has many meanings, but if it has moral meaning, it is found in resolving that the supreme test of all political institutions and industrial arrangements shall be the contributions they make to the all-around growth of every member of society. (p. 186)

Democratic structures respect, acknowledge, and sanction, as a social construct, the best form of growth for every member (Tozer, Senese, & Violas, 2012). The strengths of students within the context of democracy "must emerge from the concerns, values, habits and practices of cultural groups" (Hytten, 2009, p. 397).

That language of democracy permeates every concept practiced within the CSFE Principles. Teacher educators, classroom instructors, and teacher candidates, when well-versed in the content and practice of the Principles, foreground every instructional choice with an explicit awareness to the skills needed to function in a democracy, as interpreted through the SFE tradition. Similar to the example of students working in group contexts instead of straight rows, informed instructors situate their instructional plans so as to do democracy in the classroom.

Thus, the normative practices within CSFE Principle #2, for example, tell a first-grade teacher several significant points. She identifies that learning to read is essential for life in a democracy. However, the need to critique and judge different characters' points-of-view is also essential to do democracy. As primary students read and discuss traditional fairytales such as *The Three Little Pigs*, for example, the teacher presents content, writing activities, and group discussions to examine different variants of the same tale. Points-of-view in works such as *The True Story of the Three Little Pigs*, told from the perspective of the wolf, would be considered a staple to the instructional program. The plan devised for the lesson, its execution, and subsequent assessment, operates as the norm. Learning to read is as significant in value as learning to critique and evaluate different perspectives. The language, the dispositions, and the content implementation, rooted in the CSFE Principles, provide strategies within democratic structures as the standard. This multiplicity of skills tied to content within the frame of Deweyan democracy operates at every grade level from pre-K to 12th grade. And, most importantly, each teacher at every level would promptly communicate why the skills of learning to critique literature are as important as the ability to read text.

THE COMPLEXITY OF DEMOCRACY PRACTICED IN THE SCHOOLING CONTEXT

Kuhn (2008) identified the multiplicity of varied skills and strategies operating within community as the term "complexity." As a concept, it is "both the nature of the world and human sense-making" as "dynamic and emergent" (p. 182).

Achinstien and Barrett (2004) described complexity as the hidden aspects to teaching. They look at different styles of leadership between teachers who rely on managerial or controlling tasks to those that integrate the political and cultural aspects of content offered in the classroom.

Within the frame of Brown and Krache (2010), the specifics of complexity are delineated through the use of role-play scenarios as teacher candidates look at race, gender, and class within school experiences. From managing a group of kindergartners in an art activity to lining up fourth graders for lunch, the social aspect to learning and interacting within the schooling environment is fully questioned and analyzed. The teacher candidates have space and voice to rehearse the social complexities encountered daily in the classroom setting.

The CSFE Principles integrate multiple complexities within the context of the school day to a similar level of depth as interpreted by Brown and Krache (2010) as well as Achinstien and Barrett (2004). The intent of the CSFE is to help teachers prepare students as citizens within democratic structures. When applying, for example, Principle #5—The educator understands the full significance of diversity in a democratic society and how that bears on instruction, school leadership, and governance—the teacher acknowledges the vocabulary in which democracy is viewed as a moral activity and not solely as a government structure. Butts (1980) explained that schooling offers the opportunity to think about the position of the individual in community. Banks (2009) saw citizenship education as a way for schools to help students "develop critical and clarified cultural identities" as well as "acquire knowledgeable, critical, and analytical attachments to their nation states" (p. 107). School and democracy, contextualized within citizenship, is one form of complexity matched to the dispositions of the CSFE, expressed in the standards committed to the practice of leadership, school governance, and instruction from Principle #5.

The concept of complexity connects the content of the Principles to the operationalized language of dispositions. The essence of a rehearsed, disciplined, democratic citizen requires that students and teachers emulate qualities built within the valued constructs of the CSFE Principles, situated within the SFE frame. To develop understanding of concepts of equity, access, and opportunity, for example, critical reflection must be infused within practical, informed analysis when doing the work of the Principles, such as questioning room and building arrangements (Tindle, Freund, Belknap, Green, & Shotel, 2011).

SFE OPERATES AS A TOOL TO PROVIDE SUPPORT FOR TEACHERS

Teachers who model SFE practices document stronger instructional delivery. For example, Madda and Schultz (2009) looked at teacher scholars who live and serve in the same urban, low-income areas as the children they instruct. These instructors connect community experiences to content with an explicit effort to provide teaching within a democratic approach. Joining students and teachers from the same community bridges social context, instructional delivery, content, and scholarship within a familiar and caring experience (Murrell, 2001).

Schultz (2007; 2008) depicted the daily life of his classroom as students connected social context and academic rigor. In his portrait of his own teaching, Schultz (2007; 2008) illustrated that he does not come from the same community as the children he served. However, the children and instructor, together, questioned and critiqued the social world neighboring the urban classroom. The curriculum intersected with issues of work and life in poverty, as students learned to voice their opinions with the use of tools, such as petitions and political forums, in an effort to improve the conditions of their school.

Gutstein (2007) engaged in a similar type of work. He identified the anatomy of math instruction in urban classrooms. The content was embedded in the social world of the lives of the children served. For example, junior high students evaluated gentrification—the process in which developers purchase land at low cost in low socio-economic status communities, geographically close to the urban centers, in the hope of selling new homes at maximum financial profit. This work was not an academic endeavor removed from the lives of the students. They analyzed their own home values, as developers purchased homes and land in their own community. The students studied the math matched to social forces as they occur in real time. The study of numbers to explain the social world occurs simultaneously.

Schultz (2007) and Gutstein's (2007) rich portraits of classroom life achieve the vision sought by Giroux (1985): Schools embody a thoughtful, questioning, and socially just view of the political and cultural structures. Analysis and critique are the roots of scholarly work between students and teachers. Teachers, serving children from all economic backgrounds, need to direct and engage the social world. Content matched to students' lived experiences is a must. If the students are of color, provide quality literature representative of that culture. If a neighborhood begins the process of gentrification, ask questions such as: Why? How will this impact the home my family rents or owns? Teach the process of contacting aldermen and/or other officials to provide affordable housing for current residents.

The key to this work is the following: SFE acknowledges that schooling mirrors the society in which we live, but, simultaneously, it requires that teachers and students work to transform democratic society to question the status quo and develop as fully for the benefit of that society (CSFE Standards, 2000). The marriage of explicit standards within the CSFE Principles to the content of SFE will provide the desired professional dispositions embedded within a shared and cohesive language, which seeks to better inform teachers and structure content delivery (Laird, 1998).

How teachers express their understanding of social context within SFE in an outcomes-based assessment format is at its early stages. The work of Mueller (2006), Cochran-Smith et al. (2009), and Benchik-Osborne (2013) are first efforts to document classroom teachers' understanding of school and its relationship to society within a frame matched to the content and values grounded in the SFE tradition. These researchers saw classroom teachers connect student culture to content delivered. But, Benchik-Osborne (2013) and Mueller (2006) also identified teacher respondents who did not recognize cultural connection between content and students.

Garmon (2005) spoke of the importance of providing student teachers with diverse settings for teacher preparation with an awareness of the social world and its connection to classroom instruction. More, though, needs to be done to fully detail and document how and in what ways teachers link social-cultural context to instruction (Gay, 2000). How teachers understand social context, and how they apply that understanding to their practice, is a subject on which much less has been written (Richardson, 1996).

LOST IN TRANSLATION

The initial studies that examine outcomes-based assessments highlight some disturbing trends. Democracy, as a complex construct, does not drive classroom teacher instruction in many instances (Tozer & Butts, 2011). Support for this point comes in the frame of my own research (Benchik-Osborne, 2013). I saw a lack of teacher awareness of SFE in several contexts. Settings in which little or no connection to the CSFE Principles was evident, with students engaged daily in isolated tasks. Teacher-led discussions, for example, focused exclusively on vocabulary from a basal reader in whole group format with little or no cultural connection. In one particular classroom, the fourth graders were failing numerous test assessments and the blame fell on the children. Little or no reflection as to the content delivery offered on the part of the teacher occurred (Benchik-Osborne, 2013).

Limited grasp of SFE translates to many challenges. When I asked respondents what led them to organize and execute their learning experiences in the classroom, I encountered two common responses that bothered me a great deal. Principally, all the teachers, regardless of the degree to which they executed cultural connection to content, informed me that psychology directed their understanding of teaching, schooling, and instruction. And, subsequently, those who conducted aspects of SFE-mediated-instruction, assessed alongside the CSFE Principles, indicated that they knew they were different from other teachers in their buildings, but could not tell why they instructed with a connection to culture and context.

Thus, none of the respondents articulated a grasp of SFE or even referenced vocabulary from the field to explain what they did or why. When asked if they knew of a field connecting the social world to schooling, they did not identify or acknowledge SFE. None of them claimed to know of its existence. One referenced a course in which she studied school and law but did not see how a field such as SFE existed or could better support her as a teacher. She saw herself as isolated, with little backing from other faculty or from the academic community. The execution to develop potential most fully within a democratic structure is difficult work. To not position such work with other scholars, researchers, and teachers seems to be insurmountable as a successful endeavor. In turn, the translation of SFE within the practical aspects of the CSFE Principles could easily be lost without explicit connection to teacher preparation and daily life in a classroom

Teachers who engage in practical aspects of the CSFE Principles provide richer instruction with the study of the social context, even if they are not aware that they provide such instruction. For example, in one context observed within the frame of my study, the class examined Afghan settlement camps. This work gave the boys and girls in the sixth-grade class in Chicago an avenue to examine a community that was functioning a world away from their neighborhood. They analyzed how the camp operated, concentrating on the political will to place social restrictions on girls within the camps as well as within the villages and cities of Afghanistan. The content helped the sixth graders analyze and critique their own community experiences with a new perspective.

The travesty became most apparent, though, when the teacher, who analyzed the lives of teens from Afghanistan to Chicago, could not articulate the strength of her efforts but only voice that she was different from most of her faculty. If she could value the complexity of what she offered, her own skills and strategies could develop more fully. The concept of complexity gives student teachers and classroom instructors an appreciation for the rich level of depth required to understand the social world locally, nationally, and internationally from the lens of the SFE. The standards from the CSFE Principles provide specific strategies as to how to apply SFE in the classroom while also supporting the qualities or the dispositions needed so that teachers actually do democracy in the classroom with a clear, explicit language describing what they do in the classroom, and why they do it.

Unfortunately, the meaning of teacher practice and thought is lost much too often. The teacher may not provide substance to practice. If meaningful instruction is offered, the teacher may not be able to explain why s/he selects certain instructional practices. At worst, no substance is offered in practice. But, to another disparaging end, the educator may provide significant rich teaching and practice but not be able to explain why certain choices are made; she may engage in action but fail to explain the choice selected. Such effort is not going to sustain itself. SFE provides that much needed logic model. CSFE Principles support, within its standards, a clear explanation as to how to do SFE and how to contextualize teacher beliefs grounded within democratic thinking.

PRACTICALITY OF CSFE PRINCIPLES

Tozer and Miretzky (2005) saw the content of SFE as essential to practice. Just as psychology is viewed as a field directly related to the practice of classroom teaching, informing instructors how best to meet the needs of individual students' intellectual growth in useful and concrete ways, so too should SFE be viewed as applicable to practice. The study of schooling and society should not be seen as a liberal arts course, providing only a historical tale of schooling in the U.S. It should, instead, expand teachers' knowledge base to inform their practices and beliefs (Tozer & Miretzky, 2000; 2005).

Ideally, teachers need an internal consistency in their thinking about schooling and society. They ought to, among other educated professionals, embrace a shared set of beliefs and practices exhibiting the ideals sought in SFE. From the work of Mueller (2006) and Benchik-Osborne (2013), this is not the case currently. The respondents, in both studies, expressed markedly distinct and separate ways to describe good teaching.

Cochran-Smith et al. (2009) examined teachers' commitment to content and skill development of children that included a full grasp of the cultural backgrounds from which the students came. But, even within the frame of that study, the first-year in-service teachers did not convey a shared language or vocabulary as to how to connect care, context, democratic practices, dispositions, and content to inform curricular practice.

The CSFE Principles may provide a way to inform and assess student teachers as well as current classroom teachers, education professors, curricular researchers, and social foundations scholars alike. To be informed as to how, in what ways, and why SFE informs classroom practice needs to be explicit for all involved in curriculum planning and instructional delivery within a democracy.

Ultimately, SFE should be viewed as a practical set of strategies (Dottin, 2011). It is content, rooted in the liberal arts tradition, which needs to be tied to the national conversation of standards to inform teachers. The CSFE foregrounds this discussion:

> Recently, a number of sustained efforts have resulted in new approaches to assessing the professional expertise of beginning and experienced teachers on the basis of what they know and are able to do. With the involvement of the two large national teacher unions, such agencies as the National Council for Accreditation of Teacher Education, the National Board for Professional Teaching Standards (NBPTS), the Interstate New Teacher Assessment and Support Consortium, and state education agencies have sought to conduct assessments of teachers on the basis of evidence of teacher knowledge, dispositions, and performance. (2000)

The intent is to match SFE content to teacher practice with disciplined language in rich and detailed ways. Uniform language as to how to apply SFE to classroom practice is fundamental. To provide full transparency as to how to do SFE when teaching helps teachers apply that content within the course of the school day (Dottin, 2011). The hope is that application of the CSFE Principles provides that help.

The explicit use of SFE, embedded within the language of the CSFE Principles, supports scholars and classroom teachers to evaluate practices. As Dottin et al. (2005) offered, the work of SFE is to do just that: Question, critique, judge, and assess how such standards inform instructional practice with a critical lens. Scholars and teachers should not be limited by the standards but instead provided a vehicle to open doors to problem-solving opportunities. The uniformity of language in the CSFE Principles delivers a way to communicate efficiently among professionals as well as a way to evaluate what SFE practices look like in the classroom. The capacity to question and to critique is the very essence of strong SFE practices, which needs to be the core of such theory and practice.

APPLIED LIBERAL ARTS

SFE is a liberal arts class with practical applications. When I instruct graduate students with the SFE focus, they voice at the start of each term that history, philosophy, and the social sciences are content areas to be memorized but not necessarily practiced within classroom teaching. And, they continually voice, at the end of each semester, that they are surprised that such content areas may be able to support their instruction.

To question content taught and to instruct at a deeper level needs to be the norm. Similar to how psychology considers its own content and applicable practice, SFE also needs to be held to that same bar. The CSFE Principles may be the venue to practice critical democratic thinking and teaching. They may also be the language needed to provide structure and vocabulary to support SFE content and practices in the classroom context.

As this section comes to a close, I see the need for a text like this. The professional dispositions from the SFE lens, matched well to the CSFE Principles, provide a language and practice to support classroom teachers wisely and effectively. From my own work (Benchik-Osborne, 2013), the teachers who concerned me the most and upon whom I most reflected were the instructors that valued and practiced elements of the CSFE Principles. The concern lay not in how they executed the CSFE concepts—I was thrilled to see them rehearsed in the classroom. My greatest fear resided in the fact that the teachers were completely unaware of SFE and its community of scholars and practitioners. If these teachers, willing to take a risk to question schooling, content, and the social structure, did not see a connection between their efforts and SFE, opportunity to evolve or develop their thinking is extremely limited. Rank-and-file teachers, unaware of the content, vocabulary, and practices of SFE, may never attempt such efforts. The work of SFE, then, at best, stagnates or at worst, fails, entirely because the community of teachers and scholars does not translate its value from theory to practice.

As Tozer and Miretzky (2000; 2005) indicated, teachers are required to study SFE for certification within most of the United States. If teacher certification necessitates such preparation for educators, then application of SFE content needs to be explicitly rehearsed within practice (Tozer & Butts, 2011; Dottin, 2011). To follow, SFE should inform classroom practice. The hope is that the explicit CSFE Principles operate as one tool to connect the content of the liberal arts to frame the practices of the K-12 classrooms wisely and effectively. The resulting outcome translates to deep reflection and thoughtful practice as the norm within school cultures and classroom contexts. The key point is this: SFE, embedded within standards, translates to good teachers doing good teaching to help children both understand and practice democracy. The CSFE Principles may be the very vehicle to propel a standard form of communicating, applying, evaluating, and assessing SFE concepts in K-12 classrooms in the democratic context of the U.S. To engage in good teaching, teachers need to know what qualities and dispositions are necessary within themselves to concretely execute contextualized SFE skills and lessons. The CSFE Principles function as one tool to achieve that goal. The integration of standards from the CSFE highlight both dispositions valued within individual teachers, and, at the same time, content of SFE as a field of study. The resulting outcome may well work wisely and effectively to provide a supportive language to benefit classroom teachers, student teacher candidates, and teacher educators.

REFERENCES

Achinstein, B., & Barrett, A. (2004). (Re)Framing classroom contexts: How new teachers and mentors view diverse learners and challenges of practice. *Teachers College Record, 106*(4), 716–746.

Andrzejewski, J., Baltodano, M. P., & Symcox, L. (Eds.). (2009). *Social justice, peace and environmental education: Transformative standards.* New York, NY: Routledge.

Bailey, L. (2010). The impact of sustained, standards-based professional learning on second and third grade teachers' content and pedagogical knowledge in integrated mathematics. *Early Childhood Education Journal, 38*(2), 123–132.

Baker, P. B., & Digiovanni, L. W. (2005). Narratives on culturally relevant pedagogy: Personal responses to the standardized curriculum. *Current Issues in Education, 8* (15). Retrieved February 1, 2013, from http://cie.asu.edu/volume8/number22/

Banks, J. A. (2009). Human rights, diversity, and citizenship education. *Educational Forum, 73*(2), 100–110.

Benchik-Osborne, J.R. (2013). An empirical study: To what extent and in what ways does social foundations of education inform four teachers' educational beliefs and classroom practices? *Educational Studies, 49*(6), 540-563. doi:10.1080/00131946.2013.844150.

Brown, K. D., & Kraehe, A. M. (2010). The complexities of teaching the complex: Examining how future educators construct understandings of sociocultural knowledge and schooling. *Educational Studies, 46*(1), 91–115.

Butts, R. (1980). Curriculum for the educated citizen. *Educational Leadership, 38*(1), 6.

Butts, R. (1993). National standards and civic education in the United States. *International Journal of Social Education, 7*, 86–94.

Butts, R. (1995). Antidote for antipolitics: A new "text of civic instruction." *Education Week, 14*, 48.

Cochran-Smith, M., Shakman, K., Jong, C., Terrell, D. G., Barnatt, J., & McQuillan, P. (2009). Good and just teaching: The case for social justice in teacher education. *American Journal of Education, 115*(3), 347–377.

Council of Social Foundations of Education (CSFE, 2000), Formerly the Council of Learned Societies in Education (CLSE). *Standards for academic and professional instruction in Foundations of Education, Educational Studies, and Educational Policy Studies.* San Francisco, CA: Caddo Gap Press. Retrieved May 23, 2013, from http://www.unm.edu/~jka/csfe/standards_matrix.html

Dewey, J. (1920). *Reconstruction in philosophy.* Boston, MA: Beacon Press.

Dottin, E. (2011). Social foundations and the professional preparation of teacher education. In S. Tozer, B. P. Gallegos, A. M. Henry, M. Bushnell Greiner, & P. Groves-Price (Eds.). *Handbook of research in the social foundations of education* (pp. 399–413). New York, NY: Routledge.

Dottin, E., Jones, A. H., Simpson, D., & Watras, J. (2005). Representing the social foundations of education in NCATE: A chronicle of twenty-five years of effort. *Educational Studies, 38*(3), 241–254.

Garmon, M. A. (2005). Six key factors for changing preservice teachers' attitudes/beliefs about diversity. *Educational Studies, 38*(3), 275–286.

Gay, G. (2000). *Culturally responsive teaching: Theory, research, and practice.* New York, NY: Teachers College, Columbia University.

Giroux, H. A. (1985). Critical pedagogy, cultural politics and the discourse of experience. *Journal of Education, 167,* 22–41.

Gutstein, E. (2007). "And that's just how it starts": Teaching mathematics and developing student agency. *Teachers College Record, 109*(2), 420–448.

Hytten, K. (2009). Dewey democracy in a globalized world. *Educational Theory, 59*(4), 395–408.

Hytten, K. (2010). AESA 2009 presidential address cultivating hope and building community: Reflections on social justice activism in educational studies. *Educational Studies, 46*(2), 151–167.

Kuhn, L. (2008). Complexity and educational research: A critical reflection. *Educational Philosophy & Theory, 40*(1), 177–189.

Laird, S. (1998). Teaching and educational theory: Can (and should) this marriage be saved? *Educational Studies, 29,* 131–151.

Lubinski, C. A., & Otto, A. D. (2004). Preparing K-8 preservice teachers in a content course for standards-based mathematics pedagogy. *School Science & Mathematics, 104*(7), 336–350.

Madda, C. L., & Schultz, B. D. (2009). (Re)constructing ideals of multicultural education through "grow your own teachers." *Multicultural Perspectives, 11*(4), 204–207.

Malina, E., Plunk, D., & Lindell, R. (2006). Development of a standards-based integrated science course for elementary teachers. *AIP Conference Proceedings, 818*(1), 19–22.

Mueller, J. (2006). Does talking the talk mean walking the walk? A case for forging closer relationships between teacher education and educational foundations. *Educational Studies, 39*(2), 146–162.

Mulcahy, D. (2011). Assembling the "accomplished" teacher: The performativity and politics of professional teaching standards. *Educational Philosophy & Theory, 43,* 94–113.

Murrell, P.C. (2001). *The community teacher: A new framework for effective urban teaching.* New York, NY: Teachers College Press.

Murrell, P.C. (2002). *African-centered pedagogy: Developing schools of achievement for African American children.* Albany, NY: State University of New York.

Richardson, V. (1996). The role of attitudes and beliefs in learning to teach. In J. Sikula, T.J. Buttery, E. Guyton (Eds.), *Handbook of research on teacher education* (pp. 102–119). New York, NY: Simon & Schuster Macmillan.

Schultz, B. (2007). Living savage inequalities: Room 405's fight for equity in schooling. *Journal of Educational Controversy 2.1.* Retrieved from http://www.wce.wwu.edu/Resources/CEP/eJournal/v002n001/a001.shtml

Schultz, B. D. (2008). *Spectacular things happen along the way: Lessons from an urban classroom.* New York, NY: Teachers College Press.

Shiveley, J., & Misco, T. (2009). "But how do I know about their attitudes and beliefs?": A four-step process for integrating and assessing dispositions in teacher education. *Clearing House, 83*(1), 9–14.

Splitter, L. J. (2010). Dispositions in education: Nonentities worth talking about. *Educational Theory, 60*(2), 203–230.

Tindle, K., Freund, M., Belknap, B., Green, C., & Shotel, J. (2011). The urban teacher residency program: A recursive process to develop professional dispositions, knowledge, and skills of candidates to teach diverse students. *Educational Considerations, 38*(2), 28–35.

Tozer, S.E., & Butts, R.F. (2011). The evolution of social foundation of education. In S. Tozer, B. P. Gallegos, A. M. Henry, M. Bushnell Greiner, & P. Groves-Price. *Handbook of research in the social foundations of education* (pp. 4–14). New York, NY: Routledge.

Tozer, S. E., & Miretzky, D. (2000). Professional teaching standards and social foundations of education. *Educational Studies, 31*(2), 106.

Tozer, S., & Miretzky, D. (2005). Social foundations, teaching standards, and the future of teacher preparation. In D.W. Butin (Ed.), *Teaching social foundations of education: Context, theories, and issues* (pp. 3–28). Mahwah, NJ: Lawrence Erlbaum Associates.

Tozer, S.E., Senese, G., & Violas, P.C. (2012) *School and society: Historical and contemporary perspectives, 7th ed.* Boston, MA: McGraw-Hill.

Villegas, A. M. (2007). Dispositions in teacher education: A look at social justice. *Journal of Teacher Education, 58*(5), 370–380.

Warren, D. (1998). From there to where: The social foundations of education in transit again. *Educational Studies, 29,* 117–130.

CHAPTER THIRTEEN

Urban Teachers AND Technology

Critical Reflections in the Age of Accountability

KATE E. O'HARA

INTRODUCTION

In the current age of accountability, the use of technology for teaching and learning is an expectation in both the national teacher evaluation system as well as in the national standards for students. This use includes technology for creating, refining, publishing, and collaborating on writing, digital media to inform curriculum, conducting efficient research on the Internet, and evaluating and integrating information presented in multimedia formats. However, urban teachers face numerous challenges and obstacles that prevent them from effectively integrating technology in their practice (Groff & Mouza, 2008). These barriers include, but are not limited to: economic factors, lack of professional development opportunities, and test-driven practices. Yet, for every integration hindrance faced, there are many urban teachers armed with a positive professional attitude, determined to use technology in meaningful ways. With a belief in the potential of effective technology use in relation to their students' learning, these urban teachers work tirelessly to provide students with fair and equitable opportunities.

The in-service, New York City teachers I refer to have an important story to be told. This auto-ethnographic piece reflects my recent experiences working with them as a both a teacher educator and instructional technology specialist. I define my method of research as auto-ethnography; a critical account of my own experience as well as that of others, drawing on the work of John van Maanen

(1988), who defined ethnography as a "written representation of culture (or selected aspects of culture)" (p. 1). From this viewpoint, I analyze both the socio-cultural and ideological forces that frame my own image as a teacher, my own self-image as a researcher, and take into account my worldview and my definition of effective instructional technology.

Essentially, my reflections will be constructed from personal and observed scenarios and resituated in written form, with a continued awareness of the limits of language, as well as the non-neutrality of the words themselves. Yet despite these limitations, it is my aim that my words and representation bring to light critical insight, couched in theory, of effective technology use by urban teachers.

IT'S JUST THE WAY IT IS

It is a warm, May afternoon, and the air in the fourth-floor hallway is thick with both heat and the pollutants from the city street below. The fumes of diesel exhaust rise from a truck parked in front of the school, and the smell lingers, mixing with the bustling bodies of high school students as they squeeze down the dim, narrow hall to their next class. "Move it, move it, move it!" shouts a security guard, herding the bodies along the corridor and down stairwells. I reach my destination; the English Language Arts (ELA) classroom of a 12-year veteran teacher. She enters the room at the same time I do.

"Ugh, I hate 5th period! I have to climb three flights of stairs, and drag all this stuff." She makes a gesture with her head, nodding toward the stack of papers, books, and folders that spill out of her arms onto the desk. "How are you?" I ask her. "Ah, same ol' story here!" she laughs. Years earlier, I supported her and several of her colleagues when I was working as an instructional technology specialist. My work at that time was to support teachers in the effective use of technology. When labeling technology use as "effective," I am referring to use that in some way positively impacts and enhances teaching and learning. "Effective" use is technology use that "requires fundamental changes in the way we teach and learn in schools" (Su, 2009).

"Did you see my new SMARTBoard?" she says sarcastically. In the rear corner of the room sits an interactive whiteboard, missing a few of its pens, with a layer of dust on its plastic frame. On the white surface, someone had taped a typewritten flyer, "State Testing Schedule," and another sign, hand-written in red marker on college-lined loose-leaf, asking "Did you borrow my USB cable? Please return it!" The tape on the paper, yellow and peeling, is beginning to fall off and flap forward, obscuring the message's writing.

"You know, I'll have to say The SMARTBoard was exciting when I got it but it's been nearly impossible to use. First, I didn't get any training—which is fine because I'll play around with it myself, but I need a computer to go with it! I've brought my laptop from time to time, but now the USB cable is missing and I don't have the money to buy a new one." She shakes her head, frowning, "What am I going to do? That's just the way it is."

The scenario of the high school ELA teacher is not uncommon in urban schools. It is ironic that our United States Secretary of Education, Arne Duncan (2011), recently told teachers, "Working together, we can transform teaching from the factory model designed over a century ago to one built for the information age." A wonderfully optimistic message, but what measures have been put in place to transform teaching? Unfortunately, the factory model is alive and well in urban schools. American Federation of Teachers President Randi Weingarten (2010) explained how many public schools are still operating on an Industrial Age model or the "pedagogical equivalent of a factory by reducing the learning experience to a conveyor belt of rote prep sessions and multiple choice tests" (p. 37).

Weingarten's (2010) image of a conveyor belt is further instilled when examining the overcrowding issues many urban schools face. For example, in New York City, the nation's largest school district, nearly half of the public schools "have classrooms that are more crowded than the teachers' union contract allows" (Kuczynski-Brown, 2012, para. 1). The overcrowding, coupled with the scheduling of the typical school day, makes for less-than-optimal teaching conditions. In urban secondary schools, block period programming is rare; students move every 40 to 43 minutes throughout the day to a new class, but not necessarily a new opportunity for learning.

A middle school Science teacher explains,

> I can't stand the constant moving. It's just too many kids and teachers in too big a building trying to get from one place to the next. What's the point of trying anything? My chair just offered me a set of laptops. How cool is that, maybe finally so some project based learning? But it's a joke, really—when are we trying those out? By the time I take attendance and review homework it's time for them to go to the next class, never mind 34 kids logging onto a computer.

In addition to the aforementioned factors to consider before "transforming teaching" into a model "built for the information age" we need to focus on the tools themselves. When technology based resources are lost, damaged, or stolen, urban schools often do not have the funding to replace or even maintain existing equipment.

States often inform districts of their budgets too late (e.g., often after school has already begun) for districts to be able to properly plan how to best use resources to support students and teachers ("How Bureaucracy Stands in the Way," n.d.). However, in New York City, the largest urban district in the country, this is not the case. Rather, NYC Department of Education budgets are in place prior to the academic year, which starts in September, but money being budgeted for technology does not always happen. A former urban district technology director with over 25 years experience clarifies,

> There is definitely more flexibility than in past years for principals to move monies in budgets around, but unless it is a mandate, not much money is being moved for technology purchases or training of teachers. It has to be a priority. And really technology has never been a priority. It has always been an add-on.

He goes on to explain that the technology is too often viewed as an add-on because it is typically something "tried out" as a result of a grant or an initiative, but never truly integrated into classroom practice as an instructional tool. So, with only "pockets of good things happening" throughout urban schools by ambitious and determined teachers, there is no cohesive impact.

URBAN TEACHING: TRAINING, TESTING, AND TECHNOLOGY

"Teacher researcher pedagogy suggests that teachers teach and, properly situated, construct new knowledge in their classroom" (Anderson, 2005, p. 68). But suppose an urban school teacher is properly situated, with ample resources, available technologies, and ideal working conditions; is the teacher solely responsible for learning new teaching methods, for acquiring new instructional strategies, and constructing new knowledge? The teachers I work with operate within a system that reduces "teaching to a technical craft in the employ of government officials who appear to wish to limit the curriculum and the purposes of schooling to simple information and basic skills" (p. 68). At present in NYC, teachers are "teaching" under strict weekly schedules driven by standardized exams, as well as adherence to "Scope and Sequence" documents. These documents, created for the content areas of Mathematics, Science, and Social Studies, offer a grade-by-grade overview of all the topics that students are expected to know. In theory, it makes perfect sense to have yearly instructional goals; however, in practice, the tight pacing of topics to be taught allows for little variation in types of teaching, with a focus on direct instruction. Also, for students, a tight-pacing schedule leaves little room for exploration, understating, and application of a topic or concept.

A high school Math teacher laments,

> I feel like I want to do hands-on projects.... I guess for some of my kids I really need to do hands on projects and activities for them to understand, but following the scope and sequence calendar, I'm not sure what options I have. I got a list of things they need to know by a certain time...

He sighs and continues, "I'm always using the text and then maybe practice worksheets, but that's about it…it's pretty straightforward. I guess pretty boring for them (laughs)…. I guess boring for all of us."

Given the current scenarios, what options do teachers have for professional growth? The term "professional development" has traditionally represented opportunities for further development of practicing teachers, with a focus on instructional skills and strategies (Pinar et al., 1995). Currently, in states across the U.S., there are unique requirements for teacher licensure and certification, many of which include professional development in addition to academic degrees. For example, in New York State, all teaching certifications are considered "professional" and teachers in a public school are required to complete 175 hours of professional development every 5 years. ("Professional Development for Professional Certificate Holders," 2010). The professional development hours will maintain the validity of the professional certificate and allow an employed teacher to continue to teach in a public school.

The idea behind the state requirement is that by continually taking courses, teachers in New York City Public Schools will enrich their professional capacity, and accordingly, improve their students' academic achievement. However, will 175 hours of courses every 5 years determine one to be "professional," thus improving student achievement?

According to the American Federation of Teachers' (2002) Principles for Professional Development:

> Professional development is an essential element of comprehensive or "systemic" reform. The nation can adopt rigorous standards, set forth a visionary scenario, compile the best research about how students learn, change textbooks and assessment, promote teaching strategies that have been successful with a wide range of students, and change all the other elements involved in systemic reform—but without professional development, school reform and improved achievement for all students will not happen. (p. 2)

The above quote from the teachers' union stresses the importance of professional development and equates it with the enormous undertaking of improving "achievement for all students." Yet, if professional development is supposedly so integral to teaching, why is it so often presented as something distributed to teachers, neatly packaged, void of context, void of the realities of the urban classroom?

In *Classroom Teaching: An Introduction*, Joe Kincheloe (2005) spoke of teachers being alienated cognitively and also ontologically, which relates to the nature of one's being, the nature of one's relationship with the world. Educational reforms of standardization curriculum move teachers further from reflective practice and closer to teaching their students isolated pieces of information without regard to relationships and context, without questioning the "facts" presented. And, just as their students are expected to be recipients of objective information, urban teachers are offered few opportunities during professional development to reflect on their own thinking, their own teaching, or consider the structures and discourses that shape what it is to "teach."

For example, when New York City teachers are engaged in professional development related to instructional technology, reflective practices are atypical experiences. In fact, in urban schools, when technology equipment is purchased it is rare, if ever, that professional development in the use of the technology is also included. If technology-based professional development for teachers is provided, it is at a monetary cost to teachers, and most often is a workshop or series of sessions that teach participants basic skills about the use of a particular piece of hardware or software.

An elementary teacher explains, "When we have an hour or two hour workshop about technology I feel more confused and overwhelmed than I did before the professional development!" Her colleague elaborates,

> That is true (laughs), but we do have times that we've worked together in a small group, by the grade level we teach, learning together about something, some technology. Early this year it was about using Wikis. We even have new laptops in the building. But, I dunno. It's as if you can't concentrate or something. There's so much to do throughout the day my head is filled. You know, with all this new administrative stuff now, paperwork and reports to fill out each day. I mean, I'd love to be able to try it [a Wiki] or use the new laptop but, uh, she's right.

Shrugging her shoulders and frowning, she continues, "I'm just so overwhelmed most times…. I wish we were given some time to slow down…sit and learn and work with one another."

When providing teachers with professorial learning opportunities related to technology, "research consistently shows that factors such as a long duration, ongoing coaching and support, and a close connection to practice are essential for professional development to have an impact" (Martin et al., 2010, p. 71).

There needs to be a shift from simply buying a new technology for teachers or showing teachers a new technology-based tool. There needs to be movement to

> think beyond providing more hardware, software, and connecting schools to the Internet, but instead thinking about keeping urban schools and teachers well-informed and trained in the effective use of technology for educational purposes. Technology will fail to meet its educational promise if teachers are not equipped with the skills and knowledge needed to help the urban learner and if the urban learner does not have access to effective learning strategies as well as the relevant tools to succeed. (Keengwe & Akyeampong, 2010, p. 1267)

In spite of limited efforts within urban schools for teachers to learn about technology and effective use, the sporadic opportunities to engage in the small learning communities that exist are not necessarily guaranteed to be successful. In *Communities of Practice: Learning, Meaning, and Identity*, Wenger (1998) presented readers with a real-world scenario to exemplify the concept of non-participation:

> It is often the case that, rather than being direct boundary relations between communities and people or among communities, relations of non-participation are mediated by institutional arrangements. This is true for claims processors. The low status of the job in the company, the meager salary, the lack of encouragement of initiative, the perception of repetitiousness, the pervasive use of standardized reifications to connect with the real world, and the organization of work in terms of narrow procedures all contribute to an experience of non-participation. (p. 169)

Wenger's (1998) words describe the circumstances of a claims processor, but in reading his description, I immediately think of teachers as he describes the low status of the job, the meager salary, the lack of encouragement of initiative, the perception of repetitiousness, the pervasive use of standardized reifications to connect with the real world, and the organization of work in terms of narrow procedures, all contributing to an experience of non-participation. It is these factors that can impede the participation of teachers in worthwhile professional development opportunities aimed at developing the skills and knowledge needed to help the urban learner.

Additionally, in my role as a professional developer, I found that a short series of training sessions related to technology integration rarely leads to any impact at the classroom level. Despite the fact that the participating teachers often leave professional development sessions with new ideas and strategies, when it comes to engaging in effective implementation at the classroom level, success isn't always the outcome.

Similar to any professional development, not specific to technology, research indicates that sustained and intensive professional development is more likely to have an impact on teacher outcomes. Furthermore, "professional development that focuses on academic subject matter (content), gives teachers opportunities for 'hands-on' work (active learning), and is integrated into the daily life of the school (coherence), is more likely to produce enhanced knowledge and skills" (Garet, Porter, Desimone, Birman, & Yoon, 2001 p. 935).

Moreover, urban teachers frequently receive professional development by someone outside the urban school system; either a "trainer" from an education corporation or, if an educator, one who teaches or supports teachers in rural or suburban areas. One high school teacher I work with reflects a common sentiment of his peers:

> We rarely have PD. Then when we do, it's this ridiculous long all day thing where we have to listen to someone who is teaching in the Midwest with 20 freaking kids in her classroom. I mean, are you kidding me? I know that sounds harsh and I'll admit many of the ideas we hear about are good, but what they're selling just ain't going to happen with

35 kids and never mind no computers. But in fairness to him (the principal) I know he's trying to do something good.

When speaking with principals about the quality of professional development their teachers encounter I have heard a similar tale,

> Listen, I get pressure for our students to pass tests. I want to do a good job—and the same goes for my teachers. Yeah, I know one-shot training isn't the greatest and most times not the most interesting, but I'm going to try to get us as much help as I can, as often as I can—whether teachers think it's good or not.

And throughout urban districts, there are plenty of principals trying to do "something good" for their teachers. And they are doing so at the suggestion of a higher power. On July 2, 2009, the United States Secretary of Education, Arne Duncan, spoke at the National Education Association's yearly conference. He stressed that, "states and districts should be able to identify effective teachers and principals" (para. 22). Then, a few years after Duncan spoke at the conference, the states that were recipients of the Obama administration's Race to the Top grants were "asked to define effective teaching in terms of student achievement outcomes, aggregate teacher effectiveness data to the preparation program level, and make regular public reports of their findings" (Crowe, 2011, p. 2).

Linda Darling-Hammond (2012), nationally recognized leader in educational policy, relates the concern of schools administrators, "the principals worry that greater focus on teaching to multiple-choice tests will reduce the time for the research, writing and complex problem-solving students need to succeed in today's society" ("Should Student Test Scores Be Used to Evaluate Teachers?" para. 23).

A middle school math teacher relates a similar sentiment,

> Sure, I'd love to use technology. I have a Web site I made for my kids to review concepts. I have videos and links to online games. I even designed this equation project, but now they have to access it from home [pauses] or anyplace outside of school. They used to be able to use the laptop cart or the computer lab, but now I was told those were only available for testing.

A middle school technology teacher concurs,

> I love to do interdisciplinary project-based learning with the students. But right now they are using my computers for ELA testing. There's the actual testing, then all the re-tests or make-up tests that take up more instructional time. In total I'll be losing about 6 weeks of instructional time due to beginning, middle, and end-of-year testing.

Teachers attempting to use technology in meaningful ways to foster students' understanding of difficult concepts, or to aid in literacy development, are overshadowed by the national agenda. In theory, who wouldn't want effective teachers and principals? And it seems sensible that we look at the achievement of our students by connecting them to those who teach them—or is it? In a critically reflective way, Pierre Bourdieu's (2000) concept of "symbolic violence" permeates this scenario.

According to Bourdieu (2000), symbolic violence is an unconscious mode of cultural and social domination in which,

> Every power to exert symbolic violence, i.e., every power which manages to impose meanings and to impose them as legitimate by concealing the power relations which are the basis of its force, adds its own specifically symbolic force to those power relations. (p. 4)

Through this critical lens, the symbolic force of the federal government can be seen permeating the state and the city. It is symbolic because it is not physical, but rather situated in fields as a material force, part of everyday life in the urban classroom. The environment of scripted curriculum and standardized tests is symbolically violent because there is domination and power as the basis of these practices. However, the outward dialogue is one of equity, effectiveness, and high achievement; imposed meanings that are legitimated and perpetuated. The public transcript, the interactions between dominators and oppressed (Scott, 1990), states we support teachers and provide them with professional growth opportunities. In the hidden transcript, teachers are dissatisfied by standalone skill-based workshops, or training sessions by those who understand very little about the teachers' classroom community. But the hegemonic web is elaborately woven. The teacher quoted earlier, with symbolic forces around him, conceded that his principal was "doing something good." However, "doing something good" can also have a downside.

For example, striving for quality teachers and high student achievement can certainly be viewed as "doing something good," but unfortunately, the federal government has advanced an agenda that includes an over-reliance on high-stakes tests for students, teachers, and administrators. As Arne Duncan noted, we need to identify "effective" teachers, but what factors are taken into consideration? Do teachers teach and students learn, void of context with a neutral curriculum? Or are we shaped by political, social, and ideological forces?

TEACHERS USING TECHNOLOGY: DEDICATED AND DETERMINED

Despite the challenges encountered, there are many urban teachers that are determined to use technology with their students in meaningful ways, regardless of any mandates associated with technology use, such as teacher-evaluation practices and students meeting national Common Core Standards, or passing standardized exams. With a belief in the potential of effective technology use on their students' learning, there are urban teachers who work tirelessly to provide students with fair and equitable opportunities.

These teachers use blogs, wikis, and create digital projects that support the development of literacy, including digital and visual literacy; develop technology-based projects exposing students to issues related to copyright and fair use; engage in Internet research that uncovers multiple perspectives on a topic; and create videos and screencasts to aid in comprehension. And the examples do not end there. The teachers are often self-taught, using the technology as a true instructional tool, positively impacting and enhancing both their teaching and their students' learning.

A high school teacher relates why she designed a collaborative Web site in which students can upload multimedia projects about current events:

> I love when everybody talks about critical thinking. Yeah, right, more like read a textbook, answer questions, and then take a test. I think our site allows students' knowledge and creativity to shine. It's a place for them to show their work, show what they really know... not just a test score.

And shine it does. The site, with editing rights given to students, is beautifully designed, with original student artwork and bright, colorful and aesthetically pleasing. The projects that students upload contain text, video, and graphics. The text comprises accounts of current and historical events written from differing points of view and critiqued resources.

The teacher, in this instance, uses her own personal laptop, but is also diligent about "signing out" the laptop cart when it is not in use for standardized testing purposes. The students are engaged and motivated by the use of the technology. Their teacher elaborates,

> I can't say they all have (Internet) access at home, but somehow they find a way to work on it when they're not in school. If this was a research paper I assigned, forget it! I'd be lucky I'd get two or three handed in.

The teacher's experience correlates with findings in the field. It has been found that "technology has the potential to impact student motivation positively and, subsequently, student learning" (Heafner, p. 49, 2004). And, as for the teacher herself, she has determined value in using technology for teaching and learning, thus helping her students "achieve learning that was otherwise difficult or impossible" (Ottenbreit-Leftwich, Glazewski, Newby, & Ertmer, 2010, p. 1331).

I find the urban teachers that integrate technology into their practice to be dedicated and determined, exhibiting a professional attitude that positively impacts their students' learning and motivation, and ultimately student success (Hallam, 2009).

According to the National Council for Accreditation of Teacher Education (NCATE), the accrediting entity that determines which teacher preparation schools, colleges, and departments of education have met rigorous national standards, teachers' attitudes are part of a teacher's "dispositions." More specifically, NCATE (2012) defines professional dispositions as:

> Professional attitudes, values, and beliefs demonstrated through both verbal and non-verbal behaviors as educators interact with students, families, colleagues, and communities. These positive behaviors support student learning and development. NCATE expects institutions to assess professional dispositions based on observable behaviors in educational settings. The two professional dispositions that NCATE expects institutions to assess are fairness and the belief that all students can learn. Based on their mission and conceptual framework, professional education units can identify, define, and operationalize additional professional dispositions.

And although NCATE standards are used in developing higher education teacher preparation programs, what standards or guidelines related to teacher dispositions exist at the K-12 level? In a 2010 National Education Policy Center report, researchers identified three categories to be addressed in evaluating "good" teachers: teacher quality, teacher performance, and teacher effectiveness. Dispositions fall under the "teacher quality" category. However, "research has not as yet established the full complement of teacher characteristics that may affect student achievement" (Hinchey, 2010, p. 4), thus urging policy makers to construct their own decisions as to what dispositions should be included in the teacher evaluation process. But how do we assess something that we don't even know is needed? Unfortunately, what students, teachers, and administrators *do* know is that the Obama administration is "encouraging policymakers to define 'good' teachers as those who produce gains in student achievement, measured by gains in standardized test scores" (Hinchey, 2010, p. 1).

However, let's assume that policy makers in a particular state have asked their school districts to include professional dispositions in their teacher evaluation process. Before doing so, certain considerations are essential. According to the National Center for Education Statistics in urban-centric locale codes, "suburb" may be defined as a "territory outside a principal city and inside an urbanized area" ("New Urban-Centric Locale Codes," n.d.). Given that, should all teachers within a district, regardless of locale code, be evaluated on the same dispositions? Yes, but only when it is clear exactly which dispositions are to be included.

As defined by NCATE, ideally all teachers should have a positive and professional attitude, which includes fairness and a belief that all students can learn. But that relates to teachers within a preparation program; do the same dispositions readily apply in K-12 classroom practice? In regard to urban teachers, research has found a teacher's "high expectations as essential for teaching low income, disadvantaged students" (Boggess, 2010, p. 78).

Teachers may know their content area or even employ research-based teaching strategies, but when they lack high expectations for their students, the outcome is detrimental. Urban teachers who use technology for teaching and learning have expectations for their students regardless of their lack of resources. These teachers "avoid deficit thinking and maintain high expectations for their students, regardless of their circumstances (Boggess, 2010, p. 78). These teachers value technology as a tool, know that the technology use will benefit their students, and, with high expectations in mind, want to afford their students the same opportunities as those in districts rich in technology resources. A middle school ELA teacher who brings in her own laptop, designed her own blog, and has pooled money with colleagues to purchase an LCD projector, best explains,

> I'm so angry. I'm just so angry. My kids are held to the same Common Core Standards as kids with laptops and iPads and all that stuff? I'm not gonna let them fail. I can't do that—not as a teacher, not as a person.

SUMMARIES AND SOLUTIONS

It is essential to provide all teachers, not only urban teachers, with meaningful professional development opportunities around the use of technology. These opportunities must take into account the historical, economic, political, and sociocultural structures related to effective curriculum-embedded technology use. By taking into account the aforementioned structures, and employing a multilogical approach (Kincheloe, 2007), one is able to move beyond the narrow perception of equating a student's test score with effective, or ineffective, teachers to one that takes into consideration the impact of urban teacher dispositions in effective pedagogical practice.

Urban teachers need to take deliberate action, a collective effort, to work together in reflection and practice, to grow critically, or, as Freire (1998) suggested, teachers need to become "capable of inventing" their existence (p. 94). By building professional relationships, bound by critical reflection of both successes and challenges, teachers can begin to define themselves as well as their situation. However, this will go against what historically has faced teachers: being reduced to "docile bodies" placed in a hierarchy of ability (Foucault, 1977).

"Too infrequently are teachers in university, student teaching, or in-service professional education encouraged to confront why they think as they do about themselves as teachers—especially in relationship to the social, cultural, political, economic, and historical world around them" (Kincheloe, 2003, p. 47). As Kincheloe goes on to explain, the notion of "critical ontology" includes, but is certainly not limited to, a concept in which teachers develop new forms of self-awareness and an understanding of consciousness construction, seeing that the self is not preformed as it enters the world—that it *emerges* in its relationships to other selves and other things in the world. And the self, as it emerges and engages in and with the world, develops attitudes, beliefs, values; dispositions.

In an increasingly standardized profession, teachers are afforded few opportunities for collaboration, critical reflection, development of new forms of self awareness, and cultivation of professional values and dispositions. The grand narrative told is that teachers hold the official knowledge. When teachers are "effective," they are admired and supported. But teachers must now fit in the narrowly conceived federal definition of "effective." Like robots, teachers must transfer knowledge to students, in a neutral, context-void method, in a limited amount of time, with a limited amount of resources.

If one's notion of self is continually emerging, continually forming, it is essential that teachers distinguish the power relationships that play a role in the construction of self, or more specifically, the construction of "teacher." By doing so, teachers move to a critical consciousness with a momentum for change. Critical awareness can be an impetus for action; to speak out about the constraints and challenges faced daily in the teaching profession, with solutions offered as well. But when silenced by dominant powers, this is not an easy task.

Freire (1998) spoke of teachers who work in "solidarity" or "meet in cooperation" in order to "transform reality" (2005), yet urban teachers are rarely allowed to do so. They are told that there is not enough money to train teachers in areas other than those associated with subjects of high-stakes testing. Within urban schools, both teachers and students learn quickly the culture of what is "valued." Yet, at the state and national level, teachers are told that student exams are an indicator of student achievement and essential in determining "effective" teachers. *However, the practice is oppressive for all involved.* The oppressor has an interest to keep the oppressed isolated so as to deepen, even create rifts among them. In a repressive method, the oppressors "manipulate the people by giving them the impression that they are being helped" (Freire, 2005, p. 141).

Critical urban teachers must begin to form an alliance with one another, to construct a larger group that supports collaboration with mutual goals that prevent domination and isolation. Although groups such as department committees or teachers' unions aid in giving teachers a collective voice, oftentimes their topdown model unintentionally prioritizes issues not central to the classroom teacher. However, powerful alliances can be made at the ground level from classrooms, with teachers of all grade levels and discipline areas coming together to address issues and challenges unique to them, with shared goals of creating change and advancing an environment for advocacy within their building.

Despite the fact that teachers seek opportunities to better themselves professionally, such as enrolling in workshops, reading education journals, or attending conferences, teachers' growth cannot merely focus on the teaching profession or a particular content area. Teachers must become critical, liberating educators. But the "liberating process is not a professional growth only. It is self and social transformation, a moment when learning and changing society are joined" (Shor &

Freire, 1987, p. 50). This process of liberation doesn't just include the teacher, but the students as well. The liberating teacher moves criticality toward an "atmosphere of comradery" (p. 172) in their classrooms. This does not mean that the teacher is an equal to the students, offering no expertise or direction, but rather, the relationship of teacher-student becomes a "dialectical relationship instead of a manipulating one" (p. 173).

The use of technology as a tool for creating a critical, liberating process within classroom practice is invaluable. Technology, such as Web sites, blogs, and listservs can be used as tools for aiding teachers in forming alliances and uniting with other educators. Utilizing the benefit of technology to bridge distances, urban teachers can move beyond the physical boundaries of their school buildings and begin meeting, sharing, and engaging in collegial exchanges with educators in cities, states, or even countries that differ from their own. Online alliances created within virtual space and time, "provide a framework for experience" (Harvey, 2009, p. 214).

More importantly, using technology as a teaching and learning tool is essential not only for teachers, but also for their students. Similar to teachers, students can use technology to form relationships with peers worldwide, joining educational networks and projects that foster collaboration between learners around the world. Students can also explore their world beyond their classroom, accessing Web sites, Webinars, and online articles, learning of differing perspectives, and ways of knowing. Within classrooms, students can use technology in meaningful ways for collaboration, problem-solving, and knowledge-creation opposed to using the technology as a means for oppressive practices (Freire, 2005) such as the sole use of available computers and laptops for mandated standardized exams or practice exams.

When technology is not used for meaningful teaching and learning, students feel the impact. One study found that students felt the

> quality of their Internet-based assignments was poor and uninspiring. They want to be assigned more—and more engaging—Internet activities that are relevant to their lives. Indeed, many students assert that this "would significantly improve their attitude toward school and learning." (Levin & Arafeh, 2002, p. iv)

A high school student in Manhattan further explains, "Yeah we use the computers but just for practice tests. I wish we could do somethin' real…ya know, like research somebody in the world or somethin'."

With the use of technology as an integral learning tool, both teachers and students can gain new experiences and insights, as well as develop collaborations and create new knowledge(s). Despite the many challenges associated with using technology in urban schools, a belief in the potential of effective technology use, coupled with a belief that all students can learn, broadens the current educational view beyond the narrow definition of "effective" teaching to one that is highlighted by integrity, fairness, and equitable opportunities that are afforded not only to urban teachers and their students, but also to all teachers and students.

REFERENCES

America Federation of Teachers. (2002). *Principles for professional development* [Brochure]. Washington, DC: America Federation of Teachers.

Anderson, P. M. (2005). The meaning of pedagogy. In J. L. Kincheloe (Ed.), *Classroom teaching: An introduction* (pp. 53–69). New York, NY: Peter Lang.

Boggess, L. B. (2010). Tailoring new urban teachers for character and activism. *American Educational Research Journal, 47*(65) doi: 10.3102/0002831209358116.

Bourdieu, P. (1984). *Distinction: A social critique of the judgment of taste.* Boston, MA: Harvard University Press.

Bourdieu, P., & Passeron, J. C. (2000). *Reproduction in education, society and culture.* London, England: Sage.

Crowe, E. (2011). Race to the top and teacher preparation. Retrieved from http://www.americanprogress.org/wp-content/uploads/issues/2011/03/pdf/teacher_preparation_execsumm.pdf

Duncan, A. (2009, July 2). *Remarks of Arne Duncan to the National Education Association—Partners in reform.* Paper presented at the 2009 National Education Association Annual Meeting and Representative Assembly, San Diego, CA. Retrieved from http://www.ed.gov/news/speeches/2009/07/07022009.html

Duncan, A. (2011, May 2). In honor of teacher appreciation week: An open letter from Arne Duncan to America's teachers. Retrieved from http://www.ed.gov/blog/2011/05/in-honor-of-teacher-appreciation-week-an-open-letter-from-arne-duncan-to-americas-teachers/

Foucoult, M. (1995). *Discipline and punish: The birth of the prison.* New York, NY: Random House.

Freire, P. (1998). *Teachers as cultural workers: Letters to those who dare to teach.* Boulder, CO: Westview Press.

Freire, P. (2005). *Pedagogy of the oppressed.* (M. B. Raos, Trans., 30th Anniversary ed.). New York, NY: Continuum.

Garet, M. S., Porter, A. C., Desimone, L., Birman, B. F., & Yoon, K. S. (2001). What makes professional development effective? Results from a national sample of teachers. *American Educational Research Journal, 38*, 915–945, doi:10.3102/00028312038004915

Groff, J., & Mouza, C. (2008). A framework for addressing challenges to classroom technology use. *AACE Journal, 16*(1), 21–46.

Hallam, M. K. (2009). Why teacher dispositions are a crucial aspect of student success. *The Language Educator.* Retrieved from http://www.personal.psu.edu/lrc5081/blogs/lauren_craig_wl_ed_411/Teacher%20Dispositions%20Article%20.pdf

Harvey, D. (1990). *The condition of postmodernity.* Oxford, England: Blackwell.

Heafner, T. (2004). Using technology to motivate students to learn social studies. *Contemporary Issues in Technology and Teacher Education, 4*(1), 42–53.

Hinchey, P. H. (2010). Getting teacher assessment right: What policymakers can learn from research. Retrieved from http://nepc.colorado.edu/publication/getting-teacher-assessment-right

How bureaucracy stands in the way. (n.d.). Retrieved from http://www.broadcenter.org/how-bureaucracy-stands-in-the-way#Resources

Keengwe, J., & Akyeampong, A. (2010). The impact of technology adoption on urban school practices. In D. Gibson & B. Dodge (Eds.), *Proceedings of Society for Information Technology & Teacher Education International Conference.* Retrieved from http://www.editlib.org/p/33531

Kincheloe, J. L. (2003). Critical ontology: Visions of selfhood and curriculum. *Journal of Curriculum Theorizing,* 19(1), 47–64.

Kincheloe, J. L. (2005). *Classroom teaching: An introduction.* New York, NY: Peter Lang.

Kincheloe, J. L. (2007). Postformalism and critical multiculturalism: Educational psychology and the power of multilogicality. In J. L. Kincheloe & R. A. Horn (Eds.), *The Praeger handbook of education and psychology: Volume 4* (pp. 876–883). Westport, CT: Greenwood.

Kuczynski-Brown, A. (2012, September 26). New York class size: Nearly half of public schools have overcrowded classrooms, UFT says. Retrieved from http://www.huffingtonpost.com/2012/09/26/new-york-class-size-uft_n_1914357.html

Levin, D., & Arafeh, S. (2002) *The digital disconnect: The widening gap between Internet savvy students and their schools.* Washington, DC: The Pew Internet & American Life Project.

Martin, W., Strother, S., Beglau, M., Bates, L., Reitzes, T., & Culp, K. (2010). Connecting instructional technology professional development to teacher and student outcomes. *Journal of Research on Technology in Education, 43*(1), 53–74.

New urban-centric locale codes. (n.d.). Retrieved from National Center for Education Statistics website: http://nces.ed.gov/ccd/rural_locales.asp

Ottenbreit-Leftwich, A. T., Glazewski, K. D., Newby, T. J., & Ertmer, P. A. (2010). Teacher value beliefs associated with using technology: Addressing professional and student needs. *Computers & Education, 55,* 1321–1335.

Pinar, W. F., Reynolds, W. M, Slattery, P., & Taubman, P. M. (1995). *Understanding curriculum: An introduction to the study of historical and contemporary curriculum discourses.* New York, NY: Peter Lang.

Professional development for professional certificate holders. (2010). Retrieved from http://www.highered.nysed.gov/tcert/resteachers/175.html

Professional dispositions: NCATE glossary. (2012). Retrieved from http://www.ncate.org/standards/ncateunitstandards/ncateglossary/tabid/477/default.aspx

Scott, J. C. (1990). *Domination and the arts of resistance: Hidden transcripts.* New Haven, CT: Yale University Press.

Shor, I., & Freire, P. (1987). *A pedagogy for liberation: Dialogues on transforming education.* Westport, CT: Bergin & Garvey.

Should student test scores be used to evaluate teachers? (2012). Retrieved from http://online.wsj.com/article/SB10001424052702304723304577366023832205042.html

Su, B. (2009). Effective technology integration: Old topic, new thoughts. *International Journal of Education and Development using Information and Communication Technology.* 5(2), 161–171.

Van Maanen, J. V. (1988). *Tales of the field: On writing ethnography.* Chicago, IL: Chicago University Press.

Weingarten, R . (2010), A new path forward. *American Educator,* 37–39.

Wenger, E. (1998). *Communities of practice: Learning, meaning, and identity.* New York, NY: Cambridge University Press.

Contributors

Kelly H. Ahuna is program coordinator of the MSED Adolescent and Elementary Education Programs at Medaille College, where she prepares future teachers. Prior to her work at Medaille, Dr. Ahuna ran an undergraduate critical thinking program for 10 years. Her interests lie at the intersection of teacher and learner effectiveness.

J. Benchik-Osborne is an adjunct faculty member in the School of Education at Dominican University, where her work concentrates on the study of social foundations of education. Her research focuses on the application of SFE content and skills to expand problem-solving strategies and subject matter while also supporting students' cultures and life experiences in K-12 classrooms.

T. Jameson Brewer is a PhD student in Educational Policy Studies at the University of Illinois, where he studies Teach For America and other neoliberal movements in public education. He holds an MS in Social Foundations of Education from Georgia State University and a BSEd in Secondary Education from Valdosta State University.

Anthony Cody worked for 24 years in schools in Oakland, California, 18 of which were spent teaching science at a high needs middle school. He now lives in Mendocino County, California, and authors the widely read Living in Dialogue blog at Education Week; he also co-founded the Network for Public Education.

Susan Dunkle, an assistant professor of Adolescent Education at Medaille College, has an EdD in Educational Leadership and an MA in Adolescent Social Studies and Elementary Education, and has taught at D'Youville and Canisius Colleges. Past presentations at the international-to-local levels include social justice, equity, and educational policy.

David Gorlewski is assistant professor of educational administration at the State University of New York at New Paltz. He has served as a teacher, teacher educator, and senior-level administrator in the Western New York region. David is coeditor of *English Journal*, a publication of the National Council of Teachers of English. He has published numerous articles and chapters related to school reform and school leadership.

Julie Gorlewski is assistant professor of Secondary Education at the State University of New York at New Paltz. Her books include *Power, Resistance, and Literacy: Writing for Social Justice* (2011, Information Age) and, with David Gorlewski, *Making it Real: Case Stories for Secondary Teachers* (2012, Sense). She is currently coeditor, with David Gorlewski, of *English Journal*.

Nicholas D. Hartlep is an assistant professor of Educational Foundations at Illinois State University. His books include *The Model Minority Stereotype: Demystifying Asian American Success* (2013, Information Age Publishing) and *The Model Minority Stereotype Reader: Critical and Challenging Readings for the 21st Century* (2014, Cognella Publishing). He is a national trainer for the Haberman Educational Foundation (Houston, TX).

Pamela J. Hickey is an assistant professor of Literacy at Towson University. She has worked as an English language teacher in the United States and Eastern Europe. Her research interests include English learners' academic literacy development, classroom interaction, and teacher dispositions.

Jed Hopkins is associate professor of Education at Edgewood College in Madison, WI. He received his PhD in the Department of Curriculum and Instruction at the University of Minnesota in 2009. His teaching and research interests straddle literacy, teacher education, drama-in-education, and philosophy of education. Hopkins is particularly interested in appropriating neo-Heideggerian phenomenology and systemic functional linguistics for his work in teacher education.

Matthew J. Kruger-Ross is a doctoral student in the Curriculum Theory & Implementation: Philosophy of Education Program in the Faculty of Education at Simon Fraser University. After completing his BS in Middle Grades Education from NC State University in May 2005, Matthew stepped into the classroom at Carolina Friends School, an independent Quaker school in

Durham, North Carolina, where he taught math, music, and technology in the middle school. Matthew's research interests include philosophy of education, philosophy of technology, transformative learning, and critical studies.

Catherine Lalonde is an assistant professor at D'Youville College. She is the NCATE coordinator for the Education Department and teaches Critical Issues in Education and Multiculturalism and Cultural Diversity. Her research interests include social foundations of education, multicultural theory, critical media literacy and pedagogy, and food production and consumption issues.

Tim Mahoney is an assistant professor in the Department of Educational Foundations at Millersville University in Lancaster County, PA. The focus of his teaching and scholarship centers on urban education, with a particular interest in how beginning urban teachers develop their identities as successful educators in urban schools.

Sara McCubbins is a doctoral student at Illinois State University and works as project/office manager for the Center for Mathematics, Science, and Technology. She received her MS in Chemistry Education at Illinois State University and has published numerous books on topics relating to interdisciplinary project-based and performance-assessment-based curriculum.

Grant B. Morgan is an assistant professor of Educational Psychology with specialization in advanced quantitative methods at Baylor University. His primary research is related to estimation and other methodological issues in latent variable modeling commonly used in psychological and educational research. He also enjoys collaborating as a methodologist and analyst on interdisciplinary research projects.

Kate E. O'Hara is an assistant professor in the School of Education at New York Institute of Technology. Her research employs the use of autoethnographic studies, couched within a sociocultural framework. She is also an independent curriculum designer and instructional technology specialist working extensively with teachers in NYC and the Metro area.

Shelley Pineo-Jensen graduated from University of Oregon College of Education with a PhD in Educational Methodology, Policy, and Leadership. She is currently the chair of Eugene/Springfield Solidarity Network, a chapter of Jobs with Justice. She advocates for social justice, organizing actions in support of workers, and restoration of the biosphere.

Brad J. Porfilio is an associate professor in the Educational Leadership for Teaching and Learning Doctoral Program at Lewis University. His research interests and expertise include: urban education, gender and technology, cultural studies, neoliberalism and schooling, and transformative education.

Barbara Rose teaches courses at Miami University on educational issues and dominant privilege, and has administrative roles as department graduate studies director and in two divisional partnerships with area high schools and an urban cohort program. Her interests include diversity and multicultural education, teacher identity, and systemic issues in education.

Mary H. Sawyer is an associate professor of Secondary Education at the State University of New York at New Paltz, where she coordinates and teaches courses in the English Education graduate and undergraduate programs. She also co-directs the Hudson Valley Writing Project, a local site of the National Writing Project. Her research focuses on critical issues in the teaching and learning of the English language arts.

Timothy D. Slekar is the dean of the School of Education at Edgewood College in Madison, WI. Dr. Slekar began his career as a teacher and earned his PhD at the University of Maryland at College Park. During his studies Dr. Slekar worked with seventh- and eighth-grade teachers in the city of Baltimore. Dr. Slekar has published research in some of the top educational research journals (*Teacher Education Quarterly, Theory and Research in Social Education, Journal of Thought*). Dr. Slekar is one of the founders of United Opt Out.

P. L. Thomas, associate professor of Education (Furman University), taught high-school English in South Carolina before moving to teacher education. He is currently a column editor for English Journal (National Council of Teachers of English) and author of *Ignoring Poverty in the U.S.* (IAP). Follow his work at http://radicalscholarship.wordpress.com/ and @plthomasEdD.

John Ward is an associate professor in the Department of Educational Foundations at Millersville University in Lancaster County, PA. He believes in and studies teacher reflection on pedagogical practice and the process of student learning. His teaching centers on the idea that reflection as part of teacher preparation is often artificial and forced, but also can be experienced as practical, enlightening, even transformative.

Note: The editors gratefully acknowledge the contributions of Heather Roberts-Mahoney, whose editorial efforts and expertise were invaluable.

Index

Studies in the Postmodern Theory of Education

General Editor
Shirley R. Steinberg

Counterpoints publishes the most compelling and imaginative books being written in education today. Grounded on the theoretical advances in criticalism, feminism, and postmodernism in the last two decades of the twentieth century, Counterpoints engages the meaning of these innovations in various forms of educational expression. Committed to the proposition that theoretical literature should be accessible to a variety of audiences, the series insists that its authors avoid esoteric and jargonistic languages that transform educational scholarship into an elite discourse for the initiated. Scholarly work matters only to the degree it affects consciousness and practice at multiple sites. Counterpoints' editorial policy is based on these principles and the ability of scholars to break new ground, to open new conversations, to go where educators have never gone before.

For additional information about this series or for the submission of manuscripts, please contact:

Shirley R. Steinberg
c/o Peter Lang Publishing, Inc.
29 Broadway, 18th floor
New York, New York 10006

To order other books in this series, please contact our Customer Service Department:

(800) 770-LANG (within the U.S.)
(212) 647-7706 (outside the U.S.)
(212) 647-7707 FAX

Or browse online by series:
www.peterlang.com